Developing Client/Server Systems Using Sybase SQL Server System 10

Sanjiv Purba

A Wiley–QED Publication

John Wiley & Sons, Inc.

New York • Chichester • Brisbane • Toronto • Singapore

Publisher: Katherine Schowalter
Editor: Rich O'Hanley
Managing Editor: Maureen B. Drexel
Text Design and Composition: Publishers' Design and Production Services

Designations used by companies to distinguish their products are often claimed as trademarks. In all instances where John Wiley & Sons, Inc. is aware of a claim, the product names appear in initial capital or all capital letters. Readers, however, should contact the appropriate companies for more complete information regarding trademarks and registration.

Many of the products and applications discussed in this book are trademarks of their respective companies. Sybase is a registered trademark of Sybase, Inc.

This publication is designed to provide accurate and authoritative information in regard to the subject matter covered. It is sold with the understanding that the publisher is not engaged in rendering legal, accounting, or other professional service. If legal advice or other expert assistance is required, the services of a competent professional person should be sought.

Library of Congress Cataloging-in-Publication Data

Purba, Sanjiv.
    Developing client/server systems using Sybase SQL Server system 10
/ Sanjiv Purba.
       p.   cm.
    "A Wiley-QED publication."
    Includes index.
    ISBN 0-471-06249-9 (paper)
    1. Client/server computing.   2. SQL (Computer program language)
  I. Title.
  QA76.9.C55P87   1994
  005.75'8—dc2094-12670
      CIP

Printed in the United States of America
10 9 8 7 6 5 4 3 2

I would like to dedicate this book to my parents, Parkash and Inderjit Purba, my aunt Dr. Sudarshan Puri, my grandparents Amrit Gurcharan Singh and Rajwant Kaur Puri, my sisters Minni Coombs and Nina Jaiswal, my wife Kulwinder, my son Naveen Parkash, and the rest of my family and friends.

Contents

Preface

Welcome to enterprise client/server application development for the twenty-first century!

Sybase® System 10 from Sybase, Inc. combines enhanced versions of traditional Structured Query Language (SQL) Server products with a new suite of tools that were designed after extensive consultation with established Sybase users. An examination of the System 10 product line shows that Sybase, Inc. has done a good job listening to comments from users of distributed systems, client/server architecture, and especially SQL Server (e.g., "backup and restore of the database should be faster and online").

With System 10, Sybase, Inc. is positioned to assist businesses in evolving their current information systems (IS) environment to meet the challenges of the modern marketplace. This product line is designed to meet the requirements of an entire organization or enterprise, not just individual departments, and is referred to as enterprise computing.

Enterprise computing is often compared to departmental computing, which is characterized by the presence of a separate computer system for each department in an organization. In departmental computing, each computer system exists as an island having its own data and programs. Links between computer systems are cumbersome and not transparent or seamless. Data integrity problems are often caused by an inability to communicate data changes and rules to all the systems in the organization. Key users often do not have access to information that already exists in the organization. In enterprise computing, the islands disappear and the different computer systems do not exhibit the problems that plague departmental computing. This difference is shown in Figure I.1.

The basic philosophy behind System 10 is to leverage existing (legacy) computer systems, while building a more responsive and flexible information systems (IS) infrastructure that reflects true business requirements. This can mean many things: throw nothing away; bring data closer to the departments that use the data; support the active participation of mainframe computers in client/server architecture; support transparent and seamless connections between systems from different vendors; ensure data integrity in geographically distributed systems; support 24-hour-a-day/7-days-a-week system availability; and allow greater administrative control over enterprise-wide computer systems.

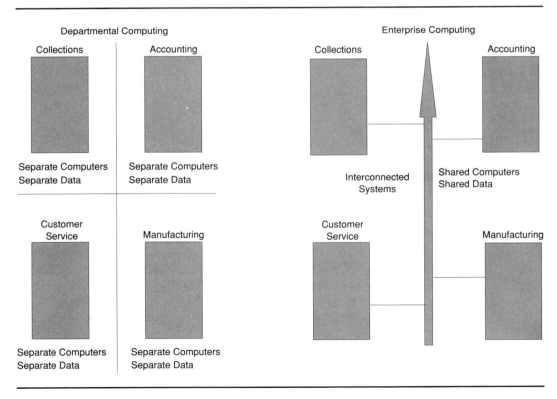

Figure I.1   Department versus enterprise computing.

System 10 promotes coexistence between different computer systems by providing tools to allow transparent and seamless connectivity between systems from different vendors (e.g., Sun Microsystems, IBM, DEC, Stratus) and with different configurations (e.g., mainframe, minis, micros). For example, a user running SQL Server on a Sun workstation can use a System 10 Gateway to execute a CICS transaction against an IMS database and update specific records only if all integrity edits in related CICS programs are applied and passed.

PURPOSE OF THIS BOOK

Since at the time of writing, Sybase System 10 consists of 7 different product groups (12 different products), each having further variations, this book focuses only on the core components required to build applications in a client/server environment.

SQL Server is the centerpiece of System 10 and, consequently, the focus of this book. The information presented here is based on the author's personal development experience using Sybase SQL Server on different client/server development projects for mission-critical application systems. Theory is included where it is helpful in explaining the benefits of SQL Server 10. The emphasis, however, is on providing the reader with practical examples of SQL Server features that can be used immediately in an application development environment. Where appropriate, examples of implemented systems are used to build examples. Two related topics are also examined, but rigorous treatment of these topics is left to two other books. These topics are SQL Server system administration, and client (front-end) tools.

After learning SQL Server 10 from this book, the reader can concentrate on learning some or all of the other components in the System 10 product line using the information contained here as a starting point. Open Client 10, Embedded SQL, and Open Server 10 are appropriate choices.

A tutorial is included to illustrate the basic steps required to build an application using Sybase SQL Server 10. Having taught at universities and colleges for a decade, the author has found that a programming application to run a Video Rental Store management system has been popular with students learning Focus, CICS, and the C programming language. This application is used in the tutorial. The Video Rental Store system was developed and tested on a Sun workstation running Sun/OS. Sybase SQL Server is portable across platforms, so this tutorial can be completed on any supported architecture. Readers who complete it should gain enough knowledge and experience to begin building their own applications using SQL Server. Readers are encouraged to modify and enhance the code contained in this book.

Two buzzwords commonly heard today are "seamless" and "transparent." The point of reference is crucial for understanding the precise meanings of these words; for example, "An SQL Server can seamlessly issue a remote procedure call to an Ingres database through a gateway." Seamless in this example refers to the user's viewpoint. The user can click on a button to access data without caring where the data is stored or how it is retrieved. The developer, on the other hand, must be concerned with storage and retrieval in order to support these seamless and transparent qualities for the user. These must be built into a system, adding complexity to the developer's job description. With the OmniSQL Gateway this situation is moved to a higher level, but now someone is required to understand this product. An overview of OmniSQL Gateway is provided in Appendix E.

INTENDED AUDIENCE

This book is intended for a technical audience of practitioners, including IS managers, system architects, database designers, DBAs, systems analysts, developers, consultants, and system integrators, and can be used by those new to Sybase and/or client/server architecture. Users of earlier versions of SQL Server (pre-System 10) can also use this book to learn the new features built into this release.

The author does not assume the reader has specific IS knowledge; however, readers who are new to relational databases and SQL may find it useful to read some of the relevant books identified in the Bibliography.

ORGANIZATION OF THE BOOK

This book has 20 chapters and 10 appendixes.

Chapters 1–3 provide an introduction to the Sybase view of enterprise client/server application systems. The different components of System 10 are presented and discussed. The architecture of SQL Server is defined in the context of the client/server model.

1 Introduction
2 Client/Server Concepts
3 Sybase Concepts and Architecture

Chapters 4–13 focus on Transact-SQL. This involves concentrating on object creation and disposition, data manipulation commands, stored procedures, triggers, and system administration commands.

The focus of Chapters 14–16 is on the client platform. This includes the Open Client application programming interface (API) and a method for sending requests to SQL Server across a network and receiving and processing information from SQL Server.

A tutorial designed to build a Video Rental Store management system is provided in Chapters 17–20.

The following appendixes are included in this book.

ACKNOWLEDGMENTS

I would like to thank many individuals and organizations that have helped me over the years. First I would like to thank Sybase, Inc. for producing an excellent product line that is serving satisfied clients worldwide in a wide variety of industries. The high satisfaction level my clients have experienced with Sybase SQL Server motivated me to write this book.

I would also like to thank Sybase, Inc. for helping me to locate a copy of SQL Server to conduct research for this book. Thanks also to Sybase staff in various departments—Technical Support, PR, Sales, Consulting, and others. Very special thanks go to Sonya Hopkins, PR Coordinator, Sybase, Inc., for all her help over the past year.

Special thanks also go to Bruce Voogel, Systems Engineer, Sun Microsystems of Canada, Inc. Both Bruce and Sun went way past the call of duty in helping me to locate hardware to run SQL Server. This helped me meet my publishing deadline.

I would also like to thank two of my colleagues for playing the lead in writing two chapters for this book. Thanks go to Bill Houston, Senior Management Consultant, for being the lead on Appendix E (an overview of the System 10 product line). I would also like to thank Len Dvorkin, Project Manager, for contributing 98 percent of Chapter 4 (Introduction to SQL and Creating Objects).

I would like to extend my thanks to the following individuals for their assistance in other areas of my career over the years.

The partners at Flynn McNeil Raheb and Associates:
Robin McNeil for hiring me out of university and cutting my learning curve by providing me with experience, knowledge, skills, and a methodology for solving problems; Mike Flynn for encouragement to write and being a powerful symbol of a professional management consultant; and Selim El Raheb for being a pioneer of client/server systems and one of the best application architects with whom I have ever had the pleasure to work.

George Ross, Director of large client/server projects

The entire JetTix project team

Lynn Reynolds, Director of Continuing Education at Ryerson University

John Pickett, Editor-in-Chief, Laurentian Technomedia

Bharat Shah, President of McCann Computer Systems

Michael Sutton, Electronic Forms expert

Ted Wallace, Networking specialist

Thanks also to Ed Kerr, Vice President, Wiley-QED Publishing Program, for encouragement, patience, and keeping this book on track.

Introduction

In this chapter a reader will learn about:

- Introduction to Sybase SQL Server 10
- Overview of Sybase SQL architecture
- Getting started
- Hardware requirements
- The Sybase environment

1.1   WHAT DOES SYBASE SQL SERVER DO?

Sybase SQL Server 10, in simple terms, acts as a guardian of corporate and application data. Sybase SQL Server accepts a request of some type from a caller (commonly referred to in the industry as a "client"), processes the request, and returns an answer, allowing SQL Server to be viewed as a "black box" in the traditional functional sense. In order to interact with SQL Server, client platforms only need to learn a method of issuing a request of some kind and interpreting a response. This process is shown in Figure 1.1.

Many things are happening in this example. The client request must reach SQL Server and be phrased in a common language. The server must be able to ascertain the identity and security clearance of the caller and only then process the request. Finally, after completing the request, the server must have the capability of returning a response to the client, which could be a message or a copy of the data that was

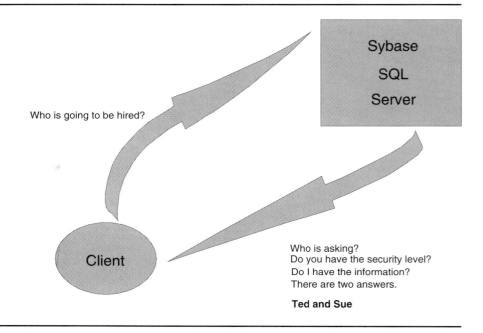

Figure 1.1   Overview of Sybase SQL Server and a client.

requested by the client platform. Of course, this is a greatly simplified view of client/server architecture.

1.2   OVERVIEW OF SYBASE SQL SERVER ARCHITECTURE

SQL Server architecture consists of several major components that can be described as follows.

The Server Nucleus This term describes the collection of software installed on a host platform that acts as a server to client platforms. It includes the SQL Server kernel, Process Manager, Query Optimizer, system databases, and application data. It does not include software and hardware that is devoted to communications. The "nucleus" is the database server black box shown in Figure 1.1.

The Client A client platform that communicates with the SQL Server nucleus must contain specific components (e.g., application programmer interfaces or APIs) that are linked with application programs and utilities or are used as standalone libraries that support client calls to

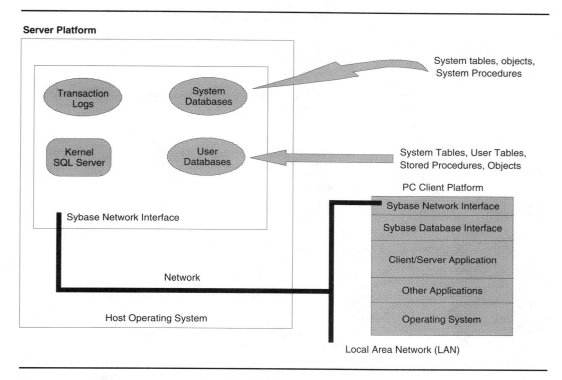

Server Platform

System tables, objects,
System Procedures

Transaction
Logs

System
Databases

Kernel
SQL Server

User
Databases

System Tables, User Tables,
Stored Procedures, Objects

Sybase Network Interface

PC Client Platform

Sybase Network Interface

Sybase Database Interface

Client/Server Application

Other Applications

Network

Operating System

Host Operating System

Local Area Network (LAN)

Figure 1.2   Simplified view of Sybase SQL Server architecture.

the server. Client platforms can be intelligent workstations or dumb terminals.

The Network The network supports communication between SQL Server and the client platforms and also supports connections between multiple SQL Servers. It is the glue that binds client/server or distributed applications. In an enterprise-wide client/server environment, the network connects systems from different departments into a seamless, heterogeneous whole.

These three components are shown in Figure 1.2. Sybase SQL Server architecture is discussed in more detail in Chapter 3.

1.3   SUPPORTED ENVIRONMENTS

Sybase SQL Server is available on many hardware platforms under a variety of operating systems, such as:

- UNIX (Digital, AT&T/NCR, Sun, HP),
- AIX (IBM RISC 6000),
- VMS (Digital), and
- VOS (Stratus).

Sybase SQL Server client platforms may be any of the following:

- MS-DOS or Windows PCs,
- OS/2 PCs,
- Next PCs,
- UNIX workstations,
- UNIX terminal servers, or
- Apple Macintoshes.

Sybase SQL Server, through the Open Client interface, supports the following popular networks:

- DECnet,
- Named Pipes,
- NetWare,
- SNA,
- TCP/IP, and
- others.

Sybase, Inc. has demonstrated its commitment to open architectures, having first published client and server interfaces for integrating data from SQL and nonSQL sources in 1989. The company is continuing to develop other tools for working in heterogeneous, multi-RDBMS environments. This approach to support multi-RDBMS environments is valuable to organizations with large investments in legacy systems.

1.4   GETTING STARTED

Sybase SQL Server is installed on a server platform using utilities provided by Sybase. Since this administrative task is performed infrequently, the author has found that many developers choose to avoid participating in the activity during development projects—possibly due to a perceived lack of time or interest. Based on the author's experience, it is useful to invest some energy in understanding the SQL Server installation process in order to learn where the different components of this powerful product reside. For completeness, Chapter 18 describes an installation and setup process for a generic Sybase SQL Server.

There are always some differences in the installation process, depending on the hardware platform, the operating system, and the version of SQL Server being installed.

A good place to start in terms of hardware capacity requirements for SQL Server is a server platform with about 35MB to 50MB of free disk space reserved to hold the program modules, the default databases, and additional user databases. In terms of main memory, an SQL Server environment variable called "memory" specifies the amount of random access memory (RAM) that SQL Server will reserve for its operation at the time of initiation. The default values for the memory variable are a good place to start and typically can range from 8MB to 12MB by default, depending on the version of SQL Server. Figure 1.3 shows Sybase SQL Server's utilization of RAM.

Following installation, SQL Server is moved from a tape/disk/optical storage medium to a server platform's disk storage. Several files are

Total Memory = 10MB

Data Cache
Procedure Cache
Devices
Active Objects
Locks
Active Database
# of Users
Overhead
SQL Server Executable

Figure 1.3   SQL Server memory utilization.

created to support the operation of SQL Server. An ASCII file called interfaces is created in the Sybase home directory. This file contains the logical and physical name of SQL Server, which by default is Sybase. In System 10, an additional entry is inserted into this file at installation time for the backup server. An errorlog file is used by SQL Server to store important system and error messages; it is a text file that can be read by a simple text editor. An executable file named isql is commonly used by developers to logon to SQL Server. Files called startserver/ runserver allow SQL Server to be initiated to run as a process in a multiuser/multiprocessor environment. Various other important files are contained in the Sybase directory structure and will be discussed in Chapters 3 and 18. Figure 1.4 shows a simplified view of SQL Server following installations.

SQL Server can be initiated by changing the current directory to /$SYBASE/install and executing the startup script. SQL Server will

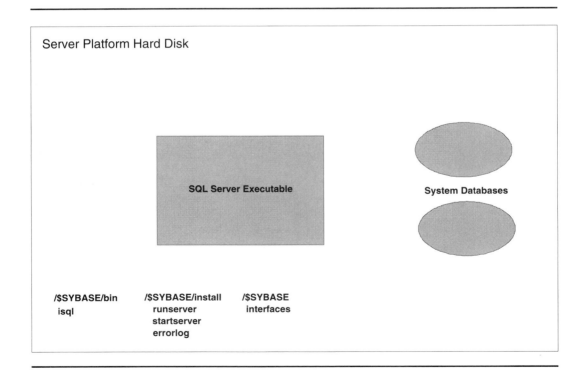

Server Platform Hard Disk		
SQL Server Executable		**System Databases**
/$SYBASE/bin isql	/$SYBASE/install runserver startserver errorlog	/$SYBASE interfaces

Figure 1.4   Simplified view of SQL Server following installation.

take a few minutes before it can serve clients. Various activities, such as automatic recovery, clearing of the *tempdb* database, and rollback of incomplete transactions, occur during this initiation process. The errorlog contains messages from the startup process.

Once SQL Server is initiated, users can logon in a number of ways. The easiest method is to use **isql** command and the name of the SQL Server from the interfaces file. The syntax is as follows:

```
isql -Uuserid -Ppassword -SSYBASE
(this assumes that 2 environment variables are set.
i.   DSQUERY is path of directory that contains Sybase.
ii. SYBASE is the network name of SQL Server as
contained in the interfaces file.)
```

On systems that can access more than one SQL Server, the interfaces file will also contain their logical/physical names. The command to logon to any server requires a simple adjustment to the previous command, as follows:

```
isql -Uuserid -Ppassword -Sserver_name
```

The general format is as follows:

```
isql -Uuserid -Ppassword -Sserver_name -Ooutput_file
-iscript_file.
```

SQL Server will run as an active process until it is shut down by a user. The basic steps to get started are summarized in Figure 1.5.

One major part of SQL Server that is visible to the user consists of

---

A summary of the steps for getting started are:

1. select server hardware environment;
2. install SQL Server;
3. initiate SQL Server;
4. logon to SQL Server;
5. perform work; and
6. shut down SQL Server.

Figure 1.5   Summary of getting started.

a set of databases and tables. Once logged on, the user can navigate between these databases, much in the same way as is done in the directory structure of operating systems like MS-DOS and UNIX. Each database has a unique name. In Sybase SQL Server versions 4.x and 10, the following system databases are available after installation:

- master
- model
- tempdb
- pubs

System 10 contains the following additional databases:

- sybsystemprocs
- sybsecurity
- sybsyntax
- pubs2 (can replace pubs)

A user is associated with a default or current database according to his or her logon id. This is shown for an SQL Server 10 environment in Figure 1.6. The concept is the same for the other versions of SQL Server.

Once logged on, users can change to another database with the **use database** command, as follows:

```
use sybsystemprocs
go
```

or

```
use master
go
```

Conversely, users can access objects in other than the default database by qualifying commands, as follows:

```
/* from sybsystemprocs */
select * from pubs2..stores
go
```

The full syntax of the qualification is: dbname.owner.object. The owner is provided if you are not owner of the object being referenced, as follows:

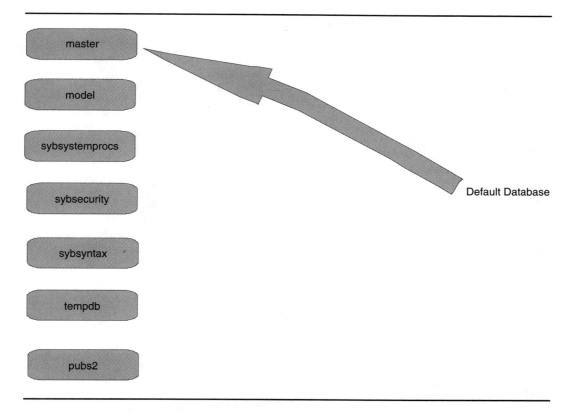

Figure 1.6   Default database.

```
select * from video.sector.sales
go
```

Figure 1.7 demonstrates the effect of changing the default database for an SQL Server 10 environment.

A variety of actions can be executed against the current database or another database. The following chapters in this book discuss these options.

1.5   SUMMARY

This chapter introduced the reader to Sybase SQL Server 10. The reader should be aware that the word "Sybase" is often used interchangeably

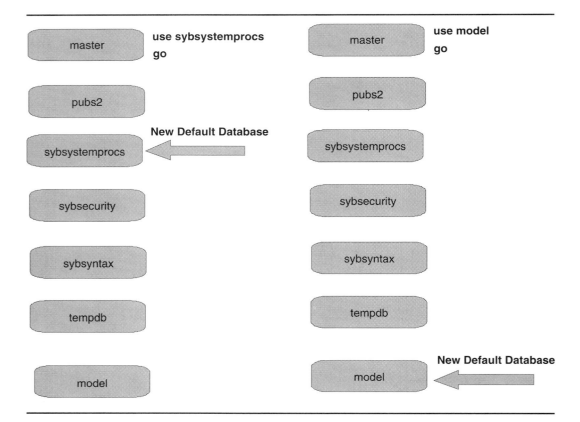

Figure 1.7   Changing default database.

to refer to the corporation (i.e., Sybase, Inc.) or Sybase SQL Server. It is not unusual for someone to ask: "Do you have Sybase experience?" This historically meant: "Do you have experience with SQL Server?" With the release of System 10, Sybase can now be interpreted to mean any number of products. To avoid confusion, this book uses the terms SQL Server and Sybase as synonyms. Other System 10 products are explicitly identified (i.e., Open Client, Control Server).

This chapter (and the preface) also introduced the reader to both the client/server and the enterprise client/server models. The next chapter focuses on client/server architecture, while Appendix E provides a discussion on enterprise client/server architecture and how it is supported by Sybase SQL Server 10. A strong case can be made that client/

server architecture was popularized by the release of Sybase SQL Server in 1987.

This chapter also provided a simplified introduction to the SQL Server environment. The installation process and some of the important files for entry into SQL Server were discussed. The basic logon command **isql** was introduced. The other chapters discuss the functionality that is available to the user after logon. Readers who are already familiar with client/server concepts can jump to Chapter 3, which begins a detailed analysis of Sybase SQL Server components.

Client/Server Concepts

In this chapter a reader will learn about:

- Definition of client/server architecture
- Three components of client/server architecture
- Relationship to SQL Server
- Earlier architectures
- "Open" concept

2.1   OVERVIEW OF CLIENT/SERVER ARCHITECTURE

Client/server architecture is discussed in this book because of its relationship to Sybase SQL Server. While SQL Server can be implemented in non-client/server mode, most implementations use the client/server model. In fact, it can be argued that Sybase, Inc. popularized client/server architecture with the release of SQL Server in 1987.

This chapter provides a definition of client/server architecture, focuses on its major components, and explores the relationship between client/server and Sybase SQL Server. The information presented is at an introductory level intended for readers who are new to client/server architecture. Advanced readers can choose to browse this chapter and then move quickly to the next one, which focuses on Sybase SQL Server 10 architecture.

2.2   EVOLUTION OF CLIENT/SERVER ARCHITECTURE (A BRIEF HISTORY)

The 1980s saw the emergence of client/server architecture as the solution of choice for many types of business applications worldwide. Several factors contributed to this evolution. The release of the IBM Personal Computer in the early 1980s gave users significant (relative to the 64K based computers[1] of the time) processing power at their fingertips. Many users eagerly accepted automation, and there seemed to be a new frontier mentality. This led to the proliferation of desktop software such as EasyWriter, WordPerfect, Lotus 1-2-3, VisiCalc, ACCPAC, and Windows 2.0. Shrinkwrap software was only effective in automating a small subset of manual procedures being used in businesses, so many users turned to customized programming solutions to satisfy their requirements.

The BASIC programming language was all the rage for PC application developers, as it offered input/output control (poke, peek), screen colors, complex file structures, bit level processing, sound, an easy-to-use compiler/linker, and a file editor. In response to growing data storage and retrieval demands, desktop database management systems (DBMS) such as dbase and Paradox gained acceptance. Many users either learned to develop applications using them or hired eager apprentice programmers to do the job. This led to islands of data stored inside standalone PCs. Users shared information by swapping files on diskettes.

The IBM PC was so successful in gaining widespread acceptance that dozens of cheaper clones with varying degrees of compatibility emerged to compete with it. This drove prices lower, further encouraging the spread of the PC in the user community. Technical advancements such as hard disks, modems, and high-quality printers improved the value offered by PCs.

Meanwhile, the mainframe and the mini were the rage of business organizations. It seemed that all large companies were automating parts of their business requirements using these large machines with incredibly powerful CPUs and large volumes of DASD, and having the capacity to support many dozens of simultaneous users through "dumb" terminals. These terminals were considered dumb because they had no local processing power. Their only function was to pass information from a keyboard to the CPU and to display information on the terminal screen. The quality of the picture was not very good; terminals were

---

[1]The popular standard before the IBM PC was the Commodore VIC 20 and the ATARI product line.

black and white, sometimes amber. Information on the screen was based on character mode (text only, no bit-mapped images), and people were impressed when someone had the patience to draw boxes and lines using the - or ¦. Reverse video was considered to be an advanced topic.

The two worlds described above largely ignored each other through mutual arrogance, or perhaps ignorance. PCs were considered to be toys by users of the big machines, who generally saw little need to use them. Users of PCs tended to be small businesses or computer hackers who could not get an opportunity to use the big machines, so they could not make a comparison.

This reality was disturbed in the early 1980s by the emergence of the local area network (LAN). Suddenly, PCs were no longer merely standalone islands of technology and data. PC users could share data, applications, and devices with others. There were problems with protocol, data collisions, response time, and occasionally with security breaches, but they seemed small when compared with the benefits that LANs offered. This was still the time when users were amused by the silliness of printing $0.00 payment checks, or fields that accepted an "O" (oh) instead of a "0" (zero). Users were far more forgiving of their computers.

Increasingly, mainframe users started using PCs for word processing and spreadsheet applications. These packages were certainly friendlier to use than many mainframe applications; in some instances, mainframe equivalents were not available. Mainframe loyalists still viewed their large machines with awe, but began to dabble with PC technology. These users accessed the best of both worlds by using their PCs for functions like word processing and accounting, while using terminal emulation software to connect to mainframes and having their PCs act as dumb terminals when the power of the mainframe was required. PC loyalists found this to be a useful ability as well, and for some time the two camps found a satisfying coexistence.

Some IS professionals started to feel troubled in this peaceful existence by the dumb use of PC computing power when the PC was emulating a dumb terminal. Furthermore, PC applications were being developed with interfaces that were getting friendlier and more graphic-oriented with vibrant colors. Nothing in the mainframe world rivaled this. But only mainframes could support intensive data applications that formed the core applications on which many businesses depended for corporate survival. For all the attraction of the PC screen interfaces, and the incredible advances in PC technology in terms of storage capacity and CPU speed, large PC systems with many concurrent users and large data volume were still not being supported. No one seemed to have the confidence to build large mission-critical systems on PC architecture.

Along came client/server architecture to fill this void. The client/server model combined the best elements of the other architectures on the market with new concepts to produce a radically new design for some types of applications. The major architectures of the 1980s can be summarized as follows.

Mainframe Systems In this architecture, shown in Figure 2.1, a mainframe computer acts as a host to connected dumb terminals. The mainframe "timeslices" its CPU power, performing all processes. The terminals serve only as input/output devices with no local processing power.

File Server Systems This architecture became popular with the development of the local area network in the mid-1980s. A PC acts as a file server by copying data files to PCs issuing a request. All processing is performed by the local PC after receiving the data file from the server PC. In large systems, a number of weaknesses in this architecture become pronounced. They are response time, concurrency control, and lack of data referential integrity. File server architecture is shown in Figure 2.2.

Databased Systems In databased systems local PCs act as dumb terminals. The server PC performs all database operations and processes.

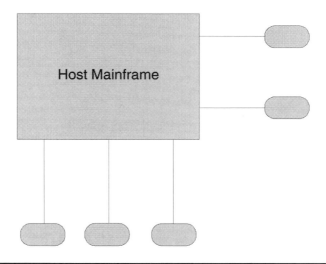

Figure 2.1   Mainframe-based systems.

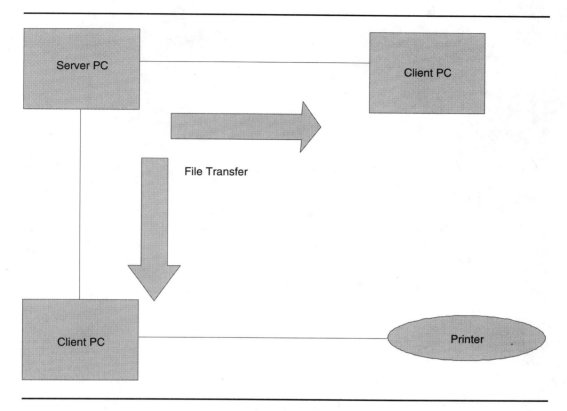

Figure 2.2   File server architecture.

This architecture is similar to the mainframe system on a smaller scale, with the same attendant issues such as not utilizing the CPU of the client PC platform.

2.3   A DEFINITION OF CLIENT/SERVER ARCHITECTURE

The simplest definition of client/server architecture involves the interaction of three components: the client (front end), the server (back end), and a network. The client includes user screens, applications, and data stored on a local hard disk. The server handles database access and access to other types of services. The network connects clients and servers to facilitate communication of requests and data between them.

The reader should notice the close parallel between this definition and that provided for SQL Server in Chapter 3. The reader should note

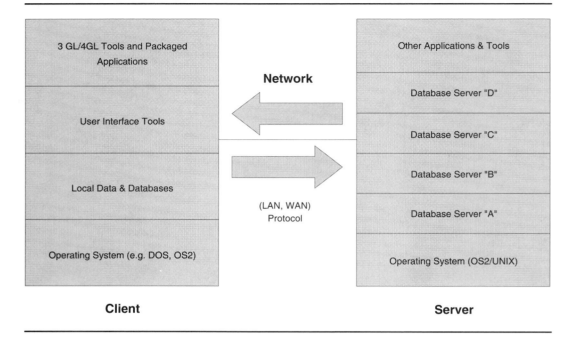

Figure 2.3   Layers in a client/server model.

that the bulk of SQL Server facilities are concentrated in a "nucleus" that consists of a set of programs and data. Additional components of SQL Server are stored on a client platform to enable communication with SQL Server. This definition is shown in Figure 2.3.

The operating systems on the client and server platforms are not required to be identical. Many installations choose Unix, SUN/OS, or OS/2 as the server operating system because of their multitasking capability. In the client/server model, hardware and software products from different vendors function cooperatively in real time.

2.3.1   The Server

More than one database server can be installed on a server platform. Servers can communicate with each other (alternating between acting as a server and a client). Remote procedure calls (RPCs) are issued by a server to make a request of another server.

In Sybase, a relational table called sysservers—stored in the master database—contains information about all other accessible database servers. Sybase offers a product called Open Server 10 that supports communication between servers. This product also allows SQL Server to execute 3GL programs from within the server itself (e.g., a C program executable).

Some platforms offer multiple CPU engines that can be dedicated to a database server, or, conversely, the CPU requirements for a single database server can be spread across multiple engines (i.e., SMP) to improve response time.

Database servers are brought up as processes in multiuser operating environments. Since other processes (e.g., a background report generation job) can be competing for CPU cycles and other resources, it is necessary to modify the database server priority relative to those others to improve response time. This is easily done in most environments (i.e., Unix, Sun/OS, Stratus VOS) using operating system commands.

2.3.2 The Client

Client platforms can transparently connect to any of the multiple database servers shown in Figure 2.4.

The client platform can contain a wide variety of products to communicate with the database server. These products can be divided into three classes.

Class 1: User Interface Development Products. This class of tools is used to develop user interfaces. The computer industry has been moving towards the use of intuitive, friendly graphic user interfaces (GUI). These interfaces communicate with database servers through layers of 3GL/4GL code, communication protocols, and network software.

Many of the examples in this book assume that the client side of the client/server equation consists of a user interface tool compiled with an application designed with C and Sybase Open Client (consisting of DB-Library and Net-Library). Some examples of products in this class are:

- Enfin from Easel
- JAM from Jyacc
- Paradox from Borland
- Powerbuilder from Powersoft
- SQL Windows from Gupta
- Visual Basic from Microsoft

Class 2: Shrinkwrap Software and Dynamic Data Exchange (DDE). This product class allows users to extract data from a database server and feed it into packaged products like spreadsheets and word proces-

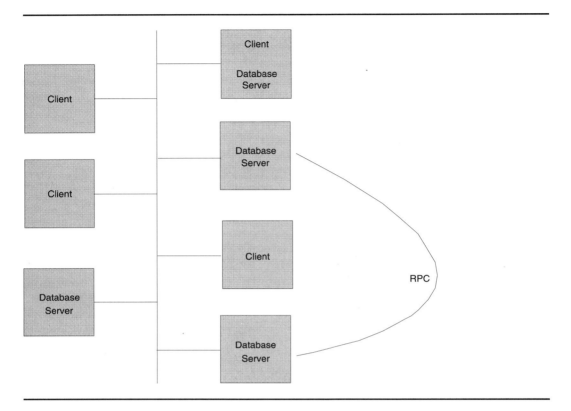

Figure 2.4   Client/server environment.

sors. This also requires layers of network protocols and software. Dynamic data exchange (DDE) allows users to pass data from one type of packaged product to another without requiring explicit conversion of the data. For example, in the Video Rental Store application in the tutorial, we may want to produce a price list that prints the photo cover of video cartridges. These images can be saved in an SQL Server database as an image binary large object (BLOB). Using DDE, this data could be extracted from a database and placed into a word processor without explicitly requiring any data conversion routines.

Some of the tools that fall into this product class are:

- Microsoft Excel
- Lotus 1-2-3 for Windows from Lotus Corporation

- WordPerfect for Windows from WordPerfect Corporation
- Microsoft Word

Class 3: Report Generators / Ad Hoc Database Access. With these tools, any users desiring access to corporate data can build their own access routines to manipulate data stored on a server machine, with minimum programming or technical knowledge. These tools allow the data to be easily formatted into reports. Some of the products that fall into this class are:

- Microsoft Access
- GQL from Andyne
- Quest from Gupta

To choose among these products for a client/server application, it is necessary to evaluate the products in terms of the following functional capabilities and relate them to application requirements.

Extent of code customization required (3GL/4GL programming language)

Style of user interface (GUI or text)

Compatibility with desired database servers from multiple vendors

Ease of modification

Ease of learning and use

Ad hoc report generation capability

On-screen statistical analysis of data

Style of screen painter

Built-in change management support

Global data dictionary support

Prototyping capabilities

Static Data In addition to user interface and application software, a client platform can also contain data in the form of flat files or a local database. Although the database server is the guardian of application data, there are several reasons to store data locally on a client platform.

Response time is the most important of these reasons. It is faster for an application to read data from a local hard disk than to issue a request to a database server across a network. In some instances, data is modified infrequently; this type of relatively static data is a good candidate for storage on a local hard disk, and it raises the issue of updating the data when it does change (i.e., tax rates go up). One solution is to store the data in a table in the database server and to download the data to the client PC when users logon to the server.

Some types of data may be unique to a client PC depending on its physical location or the type of user accessing it. An example is a PC physically located in the head office where an employee is adding video-cassettes to corporate inventory by scanning barcodes affixed to newly purchased cassettes. Since barcodes are relatively static and used by this and a few other PCs, the barcode file is a good candidate to download to the local hard drive.

Data on a local hard disk can also be used for validation purposes. For example, a client PC inside a video store that rents movie laser discs can download prices, terms, and barcodes to the hard disk. PCs in other stores do not require this data. Absence of the data on a hard disk means the PC is not authorized to rent laser discs. The ability to validate many requests against the local hard disk will save an application from issuing requests across a network and will reduce network traffic and allow the server to service a higher number of clients with faster response time.

2.3.3   The Network

The network is the glue that binds the components of client/server architecture together. The type of network software and related hardware significantly affects the overall response time, reliability, and operational costs of a system as a whole. Gateways and switching technologies are used to connect different kinds of networks and to connect platforms from different vendors to the networks. This is a good area on which to focus fine-tuning efforts to improve overall system performance, and may provide the highest relative return in client/server systems.

Some issues to consider in establishing a network for a client/server application are:

- Protocol and software requirements (e.g., TCP/IP and Ethernet/Token Ring)
- Cost and availability of communication cards
- Communication vehicle for wide area networks (WANs)
- Protocol converters
- Required release versions of the different products

In general, the protocol and software on a local area network (LAN) is consistent; however, this is not necessarily so across a WAN.

Many client/server products are being designed to allow application portability across different network environments by allowing easy replacement of a Net-Lib component without requiring any other changes. This means that applications can be developed under one network architecture and later be deployed under a different architecture without requiring significant application changes.

An optimal method for selecting the network components is to begin with the database server, the server platform, and then involve the vendors in establishing and evaluating the supported network components. Not all client/server products support all protocols and network software. The author's recommendation is to allow the choice of the database server/platform to drive the selection of the network, and not vice versa.

2.4 GETTING STARTED WITH A CLIENT/SERVER DEVELOPMENT PROJECT

Organizations can start development using the client/server model in one of two basic ways: by migrating legacy applications, preferably in manageable pieces, or by developing new applications (including mission-critical systems) that were previously not feasible with the available technology.

Organizations should be careful not to overextend on their first client/server project. In practice, choose an application that can be developed in six months or less, has a high degree of succeeding, and will gain converts for client/server architecture within the organization.

An effective method of proceeding is to involve outside consulting expertise for the first client/server project and build in a skills transfer project. It is important to begin training key staff members in client/server issues and the development experience of other companies. Courses, symposiums, seminars, books, and magazines are good ways of starting this process.

A New Development Approach In the author's experience, client/server development should not be pursued using the same development methodologies as traditional development projects. There are key differences that can cause great frustration if not managed properly. For instance, there are generally many different vendors providing products to a client/server initiative. Compatibility between different products should be tested as soon as possible during a project development cycle. Product vendors should become part of the project plan and be regularly informed of milestones, expectations, and major events. It is beneficial to hold meetings with all the product vendors in one room so that expectations are out in the open. As products continue to emerge in the marketplace, compatibility between the products becomes more of an issue than the products themselves.

As an example of the variety of products required in a "typical" client/server project, consider the following architecture almost as a minimum.

> Sybase SQL Server 10 (in SMP mode) running on a Sun Sparc Station with 15 processors under Sun OS/C Shell. 150 PC clients are attached to the server through 3Com cards under TCP/IP, Ethernet, and Open Client 10. Each client PC supports Microsoft Windows. An application is developed using Powerbuilder, C, and the Sybase DB-Library routines to issue calls to SQL Server. Several other products are supported on the client platforms, such as Microsoft Access, Lotus, and WordPerfect, and must also have access to the server data.
>
> Some of the client platforms are attached to laser printers to print invoices, others are connected to thermal printers to print receipts, and others are attached to ordinary printers. All the client platforms support barcode scanners. Some of the client platforms are located at remote geographic sites, and are linked via a wide area network (WAN).

Even in this minimal configuration, the number of products that must be integrated becomes enormous. Getting the vendors involved becomes all the more important.

Client/server projects are well suited to follow a "rapid application development" (RAD) methodology. The caveat here is that this methodology must be followed correctly. Although RAD is a largely iterative process, some major activities can be defined as follows.

1. Write a Mission Statement of the project requirements.
2. Interview users and study documentation.
3. *Understand* full business requirements.
4. Complete analysis activity.
5. Build a data model, a process model, and an Entity Relationship Diagram.
6. Build a prototype. (It is here that many advocates of RAD differ in their definition. Exactly what is a prototype? In the author's experi-

ence, a successful prototype completely captures the business requirements electronically, but in fact does nothing.)

7. Walk users through the prototype and iteratively fix it.
8. Get user acceptance of the prototype before building anything else.
9. Select products, put together a project team, and build a project plan.
10. Develop.
11. Test.
12. Accept.
13. Implement application components.
14. Review.

Client/server projects should be planned to build systems in manageable pieces. This allows users to get products sooner than if they had
to wait for the whole system to be developed and also allows greater
user participation and buy-in of the process, the advantage of which
cannot be overstated. The author has seen many projects saved after
the budget was cut, simply because the user community had fallen in
love with an application prototype (if managed properly, the users
should have made large contributions in its design) and they demanded
that more money be allocated to allow the system to be developed. If the
users had not developed an emotional stake in the application because
of their hands-on involvement in the prototype planning process, it is
doubtful that they would have fought so strongly to save the system.

Design Considerations This section provides a checklist that can be
used to trigger decisions to get started in a client/server project. A product must be selected for each item under the following headings using
the considerations as a guide.

Server Platform

1. *Database server (and number)*
Having chosen to write a book on Sybase, the author's choice is clear
and based on experience. Some objective issues to consider are the
number of supported users, throughput, performance under different loads, database server programmability (i.e., stored procedures),
referential integrity, internal security and permissions, administrative capabilities, backup/recovery, and disaster recovery.

2. *Platform*
Considerations include the cost of the platform, support agree-
ments, maintenance costs, and the track record of the selected database server. Before choosing a platform, always ask for references
from organizations using a platform running a similar application.

3. *Platform features*
    Some desirable features to look for are fault tolerance, multiple CPUs, and disk mirroring. Determine the application requirements. Ask for and check references.

4. *Server operating system*
    Common characteristics are: multiuser; multithreaded; multicompiler.

5. *Communication cards / software*
    Configure to support the maximum number of users.

Client Platforms

1. *Application programming interface (API)*
    Generally packaged with the database server. Other considerations include:
    *   Accessing other database servers
    *   Executing 3GL programming code
    *   Amount of customization that is acceptable
    *   Performance
    *   Flexibility and portability
    *   Network parameters

2. *User interface tools*
    Considerations include the following:
    *   Ease of use, intuitiveness, and friendliness
    *   Object-oriented
    *   Text-based vs. GUI-based
    *   Runtime costs
    *   Central data dictionary support

3. *3GL language*
    Considerations include the level of programming that is acceptable, the response time of the application, and the complexity of the application.

4. *Shrinkwrap software*
    Considerations include the type of user and business requirements.

5. *Operating system*
    Considerations include the type of user interface and multiuser vs. single-user requirements.

6. *Platform vendor*
    For considerations, see the server platform issues previously discussed. Several platforms from different vendors can be selected to serve as clients.

7. *Communication cards / software*
Considerations include the choice of network architecture and the availability of replacement components.

Network

1. *Protocol*
Based on database server and platform.

2. *Network Software*
Based on LAN/WAN requirements.

3. *Network operating system (NOS)*
Based on LAN/WAN requirements.

4. *LAN / WAN*
Based on geographic distribution of the application.

5. *Physical implementation*
This refers to the actual cabling and connections. Choices should be made for reliability and optimal response time, which can be determined through benchmarking and reference checking.

Data

1. *Data model / ER diagram*
Convert the logical model to physical implementation under Sybase using information in this book.

2. *Division of data between server and clients*
Position data in the server. Data that is nonvolatile can be moved closer to where it is used to improve response time. For example, experience has shown that moving a code table from a server to flat files on a client platform can reduce response time from three seconds to two seconds for the same type of application (a major improvement in online transaction systems).

Application (division of application between server and clients). Most IT professionals who are familiar with client/server architecture can tell you that the application is divided between the server and the client platforms, but how is this division determined? Some guidelines follow:

Run an application where information is captured. Edit data captured from the user before sending it to the database server. Summarize and group data from the database server before sending it to the client.

Use the client platforms to maintain the user screens.

All processing that will affect many clients should initially be integrated with the database server.

The reader should realize that the preceding list is not exhaustive and is intended only to serve as a starting point for making selections in a client/server environment.

2.5 SUMMARY

This chapter provided a brief history of application architectures that have evolved or have contributed to the development of the client/server model. The chapter focused on a definition of client/server architecture that included three main components:

1. database server;
2. client(s); and
3. network.

Client/server architecture is supported by the emergence of LAN technology, the widespread use of PCs, and the success of database servers. Sybase SQL Server is a database server. Other products, such as Oracle, Informix, Ingres, and Interface, can also satisfy this role.

A wide variety of products can be used on client platforms. This chapter divided these products into three main classes: (1) user interface development products, (2) shrinkwrap software packages and dynamic data exchange, and (3) report generators/ad hoc database access. This chapter also provided a checklist for getting started with client/server development.

Sybase Concepts and Architecture

In this chapter a reader will learn about:

- Sybase SQL Server 10
- Open Client 10
- Network issues
- Sybase SQL Server 10 architecture

3.1   GETTING DOWN TO BASICS

Recall from Chapter 1 that Sybase SQL Server architecture can be categorized into three major components, which are the server nucleus, the client, and the communication network. This chapter provides details on these components and begins with a brief discussion of Sybase SQL Server architecture. The following two sections discuss the SQL Server software that resides on a host platform and on the client platforms. The next section focuses on communication issues between the server and the client. The remaining sections in this chapter focus on Sybase utilities and Transact-SQL.

Upon finishing this chapter, the reader will be familiar with the theoretical framework of Sybase SQL Server's architecture and operations and will have a conceptual understanding of how it functions. Later chapters will demonstrate how this theoretical knowledge is applied toward satisfying practical business requirements.

Server Platform

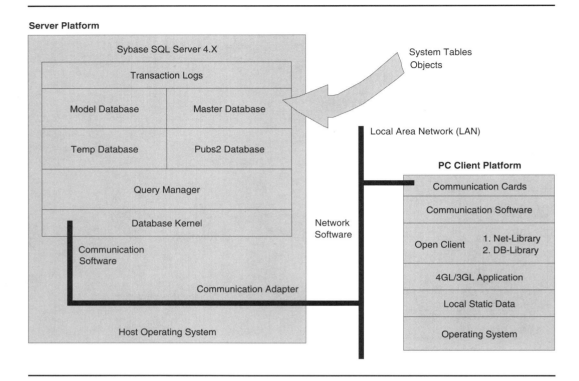

Figure 3.1   SQL Server architecture and environment pre-System 10.

3.2   DETAILS OF SYBASE ARCHITECTURE

Figure 3.1 shows the architecture of SQL Server versions 4.x.

SQL Server System 10 has expanded functionality, as shown in Figure 3.2.

3.3   THE SQL SERVER NUCLEUS

Readers new to Sybase SQL Server will find it useful to understand the manner in which information, at the system level as well as application data, is organized and saved in tables. Developing this foundation will allow users to save time during development.

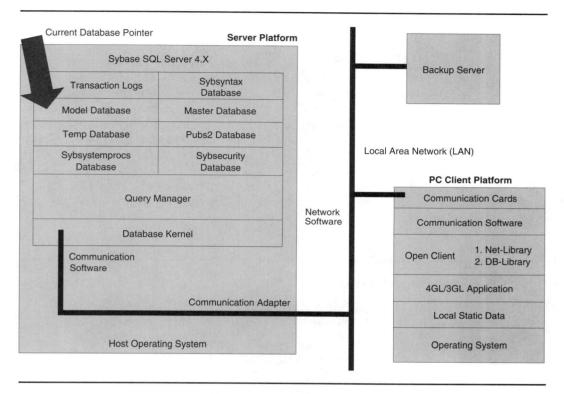

Figure 3.2 SQL Server 10 architecture and components.

SQL Server organizes data based on the relational[1] data model. The logical view of data in this model involves relations between groups of tables. Each table contains attributes that describe aspects of an entity or object; a collection of tables comprises a database. SQL Server supports many databases. Some of these can be called "system" databases in that they contain information relevant to the control of SQL Server as a whole. The other type of databases supported by SQL Server can be called "user" or "application" databases, because they are cre-

[1]The other data models are hierarchical and network. The difference between these models involves the physical storage of application data, relations between data, and the manner in which data is accessed (traversal path).

ated to manage information for user applications. A logical view of these databases is shown in Figure 3.3.

SQL Server supports the concept of a "current" or "default" database (similar to a MSDOS/UNIX subdirectory). Most commands affect the current database unless explicitly directed to affect another database (i.e., *master..tablename*). Users are assigned a "home" database at logon time based on a value stored in the master..syslogins table, or users can move to a database with the "use database" (e.g., **use sybsystemprocs**) command (assuming the user has permission to access the desired database). The stored procedure, **sp_helpdb**, lists the databases defined to SQL Server.

Sybase housekeeping, administrative tasks are generally applied at the database level. Examples are the **dump database** command to

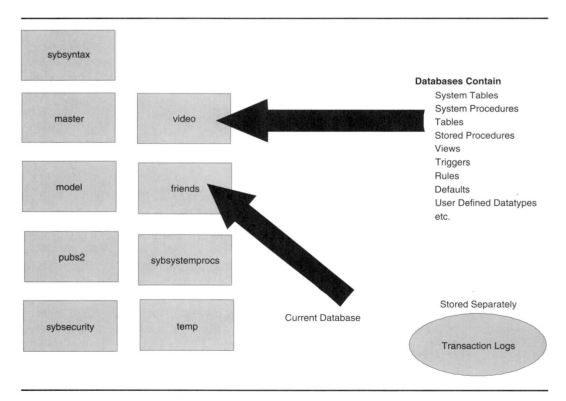

Figure 3.3   SQL Server 10 databases.

make a backup copy of a database and the **dbcc** command to test the integrity of a database. The system databases are described in the sections that follow.

3.3.1   The System Databases

SQL Server can be installed with a variable number of databases. The **master** database contains information for system administration and overall control of SQL Server and the other databases through a set of system tables.

The **model** database serves as a template for creating other databases in SQL Server. When the **create database** command is issued, the contents of the *model* database are copied to the new database.

The **sybsystemprocs** database was added to the System 10 release to hold system procedures that used to reside in the **master** database in prior releases. These stored procedures can be executed, without qualification, from any of the other databases.

The **sybsecurity** database was also added to the System 10 release. Its installation is optional and can be ignored in order to save space. This database contains two specific system tables (sysaudits, sysauditoptions) that maintain an audit trail of major events occurring in SQL Server.

The **sybsyntax** database provides help for command syntax and information about Sybase tools.

The **tempdb** database serves as intermediate storage for running applications and Transact-SQL commands. Tables are explicitly created in the *tempdb* database and subsequently disappear at specific points of SQL Server operation. Some Transact-SQL commands such as the "order by" clause also use the *tempdb* database.

The optional **pubs2** database contains a sample application that contains data and tables that can be used for testing SQL Server. Some users choose to save disk space by skipping installation of the **pubs2** database; however, some of the examples in this textbook rely on objects in **pubs2**.

The system databases are described in further detail in the following section.

Master Database The **master** database contains information about the SQL Server environment as a whole. Significant examples of this information are: the number of databases in SQL Server, configuration parameters, device information used for storing databases/transaction logs/dump devices, related physical disk information, engine information, active locks, user roles, user account information, system messages and errors, active processes, and remote servers.

This information is organized in the form of relational tables, called "system" tables. The **master** database exclusively contains the system tables listed in the following table, in addition to the system tables contained in the **model** database.[2]

System Table Name	Description
syslogins	Contains data about user accounts.
sysservers	Contains the ids of other servers with which this server can communicate.
sysprocesses	Information about currently active processes.
sysconfigures	List of variables that users can define and use in their SQL[a] programs.
sysmessages	List of error messages and warnings used by the system.
sysdatabases	Information about all databases within this server.
sysusages	Physical disk allocations for each database.
syslocks	List of active locks in the system by database and table.
syscharsets	Supported character sets or sort orders.
syscurconfigs	Configuration parameters.
sysengines	Number of active engines.
syslanguages	Information about supported languages.
sysloginroles	Information about system-defined roles.
sysremotelogins	Information about remote users.
syssrvroles	Information about server-wide roles.
sysdevices	Information about database devices and dump devices.

[a]There are several ways of programming in SQL. These topics are discussed rigorously in Chapter 4.

The information in these system tables can be viewed with a command similar to the one shown in Figure 3.4.

This command retrieves the information shown in Figure 3.5 from the database server.

---

[2]Source: *Sybase Administration Guide.*

```
select * from sysdatabases
```

Figure 3.4   Extracting information from a system table in the master database.

The reader is encouraged to use this command on the other system tables to become familiar with the information they contain. SQL Server also provides a set of system procedures, prefaced with sp_, that retrieve and format information contained in these tables. For example, the **sp_helpdb** command could have been used instead of the previous **select** command to extract information about the databases defined to the SQL Server environment. In general, the following commands can be used to retrieve information from these tables.

```
-use database_name.     (i.e., use pubs2)
 go.

-sp_help      /* displays a list of object names in
                  the default database */
 go

-sp_help sysobjects   /* displays table fields */
 go

-select field 1, field 2,... field n from
 systable_name  /* display fields of interest */
 go
```

name	dbid	suid	mode	status	version	loqptr	crdate		dumptrdate
sector_db Jun 7 1993	4	3	0	2	1	8749	Jun 20 1991	8:44AM	9:56AM
master May 17 1993	1	1	0	2	1	1145	Jan 1 1990	12:00AM	6:47PM
model May 17 1993	3	1	0	2	1	141	Jan 1 1900	12:00AM	6:47PM
tempdb Jun 8 1993	2	1	0	4	1	143	Jun 7 1993	1:23PM	9:54AM

Figure 3.5   Information about supported databases.

model Database SQL Server uses the **model** database as a template for creating databases[3] for users. The following system tables exist in the **model** database,[4] and consequently, are copied to all user databases when they are created. Changes made to the **model** database are propagated to all databases created after the changes were made.

System Table Name	Description
sysalternates	Mapping between SQL Server users and database users.
syscolumns	Information about all columns in tables and views, and for parameters in procedures.
syscomments	Information about views, rules, defaults, and triggers.
sysdepends	Cross-reference of procedures, views, tables that are invoked by other procedures, views, and triggers.
sysindexes	Information about: clustered or nonclustered indices; tables with no indices; rows containing text or image data.
syskeys	Primary, foreign, and common key information.
syslogs	Transaction log for the database.
sysobjects	Information about all tables, views, procedures, rules, and trigger default log.
sysprocedures	Information about each view, rule, default, trigger, and procedure.
sysprotects	Information about user permissions.
syssegments	Information about segments.
systypes	Information about system-supplied and user-defined datatypes.
sysusermessages	Information about user-defined messages.
sysconstraints	Information about table/column check constraints.
syslabels	Information about labels.
sysreferences	Information about table/column referential integrity constraints.
sysroles	Information about roles.
systhresholds	Information about thresholds (used for triggering transaction log housekeeping).
sysusers	Database user information.

---

[3]This is done by invoking the **create database** command.
[4]Source: *Sybase Administration Guide.*

The **select** command can be used to display the information contained in these tables. A suite of system procedures (prefaced with sp_) are loaded into the **sybsystemprocs** database after Sybase SQL Server installation to allow manipulation of these tables.

sybsystemprocs Database The *sybsystemprocs* database is an addition to Sybase SQL Server 10. In prior releases, the contents of this database, namely, system procedures, were stored in the *master* database. System procedures are prefixed by sp_ and perform housekeeping functions on system tables (as previously described under the **master** and **model** databases) and the Sybase environment in general.

System procedures can be executed while any database is established as the default. SQL Server is programmed to look for system procedures in the **sybsystemprocs** database.

Some examples of system procedures commonly used by developers are as follows:

- sp_help   Displays information about database objects.
- sp_helpdb   Displays information about databases.
- sp_helpindex   Displays information about indexes on tables.
- sp_helptext   Can be used to display the code for stored procedures, triggers, rules, and views that is compiled into the SQL Server data dictionary.
- sp_lock   Displays information about active locks.
- sp_who   Displays information about active users.

sybsecurity Database The *sybsecurity* database supports new SQL Server functionality introduced in System 10. In addition to the System tables contained in the **model** database, **sybsecurity** also contains two specialized system tables, namely:

- sysaudits
- sysauditoptions

These tables allow SQL Server to record audit information about significant events occurring in the Sybase environment, and include the following examples:

- Logins/logouts
- Trace of activity (i.e., deletions) on databases and objects
- Audit trail of a user's activity
- Trace of activity on other database objects

sybsyntax Database   This database serves as system help. A stored procedure, **sp_syntax**, is available to extract syntax and product information.

Examples

1. sp_syntax sp_who
2. sp_syntax sp_helpdb
3. sp_syntax sp_syntax

Temporary Database (tempdb)   Some readers may be familiar with IBM's CICS transaction buffer that is shared by users of a CICS system. The **temporary** database in SQL Server is functionally similar to this. The **temporary** database contains two types of objects:

1. Temporary tables created by users while logged into any of the other databases in the server.
2. Temporary working space for some Transact-SQL commands.

These objects are cleared from **tempdb** when the user, command, or application that created them exits the server or completes a task normally. Rebooting the database server also flushes the contents of **tempdb** and copies the contents of the **model** database. This book discusses commands that manipulate the **temporary** database.

pubs2 Database (a Sample db)   This database is packaged with Sybase SQL Server and should be installed[5] only if users need to use it as a training aid. System storage space can be saved by forgoing installation of the **pubs2** database.

   pubs2 contains a relational database application designed to allow a distribution company to maintain information about publishers, authors, stores, and royalties. This sample database contains 11 tables, as follows.

1.	publishers	Contains information about publishers (Each row in the table describes one publisher and is uniquely identified by a "publisher identification field (pub_id)").
2.	authors	Contains information about authors (Each row in the table describes one author and is uniquely identified by an "author identification field (au_id)").

---

[5]See "Installation Instructions" in the Video Rental Store tutorial later in the book. There is an option to do this.

   3. titles: Contains information about book titles.

   4. titleauthor   Cross-references authors and titles.

   5. au_pic   Contains pictures of authors.

   6. salesdetail   Contains detailed information about orders received at the store level.

   7. sales   Contains header information about an order.

   8. stores   Contains information about stores.

   9. discounts   Contains information about discounts.

 10. roysced   Contains information about royalty schedules applied to book titles.

 11. blurbs   Contains textual information for authors.

3.3.2   Other Objects in a Database

The reader has been introduced to one type of object contained inside a database thus far, namely tables. A more comprehensive listing of objects contained in databases follows.

Relational Table. This is a structure composed of columns and rows and containing information about an entity. Each column in the table corresponds to a field that describes the entity. Each row corresponds to one data record. Tables are related to other tables via relations between specific columns (key & foreign key).

View. A table can support multiple views of the data contained within it or across a set of tables. For example, a table that contains information about a movie could consist of the following fields (movie_number, title, director, release_date, actor1, actor2, actor3, spoken_language, and genre). One view could be to look at only the movie title and the spoken_language. Another view could be to look at only the director. Still another view could cross multiple tables and select a movie_title and all the stores that carry it.

Index. SQL Server supports clustered and nonclustered types of indexes. These are used to traverse relational tables with minimal reads, thereby increasing efficiency and response time. Maintenance requirements of indexes are minimal in SQL Server and are managed by the database server software.

A table, by definition, can have only *one* clustered index. In a clustered index, the physical order of the data records is identical to the sort order specified by the clustered index.

A table may have many nonclustered indexes. This type of index allows table data to be accessed in different orders without actually changing the physical order of the records in the table.

Procedure. A group of Transact-SQL[6] commands stored under a procedure name are referred to as a "stored procedure." The procedure is executed via the **exec procedure_name** command and is capable of accepting parameters and returning results inside parameters.

Stored procedures are a powerful option in SQL Server. System procedures (function names preceded by sp_) are themselves stored procedures.

Trigger. Triggers are similar to stored procedures but are attached to a specific table field[7] and invoked when actions such as **insert**, **update**, and **delete** are performed on the designated field. All triggers are stored procedures, but all stored procedures are not triggers.

Rule. Tied to columns in a table or user-defined datatypes, rules restrict the type of data that can be stored in the designated column. For example, a rule can be attached to a column called "sex" to restrict the acceptable values to **M** and **F**.

User-Defined Datatypes. These are user-defined to narrow acceptable data ranges, designate default values, and attach rules. User-defined datatypes are stored in the systypes system table that is contained in all databases. (See the previous rules discussion).

3.3.3   Transaction Logs

Although application developers are not required to program specifically to accommodate transaction logs, these logs must be carefully managed in a production environment to allow applications to interact optimally with SQL Server. Transaction logs serve several important functions in Sybase:

1. Changes to data managed by Sybase (i.e., with an **update** or **delete** or **insert** command) are first written to the table's transaction log before being written to a database. Many changes are usually

---

[6]This is a superset of ANSI-standard SQL and is described in more detail later in this chapter.
[7]Also referred to as "column."

batched together before being written to the actual database. This approach allows better performance than does writing each change to the database immediately as it is made. The size of the time delay is controlled by events called "checkpoints."

A transaction log containing changes that have not yet been written to the actual database is referred to as having "dirty" pages.

2. Support automatic recovery of the database in the event of a system crash. All transactions[8] that are performed in the respective databases are recorded in their own log file. In the event of a system failure, the transaction log is used to reapply all the transactions that were originally applied to the database.

3. Support manual recovery of the database in the event of a severe or hardware crash.

Overall system response time, system availability, and recoverability are affected by the effect that various Transact-SQL commands have on transaction logs.

Every SQL Server database is created with a transaction log, called the syslogs system table. A Sybase DBA has the choice of where the log is stored, how big the transaction log is going to be, and how it is administered. Although the syslogs system table is a part of a database, it should be stored in a separate physical location to reduce the likelihood of a physical disk error damaging both a database and the associated transaction log (see the following section). System response time can also be improved by this if different read/write heads are available to write to the database and the related log file.

A visual scan of the syslogs file shows cryptic information. There should never be a need to manually decipher this file; Sybase SQL Server handles this chore.

3.3.4   Physical Storage Devices

SQL Server requires physical storage, referred to as "devices," to save the objects described in this chapter. Devices can be operating system files, designated raw partitions, tape drives, and other media.

Physical location or device information for database storage is included in the sysdevices system table. The names of these devices are

---

[8]In data processing terms, a transaction refers to a discrete unit of measurable work, such as the insertion of a record, or the deletion and insertion of a related group of records.

used as part of the syntax needed to create a database. Database placement affects the read/write efficiency and the recoverability of a database following a system failure. The size of the database, of course, affects the amount of information it can store and the length of time recovered to back up and recover.

System administrators have access to numerous system commands that allow databases to be positioned on specific devices, and for increasing the size of a database after creation. System 10 provides Control Servers and Configurator to monitor and optimize size parameters.

The sysusages system table contains information that relates to the sysdevices system table and shows the amount of space allocated for each of the databases maintained by the SQL Server. Related tables are syssegments and sysindexes.

System response time is significantly improved by splitting database objects (i.e., tables and related indexes) for a specific database across several physical devices that have their own controllers. This is the theory behind Navigation Server.

3.3.5   Backup

Regular backups of databases are necessary to protect users against system failures. These can arise from several sources:

physical disk failure,

database corruption caused by software errors, and

unexpected system shutdowns.

SQL Server supports a few different flavors of the **dump** command that allow databases and transaction logs to be backed up to tapes or disk. Backups copy everything associated with a database. SQL Server theoretically allows active backups that can be completed while the database server is actively servicing users. In practice, the "backup" command is slow, and even though the server is active, client response time is affected. System 10 has introduced a Backup Server to alleviate this situation.

The **dump** command takes two forms, **dump database** and **dump transaction**. These make copies of the database or transaction log to a dump device that must be identified in the "sysdevices" system table.

The length of time taken to complete a backup is directly proportional to the size of the object being backed up. For this reason, some organizations intersperse full database backups (lots of data) with a series of transaction log backups (changed data). For example, a database can be backed up on Friday night. For the next week only the database's transaction logs are backed up (only possible if the transaction log was positioned on a device separate from the database itself).

3.3.6 Recovery

SQL Server supports two types of system recovery, automatic and non-automatic.

Automatic Recovery This type of recovery is initiated when a server is restarted after a system crash. The transaction logs for each database are used to reapply all transactions that were completed prior to the server crash and to roll back transactions that were incomplete. This type of recovery requires no manual intervention; it has happened to the author on many occasions (e.g., caused by a building-wide power failure). The SQL Server was able to recover with no side effects.

A log of this sort of activity is saved in a flat file (i.e., error_log) in the host operating system and can consequently be tracked by DBAs.

Nonautomatic Recovery In the event of a disk crash, it is necessary to rebuild the model and the user databases. It is done by using backups of the databases to reload the database, and then manually reapplying transaction logs in the order of the original transactions (assuming there were several transaction log backups between database backups). This is an administrative function that requires specialization and is not required knowledge for most developers.

3.3.7 Putting Information into Databases

Bulk Copy (bcp) This utility is used to transfer data in binary or character format into and out of SQL Server databases. Transfer of data out of SQL Server gives a variety of programs such as word processing packages, spreadsheets, and 4GL application generators access to Server data. Transfer of data into SQL Server databases allow tables to be initialized to a predefined state, which is ideal for testing, benchmarking, and conversions.

Bulk copy can be executed in fast or slow mode to load Sybase tables. Fast mode requires objects such as indexes, rules, and triggers to be dropped on recipient tables before running bcp. These objects are rebuilt after bcp completes successfully. Before running bcp in fast mode, an assessment should be made to determine whether the cost incurred by these additional steps makes it worthwhile.

SQL Commands SQL Data Manipulation Language (DML) commands such as **insert** can also be used to insert data into database tables.

3.3.8   Transact-SQL

This is a superset of ANSI-standard SQL. Some of the enhancements in Transact-SQL (e.g., stored procedures) allow SQL Server to be a programmable database server. Transact SQL supports the following features.

ANSI SQL. This includes constructs from the industry Standard Query Language (SQL) such as **table create**, **delete**, **insert**, **update**, and **select** commands.

Stored Procedures. This is a significant innovation introduced by Sybase in its first SQL Database Server release in the late 1980s. These procedures have since been incorporated into database servers offered by other vendors.

Stored procedures allow programs to be written using ANSI SQL commands combined with standard programming constructs such as **while** and **if-else**. Stored procedures accept and return parameters, support local variables, and can be invoked by name (e.g., **exec calculate_income**).

Triggers. A subset of stored procedures that are invoked as a result of SQL operations (such as **insert**, **delete**, **update**) on table fields. Triggers are used to maintain referential integrity in a database.

String Operations. Built-in functions that allow manipulation of string variables. An example is the **substring** function that returns a subset of specified length from a larger string.

Math Operations. Functions that allow spreadsheet-like mathematical operations. For example, the standard mathematical operators (+ for addition, - for subtraction, * for multiplication, and / for division) can be freely used in stored procedures or during interactive sessions.

Date / Time Functions. Functions are available to support a variety of date and time formats. For example, the function **getdate()** returns the current date, and **dateadd** allows constants to be added to a date (i.e., what is the current date + 307 days?). Parsing functions such as **datepart** allow parts of a date to be formatted (i.e., Question: What is the day of the week on Aug. 6, 1993? Answer: Sunday).

System Procedures. These useful functions all begin with sp_ and are used to manipulate system tables and database objects. Some examples are:

- sp_help   Display the names of all objects defined in a database.
- sp_helptext   Extract the source code for stored procedures from the database server. This command can be used to reconstruct the current contents of a stored procedure into an ASCII file for subsequent modification (e.g., **sp_helptext get_customer**).
- sp_who   Produce a listing of all users currently logged onto SQL Server and show the status of the last command, default database, deadlocks, the last command, and an internal process id.

These commands can be real time savers during development and ongoing maintenance. For example, **sp_spaceused** can be used to monitor the size of different tables and databases and will allow a system administrator to identify which tables are allocated with too much space and which ones are getting filled up.

3.3.9   Cursors

Prior to System 10, developers did not have a convenient method of traversing database tables one record at a time. Take the following example as an illustration of this point. Suppose a table called "movies" consists of many data records. A field in the record is called "movie_genre." Now suppose we initiate an SQL request to select all science fiction movies. The command to do this is as follows:

```
select * from movies
   where movie_genre = "SCIFI"
go
```

Now suppose that we want to read, process, and (possibly) update each record in this retrieved set. The command, as given, would retrieve all records that have "SCIFI" in the movie_genre field at once. Our desire is to get them one at a time. The answer is to use cursors. Cursors have been implemented in System 10 to give developers the convenient ability to walk through records one at a time.

3.3.10   Inside the SQL Server Engine

Basic Design   SQL Server 10 is compliant with the ANSI SQL89 standard and the ANSI SQL92 Entry Level Standard. It has highly sophisticated methods of ensuring database integrity and security. SQL Server 10 is compatible with Level C2 (Controlled Access Protection) for secure databases (as established by the U.S. Government Trusted Computer System Evaluation Criteria, or the "Orange Book") and can be upgraded to Level B1 (Labeled Security Protection).

SQL Server has a single-process, multithreaded architecture. All connected clients are viewed as tasks within a single process, as are all other activities (such as automatic backup and recovery), meaning that each additional client that connects to the server requires an additional 48K of main memory (a subset of the memory requirements of a process) instead of the total memory required for a single process (which can be as high as 2MB). This allows SQL Server to support a larger

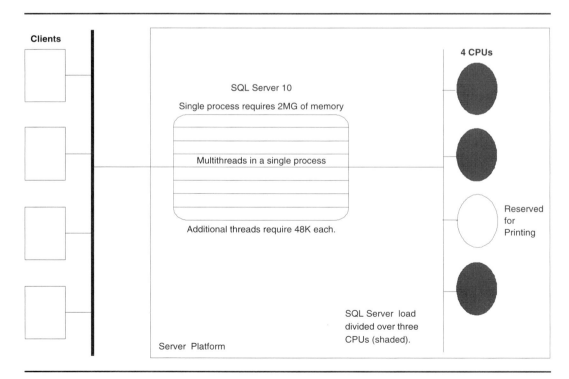

Figure 3.6   Sybase SQL Server SMP design.

number of users than database server kernels designed around "a single process per client architecture."

Since 1991, SQL Server has supported SMP (Symmetric Multiprocessing), which allows it to take advantage of computer platforms that have multiple CPUs (e.g., duplexed fault-tolerant Stratus mainframes). It is done by spreading work that would normally be done by one CPU across multiple CPUs. Unlike some other products that support SMP, the multiprocessor version of Sybase SQL Server can be programmed to use specific CPUs on a platform. This allows other jobs (e.g., nightly batch reports) to be scheduled to run on a specific CPU with regularity, and is shown in Figure 3.6.

The SQL Server kernel also handles cache management. System administrators can establish the size of a data and procedure cache. Caching can significantly improve the speed of SQL Server processing.

Query Manager This component of SQL Server is responsible for accepting a request made by a client of the SQL Server and parsing it to ensure its syntactical correctness. A syntactically correct request is then compiled and stored in the data dictionary.

A query optimizer is responsible for finding the most efficient manner of satisfying a compiled request. It involves weighing the costs of various opportunities such as which index to use in reading a table and costing out I/O options (e.g., the optimal disk drive to read).

3.4 THE CLIENT

Sybase SQL Server supports two types of clients, PC workstations and dumb terminals.

3.4.1 Intelligent Workstations

Figure 3.7 shows a representation of an intelligent workstation set up to communicate with SQL Server.

Intelligent client workstations typically contain an application developed with a programming language, a 4GL, some type of screen painter/manager, or a software package. This application is not a part of the Sybase SQL Server architecture. but is able to communicate requests and receive information through SQL Server components that are installed on the client workstation. These are:

Open Client 10 Open Client consists of the following two components, DB-Library (DB-Lib) and Net-Library (Net-Lib).

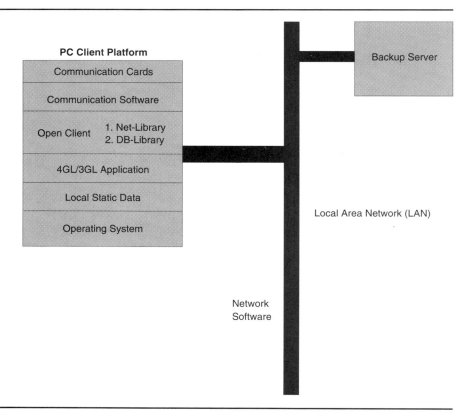

Figure 3.7   Architecture of an intelligent "client."

DB-Lib. This is a software library containing functions that allow clients to communicate with SQL Server. **DB-Lib** functions must be compiled with an application. A DB-Lib is specific to the programming language being used in an application. This allows applications to be ported to other environments by simply changing the DB-Lib component and leaving the programming code unchanged. Some functions contained in DB-Lib for the C programming language[9] are:

1. dblogin   Sets a pointer to a structure that is used to log on to a
                       SQL Server. Use the DB-Lib commands **DSETLUSER**,
                       DSETLPWD, and **DSETLAPP** to fill the structure. An
                       example is shown in Figure 3.8.

---

[9]Also compatible with COBOL, Pascal, and other languages.

```
/* program segment */
logon_ptr = dblogin()
DBSETLUSER   (logon_ptr, "neil");
DBSETLPWD(logon_ptr,"Sector");
DBSETLAPP(logon_ptr"video");
```

Figure 3.8   Setting up a login record using the C programming language.

2. dbopen   Opens a connection between a specified SQL Server and
              an application.
3. dbcmd   Places commands into a structure called DBPROCESS.
4. dbsqlexec Sends the contents of the DBPROCESS structure to the
              connected SQL Server for execution.
5. dbresults Processes messages and data returned by SQL Server
              in response to a **dbsqlexec**.

This book will later relate several experiences that can save the reader time and effort in implementing DB-Lib commands in applications.

Net-Lib. Net-Lib is a software module that allows a client to communicate with network software. This is discussed under "Communication Components" later in this chapter.

ISQL This program is installed on the client platform and grants interactive access to the SQL Server environment. It is frequently used for system administrative functions and ad hoc inquiries. ISQL is also available on the host platform for interactive connection to SQL Server.

Embedded SQL Calls This is an alternative to the DB-Lib facility. An example of this method is seen in command-level CICS programming with COBOL or with Pro *C and Oracle[10] programming. In these examples, the embedded calls are included in the source code, and the program is run through a two-stage compile process. The first stage involves a precompiler stage followed by a full compile. Many developers do not favor this method because of the intermediate modification to their code, which sometimes makes debugging difficult.

DBping This program is packaged with DB-Lib and is used to test the connection between a client platform and SQL Server, as seen in Figure 3.9.

[10]Pre-Oracle 7.

// server_address is the SQL
// Server address stored in a
// hosts file.

dbping server_address

Figure 3.9   Testing the connection between a PC and SQL Server.

Most network software has a related utility called PING that is used to test the connection between a PC workstation and a host machine running SQL Server. The syntax to run this utility is similar to that of the DBping, except that the network address of the host machine is used.

Readers will find that busy SQL Server work environments are fertile ground for problems to happen, such as the unplugging of key cables and wires without warning. Both of these utilities are diagnostic aids that can save hours of needless program debugging when a problem is actually being caused by hardware.

3.4.2   Dumb Terminals

Dumb terminals can also be used to issue requests to SQL Server. In this instance, a single application resides on a host platform and manages all requests to the server, processing of responses, and interfacing with specific dumb terminals, shown in Figure 3.10. The information contained in this book for clients is specific to (but not limited to) intelligent clients, unless otherwise stated.

3.5   COMMUNICATION COMPONENTS

SQL Server communicates with client platforms through network software and to dumb terminals through communication protocol software. Choices for both of these are plentiful and could be, for example, TCP/IP, Banyan Vines, DECNET, and Named Pipes.

SQL Server was designed to be scalable and portable. This means that most applications can be developed for a certain type of hardware configuration and be ported to a new configuration with minimal program changes (e.g., porting an SQL Server application from a Stratus VOS environment to a VESA 486 PC, UNIX environment). SQL Server

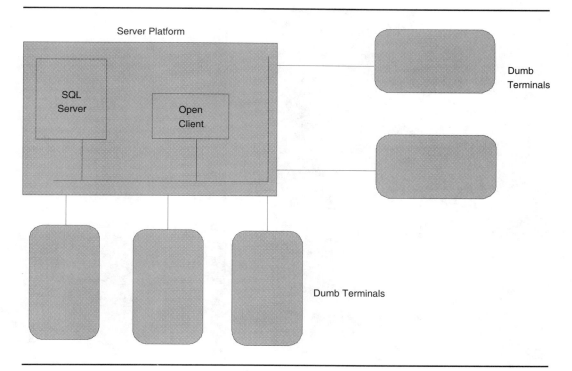

Figure 3.10   Architecture of a dumb "client."

makes this possible by communicating through modules that reside on the host machine as well as on the client machines. One of these modules (DB-Lib) was discussed previously. DB-Lib allows programming language and operating system independence by enabling easy replacement of DB-Lib versions whenever a programming language or OS changes.

As Figure 3.11 shows, there is another piece of software (mentioned earlier) called Net-Lib that is installed on client platforms. Like DB-Lib, Net-Lib is available in different operating versions, depending on the communication protocol being used to communicate with SQL Server. In Sybase SQL Server releases after 4.x, a Net-Lib can be replaced without requiring the application to be recompiled, which is extremely beneficial in applications that are serving businesses around the clock and cannot be shut down for very long. As Figure 3.11 shows, the communication protocol can be changed by making a replacement on the host machine and on the client machines.

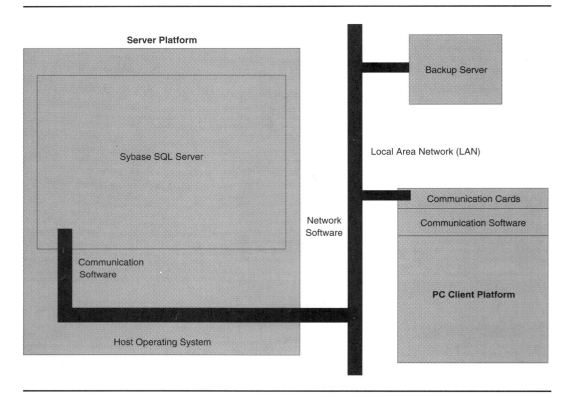

Figure 3.11   Communication between SQL Server and client platforms.

3.6   SUMMARY

This chapter introduced the reader to key Sybase SQL Server concepts and architecture in order to develop a theoretical framework for subsequent chapters. The chapter focused on concepts and architecture components that readers can affect to their advantage and that are necessary for developers, users, and management to understand in order to use SQL Server to solve business problems.

A single SQL Server consists of many databases. Each database consists of various objects, including tables, indexes, rules, views, and user-defined datatypes. This chapter divided SQL Server into three main components: the nucleus, the client, and communication network. Readers will find it useful to learn SQL Server in this order.

SQL Server is packaged with four basic databases: **master**, **model**, **tempdb**, and **pubs2**. Users define databases by using the model database as a template.

The *master* database contains system tables that are used to manage the environment of the server and store data for the other databases in the Server. All the other databases contain two types of tables. Database system tables contain administrative and other information about the database itself, such as completed transactions, the names of all objects in the database, and Transact-SQL logic in all stored procedures saved in the database data dictionary. Users can also define tables to contain data in the logical form of the relational data model. Examples of user-defined tables are found in the *pubs2* database.

Databases can also contain objects other than tables. Some of these can be user-defined datatypes, rules, indexes, views, and triggers. Advanced database server concepts such as database security and data integrity are handled through the manipulation of these objects. For example, SQL Server offers two levels of security. The first level consists of a user_id and password to the SQL Server environment. This information is stored in syslogins system table in the **master** database. The second level of security involves assigning permissions to users that can access a database and allowing them the use of certain commands only. This information is stored in the database system table sysprotects. Security can also be implemented at the network level, the physical level, and in stored procedures, triggers, and views. Data integrity is ensured through user-defined datatypes, stored procedures, and triggers.

This chapter also introduced the SQL Server kernel and related concepts of optimization and disk caching. These topics and how they can be used to improve the performance of an SQL Server application will be discussed in Appendix C: Performance Considerations.

Introduction to SQL and Creating Objects

In this chapter a reader will learn about:

- SQL commands
- Creating databases
- Insert/update/delete commands
- Creating objects

4.1 STRUCTURED QUERY LANGUAGE AND TRANSACT-SQL

Structured Query Language, commonly known as SQL (and pronounced "sequel"), was originally developed by IBM in the late 1970s and used in their mainframe relational database DB2. SQL was a significant departure from the programming languages that were then in use, because SQL was not a "procedural" language. Procedural languages like CO-BOL, C, or BASIC have in common the fact that the programmer using them gives specific instructions about the procedure to be used in order to retrieve data from the computer system. For instance, imagine writing a program that reads a student_grade file and returns the total number of students whose English grades are above 75 percent, along with their overall average. In a normal programming language, the code would direct the system to read each record in the file, discard it if the grade is 75 percent or less, and otherwise count it and begin to compile an average, as shown in Figure 4.1.

```
set student_count, total_grade, average_grade = 0

read a student record

while not end-of-file
     if subject is English and grade > 75
          add 1 to student_count
          add grade to total_grade
     end-if
     read a student record
end-while

average_grade = total_grade / student_count
print "Number of students with 75% or better in English:
",
student_count
print "Their average grade is: ", average_grade
```

Figure 4.1   Procedural code to count English students scoring 75 percent or better.

SQL offers an alternative to the procedural approach to programming. One of its basic principles is that the programmer should be more interested in *what* data is being retrieved than in precisely *how* it is retrieved. SQL does not necessarily add functionality, but it can save several lines of code; for instance, the same function performed by the code in Figure 4.1 could be rewritten in SQL as the simple **select** command shown in Figure 4.2. This **select** command provides access to data stored in a relational model. The relational database model, first invented by Dr. E.F. Codd, requires a large number of complex rules to describe it, but is summarized informally by C.J. Date using the following definition of a relational database management system:

- It represents all information in the database as tables.
- It supports the three relational operations known as **selection**, **projection**, and **join**, for specifying exactly what data you want to see (and it can carry out these operations without requiring the system to physically store its data in any particular form).[1]

---

[1]Quoted in Emerson, Darnovsky, and Bowman, *The Practical SQL Handbook*, p. 13.

```
select count (*), avg (grade)
from student_grade
where course = "English"
  and grade > 75
```

Figure 4.2   Standard SQL code to count English students scoring 75 percent or better.

While the power of this relational approach to programming can have its pitfalls in terms of optimization and performance, it allows the programmer to pay more attention to the requirements of the program, and less to the technical nuts and bolts of data access. Virtually every standard implementation of SQL has the basic **select**, **insert**, **update**, and **delete** operations, along with a powerful syntax to allow precise specification of the data records to be affected by the operation. While most real-life SQL applications still make use of other programs to process the database information retrieved, SQL's ability to take over the low-level data functions can substantially reduce programming effort.

In comparison to standard SQL[2], however, Sybase's SQL Server takes things a significant step further with its Transact-SQL language. Transact-SQL combines procedural logic with relational data manipulation commands, thus allowing the programmer to create true standalone programs (called "stored procedures") to carry out business functions, rather than embedding SQL statements into driver programs to process the data retrieved.

Readers who are familiar with SQL will have noticed that the select statement is not a true replacement for the related procedural program since there is no provision for storing or printing the calculated data totals. This problem is rectified in the Transact-SQL stored procedure shown in Figure 4.3.

---

[2]Two international standards organizations actively promote standards within the SQL world: ANSI (the American National Standards Organization), and ISO (the International Standards Organization). Each of these organizations defines certain minimum standards for implementations to follow in order to be considered "true" SQL. In the past, most vendors of SQL-based products have added customized extensions to the standard in order to achieve competitive advantages. The current ANSI standard, SQL-92, runs over 700 pages (compared to the 120 pages of its predecessor), and the next update is expected in 1995 with "SQL3."

```
create procedure count_students
as

declare @student_count   int
declare @average_grade   float

select @student_count  = count (*),
       @average_grade  = avg  (grade)
from student_grade
where course = "English"
  and grade > 75

print "Number of students with 75% or better in English: " +
      convert (varchar,student_count)

print "Their average grade is: " + convert (varchar,average_grade)
go
```

Figure 4.3   Transact-SQL stored procedure to count English students scoring 75 percent or better.

The power of SQL Server's Transact-SQL is significant for several reasons:

- It allows logical functions to be processed in a single block of homogeneous code, rather than being split between a procedural coding language (to process results) and embedded SQL statements (to maintain data).
- It improves system response and performance, because stored procedures can be "compiled"[3] into the SQL Server database and thereby skip the regular parsing, execution planning, and optimization steps required by a normal ad hoc SQL statement.

[3]Sybase's compilation of stored procedures into the database is not a compile in the regular sense of the word. While the stored procedure is not tokenized or converted to any form of machine language, the compilation step filters out syntax errors in advance and creates an execution plan that guides the database server to use (hopefully) the most efficient indexes when the stored procedure is invoked. Since this work must only be done once, each runtime invocation of a precompiled stored procedure is significantly faster than running the equivalent ad hoc statements.

- It can handle input parameters, return values, and local variables, and pass them to or receive them from other stored procedures.

Transact-SQL and stored procedures are ideal for building true client/ server systems. They allow data logic to be stored together with data on the server machine and can provide structured responses to transactions submitted from a client.

This chapter reviews the principal data definition and data manipulation commands of Transact-SQL in realistic working scenarios. Rather than exploring every syntactical variation of each command, it focuses on how the command is normally used, and why. The next chapter, covering stored procedures, discusses the control flow language used to tie these commands together into actual stored procedures.

4.2   DATA DEFINITION COMMANDS

The first set of commands that the SQL Server developer should become familiar with is the group used to create and maintain the database. One key concept to understand when creating a relational database is that the developer or database administrator need not pay direct attention to the physical placement of individual elements (tables, stored procedures, etc.) within the database.[4] Once space is allocated for the entire database, internal procedures within Sybase take care of managing that space.

It is common to refer to the commands used to create databases, tables, and other database objects as the "data definition language" (DDL).

4.2.1   Databases

Recall from Chapter 3 that, when an SQL Server is first installed, it includes the following three built-in databases at a minimum.

master is a database used to control the SQL Server process and all other objects within it, including all other databases on the server.

tempdb is a temporary database used to satisfy requests to create temporary tables as part of a query. These tables are automatically eliminated once their invoking process has completed, but if insuf-

---

[4]Sybase does provide some advanced tuning options that allow a degree of control over the placement of physical elements of the database.

ficient space is available to satisfy concurrent processes using temporary tables, serious performance problems can arise.

model is the template of a standard database used by SQL Server to create other user databases.

The basic syntax for creating a database is:

```
use master
go

create database database_name
on default = size
log on database_device = size
```

The database name is user-definable, subject to standard SQL Server naming conventions. This command will update the master..sysusages and master..sysdatabases tables. Issue the **sp_helpdb** command to see that a database is created. The maximum database default size = 8,388,608 MBs or up to 32 segments. SQL Server 10 can hold up to 32,767 databases in all.

Although not mandatory, it is usually a good idea to specify the database and transaction log sizes and locations in order to properly allocate data space and to avoid contention between the database and its transaction log. For instance, depending on the host platform, it is common to place the database and transaction logs on different devices (which could be different files, partitions, or disks) to allow concurrent I/O to take place on both objects.

Regardless of the hardware or operating system platform, SQL Server immediately allocates for itself all of the space with which it is configured, even if it does not contain enough data to fill up that space. In general, it is relatively easy to allocate additional space to a database through system procedure commands (while SQL Server is running and supporting online requests). Removing unused space from a database requires several steps.

SQL Server supports the following types of things, or "objects," within its databases: tables, rules, defaults, stored procedures, triggers, and views.

4.2.2   Tables

Recall from Chapter 3 that tables are the database objects that store the actual data in a database. They can be compared to flat files in nonrelational systems, although there are some important differences.

Table name: student_grade

	Columns				
	student ID	Student Name	Course	Grade	Term
First row →	123	Jones	English	79	Spring 94
Second row →	124	Smith	Math	67	Spring 94
Third row →	124	Smith	Physics	88	Summer 94
Fourth row →	127	Brown	English	70	Spring 94
Fifth row →	127	Brown	Physics	80	Summer 94

Figure 4.4   Illustration of relational database tables with rows and columns.

An SQL Server table is defined as having a number of "columns," each of which has its own defined datatype (integer, character, float, etc.). Data is created as table "rows," which define values for some or all of the columns. Traditionally, database rows and columns correspond to file records and fields, and it is not uncommon to hear even experienced relational database developers refer to them in that way. Figure 4.4 illustrates the relationship between database tables and their rows and columns.

Note that there is no intrinsic ordering of table columns assumed in a relational database. The columns are referred to by name only, and may be defined, selected, and updated in any order without affecting the inner workings of the database. This is very much in contrast with a traditional flat file, where the physical ordering of fields in a record is rigidly specified for reading and writing records.

The basic syntax for creating a table is:

```
create table table_name
        (column_name  datatype,
         column_name  datatype,
         . . .

        )
```

SQL Server 10 provides the **create table** command with some additional options, as shown in the following syntax:

```
create table table_name
        (column_name   datatype identity,
         column_name   datatype,
         ...

         constraint cons_name
         )
```

The **table creation** command defines the desired table name and column name and, subject to some very large limits, the number of columns in the table. SQL Server 10 support 2 billion tables/database and 250 columns/table. Each row in a table can hold 1962 bytes of data.

Sybase provides a variety of datatypes, and others may be created by the user if required. For example, the DDL for creating the student_grade table could be written as follows:

```
create table student_grade
        (student_id    int,
         student_name  char(25),
         course        char(20),
         grade         tinyint,
         term          char(15)
         )
```

Experienced system developers are familiar with this syntax and use it frequently to add or modify tables in the database. Since a real-life application database will consist of several tables, it is useful to include all of the **create table** commands used to create the application database into a single script file that can be run to re-create consistent images of the application database as many times as necessary.

It is worth noting here that columns may be defined as "NULL" or "not NULL," depending on whether the column must have a value. Defining a column as NULL has certain advantages (see the discussion of the **insert** statement later on in this chapter), but there can also be some associated performance penalties when updating NULL columns, which are revisited in Appendix C.

The "identity" option can be associated with a maximum of one column per table. The column should also be declared with a "numeric" datatype. Records added to the table do not need to explicitly insert a value into the column tagged with the identity keyword. Instead, SQL Server automatically inserts a sequential number into the column. For example, the first record is inserted with a value of 1. The next record that is inserted has a value of 2, and so on. The following example demonstrates the use of identity:

```
create table invoice
(
  invoice_number        numeric          identity,
  customer_number       int,
  product_code          char(20)
)
go

insert invoice
( customer_number,  product_code)
values
( 12, "old movie")
go

insert invoice
( customer_number,  product_code)
values
( 12, "new movie")
go

insert invoice
( customer_number,  product_code)
values
( 12, "pop")
go

sp_help invoice
go

select * from invoice
go
```

4.2.3   Indexes

Once a table has been created, the next step is usually to create one or more indexes on its data. An index is a mechanism used to order the data rows in such a way as to speed up access to the data. Although a table can be created without indexes, it would be impractical from a response time point of view unless the number of rows in the table was extremely small.

As described in Chapter 3, there are two types of indexes supported by SQL Server:

1. The "clustered" index of a table (there can only be one per table) is used to dictate the physical ordering of the table's rows. As new rows are inserted into the table, they are forced into clustered index order, which will sometimes result in page spawning, or splitting, in order to insert a row into its correct location. Clustered indexes require 120 percent of the size of the corresponding table.
2. The "nonclustered" indexes of a table (there can be several) are used to provide access to the table's data in an alternate order. Although access time via this type of index is not quite as good as by using the clustered index, nonclustered indexes allow the user to look at the table's data in more than one way. Sybase supports up to 249 nonclustered indexes per table.

An important feature of indexes in SQL Server is the fact that they can be composite in nature. A composite index is composed of more than one table column in a user-specified order. The rows are normally ordered by the first column in the composite index, but when more than one row has the same values for this column, the second column in the composite index is used to further order the rows, and so on. A composite index typically comprises as many as 5 or 6 columns, up to an SQL Server limit of 16. Composite index key length cannot exceed 256 bytes.

Indexes can be specified as "unique" in SQL. This means, simply, that no two rows can have the same values in the column(s) that make up a unique index. The choice of whether to use a unique or nonunique index generally depends on the type of data being indexed. For instance, some types of transaction identifier codes would never be reused and could therefore be suitable candidates for unique indexes. A surname field, on the other hand, would very likely have duplicate entries and would not make a good unique index (imagine how many Smiths exist out there). If a user attempts to insert a new row into a table with the same index column values of an index defined as unique, SQL Server returns an error message, and the insert fails.

To return to the student_grade table example, assume that quick access to the table would be required in three ways: to display all information regarding a particular student, to display all students from a given course and term, and to search for students with a particular name. This would lead to the creation of three indexes in our DDL script in Figure 4.5. With these indexes in place, quick access is possible for many purposes. For instance, a selection of a particular student by

```
create table student_grade            /*Create the table*/
      (student_id int,
       student_name        char(25) ,
       course              char(20) ,
       grade               tinyint,
       term         char(15)
      )

create clustered index student_id     /*Create the first
                                         (clustered) index*/
      on student_grade (student_id)

create nonclustered index student_course  /*Create the first
                                             nonclustered index*/
      on student_grade (course, term)

create nonclustered index student_name    /*Create the second
                                             nonclustered index*/
      on student_grade (student_name)
```

Figure 4.5   DDL to create the student_grade table (first attempt).

student id would use the clustered index, while selections of students by name would use the second nonclustered index.[5] See Figure 4.5.

The first nonclustered index in the DDL is a good example of the use of a composite index. It is not sufficient to specify the course name to generate a class list, since the same course may be offered over several terms. The composite index will order the rows first by course name and, when the course name of two records is the same, by term. Note that if two rows have the same course and term, there is no par-

---

[5]Sybase indexes and the Optimizer: Appendix C of this book deals with optimization and tuning aspects of Sybase in more depth, but it is worth mentioning here that the Sybase Optimizer assigns a "query path" to all SQL table access based on the selection clauses and available indexes. While the Optimizer generally makes reasonable choices as to which index will result in the fastest query, the performance-oriented programmer will ensure that most or all table access uses "where" clauses that point unequivocally at a single, predefined index. It's nice to have the Sybase Optimizer available when necessary, but it's usually better not to rely on it: It has been known to occasionally become a "pessimizer"!

ticular ordering implied by the index. If there were a frequent need to generate alphabetical course lists, it would be reasonable to place the student_course index on the student name as well so that it would be created as

```
create nonclustered index student_course
/*A better index for alphabetical class lists*/
    on student_grade (course, term, student_name)
```

Note that each index occupies one row in the sysindexes system table within the database.

4.2.4 Datatypes, Rules, and Defaults

When creating a table, SQL Server needs to know the type of data that will be stored in each table column. Data can have several different types, from alphanumeric abcde to numeric 2.589 to date/time December 31, 1979. SQL Server has a large number of built-in datatypes that can be assigned to these columns, and user-defined datatypes can also be created if necessary.

Built-in Datatypes Built-in datatypes in SQL Server fit into seven different categories, as displayed in Figure 4.6. In many cases, the "base" types have modifiers allowing definition of columns that take more or less space. For instance, columns defined with the int datatype can hold numbers up to ±2,147,483,647 and require 4 bytes of storage, while the tinyint requires only 1 byte of storage but cannot handle numbers outside of the range zero to 255. In other cases, a datatype can be defined to a fixed length (e.g., char(n)) or a variable length (e.g., varchar(n)).

User-Defined Datatypes, Defaults, and Rules Sometimes there are advantages to defining new datatypes in SQL Server so that customized rules and defaults can be attached to them. For instance, imagine that the student_id field from our example has the following characteristics:

1. The student id must be numeric.
2. If not known, use a generic student id 111111.
3. The student id must be five or six digits. Numbers between 700,000 and 999,999 are reserved and cannot be used for student id's.

It is easy to satisfy the first characteristic using the regular SQL Server built-in int or smallint datatypes. However, the second two re-

Character data:	*char(n), nchar(n), varchar(n), nvarchar(n), text*
Exact numeric:	*decimals numeric(p,S), decimal(p,S)*
Binary data:	*binary(n), varbinary(n), image*
Integer:	*int, smallint, tinyint*
Floating point:	*float, real, double precision*
Money:	*money, smallmoney*
Date and time:	*datetime, smalldatetime*
Other:	*bit, timestamp, sysname*

Source: *Transact-SQL User's Guide*, Document 32300-01-0491-01, Page 7–13.

Figure 4.6   SQL Server built-in system datatypes.

quirements need tighter control than is available through the normal datatypes. These requirements could either be supported by specific application code or, especially if more than one application can access the table, via SQL Server defaults and rules. Defaults and rules cannot be attached to the built-in datatypes, so a user-defined studentid_type datatype must first be created.

Requirement 2 would best be supported by an SQL Server default. A "default" represents a standard value that will be given to a column if no other value is inserted. The syntax for creating and binding defaults to datatypes is

```
create default default_name
   as constant_expression
sp_bindefault default_name, "datatype"6
```

Requirement 3 would best be supported by an SQL Server rule. A "rule" represents integrity constraints on the values that can be accepted by a column. The syntax for creating and binding rules to datatypes is

---

[6]Sybase provides a number of built-in system procedures, all beginning with sp_, that serve as predefined shortcuts for accomplishing system administration functions. The system procedure **sp_bindefault**, for instance, is simply a stored procedure that attaches one object (the default) to another object (a datatype or column) in the system tables. For the masochistic system administrator, the **sp_bindefault** procedure is not necessary, as it could be replaced by the equivalent SQL commands affecting the database's system tables. For the rest of us, the system procedures help to quickly and accurately perform fairly difficult system table operations and are frequently used in DDL scripts.

```
create rule rule_name
    as constant_expression

sp_bindrule rule_name, "datatype"
```

These two database objects can be added to our original DDL script and revised in Figure 4.7. Note that a default or rule can be bound to either a user-defined datatype or directly to a specific table column. In both cases, the order of commands is important. Both the default/rule and

```
/* Create user-defined datatype */
    sp_addtype studentid_type, "smallint"

/* Create defaults and rules */
    create default studentid_default as 111111
    sp_bindefault  studentid_default, "studentid_type"

    create rule    studentid_rule   as @id between 100000 and 699999
    sp_bindrule    studentid_rule, "studentid_type"

/* Create table and indices */
    create table student_grade                      /*Create the
                                                    table*/

            (student_id        studentid_type,
             student_name      char(25),
             course            char(20),
             term              char(15)
            )

    create clustered index student_id          /*Create the first
                                               (clustered)index*/

        on student_grade (student_id)

    create nonclustered index student_course   /*Create the first
                                               nonclustered index*/

        on student_grade (course,   term)

    create nonclustered index student_name     /*Create the second
                                               nonclustered index*/

        on student_grade (student_name)
```

Figure 4.7   DDL for student_grade table, with rules and defaults.

the object to which it will be bound must exist before using the **sp_bindrule** procedure.

Recall that both defaults and rules are automatically enforced for inserts and updates to the database columns/datatypes to which they are attached—no application code is necessary to enforce the rules. This makes them extremely useful features when more than one application can freely access the database and change the data it contains. There is a tradeoff in response time to enforce these rules, though, so it is common to make only light use of them in single-application databases having a single access point that has been built with an awareness of the rules and that does not rely on their presence to maintain database integrity.

4.3   DATA MANIPULATION COMMANDS

Once a database has been defined using DDL commands, it is time to start working with that data. Standard SQL supports four basic data access commands:

Select allows retrieval of data rows.

Delete allows table rows to be removed.

Insert allows addition of new table rows.

Update allows changing of data rows.

These four commands, which appear deceptively simple at first glance, comprise the core of SQL's "data manipulation language" (DML).

4.3.1   Retrieving Data: The select Command

The **select** command in some ways forms the foundation of the Structured Query Language. It epitomizes SQL's ability to focus on what data is required instead of how it is retrieved. With a single **select** command, it is possible to perform a wide variety of functions, either individually or together, including (but not limited to):

- Retrieving selected columns of a single table
- Reformatting retrieved results, and using computation to create "derived" columns
- Avoiding retrieval of the same column values more than once
- Retrieval of results that relate different tables to each other
- Adding logical constraints that limit the rows that are retrieved
- Automatically reordering retrieved rows
- Producing summary totals of retrieved data

The full syntax of the **select** command is extremely long and complicated, and most everyday uses of the command will only use a relatively limited subset of the clauses, virtually all of which are optional.

In its most common usage, the **select** command is written as

```
select select_list
from table_list
where search_conditions
```

The select_list is a list of columns from tables that can be combined with constants, local Transact-SQL variables, Transact-SQL functions, and mathematical equations. Instead of naming specific columns, using "select * from ..." retrieves all columns from the relevant tables.

The select_list gives an enormous amount of power to combine operations in a single retrieval command. For instance, we could create a (rather perverse) **select** command against our student_grade table that would return a variety of results:

```
select count(*),          /* Total rows in table */
       "rows in table",   /* constant text */
       student_name,      /* column */
       grade / 100,       /* decimal expression of
                             grade */
       max(grade)         /* highest grade value in
                             table */
from student_grade
```

and that would return the following selection of rows, given the data in Figure 4.4 (assuming that 5 records had previously been inserted into the table).

```
5, "rows in table", "Jones", .79, 88
5, "rows in table", "Smith", .67, 88
5, "rows in table", "Smith", .88, 88
5, "rows in table", "Brown", .70, 88
5, "rows in table", "Brown", .80, 88
```

The table_list is a list of tables from which data can be selected. In many cases, particularly when a database has been fully or partially normalized[7], it is not possible to retrieve all of a query's required data

---

[7]Normalization and the five widely accepted normal forms fit into the realm of data modeling, and entire textbooks have been written on the subject. For our purposes, it is enough to say that normalization of a database eliminates data redundancy by isolating data belonging to different classes of items into separate tables.

from a single table. Rather than issuing two **select** commands and merging the results through application code, more than one table can be specified in a **select** command (a **select** command from more than one table is commonly called a "join") and combined results are returned.

To continue our previous example, imagine that there was a requirement to list the names and addresses of all students who took Physics in the Summer 94 session. We notice immediately that student addresses are not stored in the student_grade table. Instead, they are stored in a separate student table that contains extra demographic information:

```
create table student
      (student_id            int,
       student_name          char(25),
       address_line1         char(25),
       address_line2         char(25),
       city                  char(20),
       state_or_province     char(2),
       country               char(20),
       zip_or_postal_code    char(12),
       telephone_number      char(15)
      )
```

There is a common field in both the student and student_grade tables, namely the student_id field. By using SQL joins, it is possible to take advantage of this fact by selecting the students who took Physics in the Summer 94 session from the student_grade table at the same time as the address information from the student table. See Figure 4.8.

```
select  sg.grade,
        st.address_line1,
        st.address_line2,
        st.city,
        st.state_or_province,
        st.country,
        st.zip_or_postal_code
from student_grade sg, student st
where sg.course      = "Physics"
   and sg.term       = "Summer 94"
   and sg.student_id = st.student_id
```

Figure 4.8   Illustration of a table join.

There are two things in particular to notice about this join:

1. It doesn't matter in which order the tables are specified in a join. The Sybase Optimizer will (attempt to) choose the indexes in each table that will make the database work as efficiently as possible.
2. Sybase will not accept a multitable **select** command with an ambiguous select list (i.e., where a column name exists in more than one of the joined tables). For that reason, it is necessary to preface any ambiguous column names with the table name from which Sybase is to take the information. This represents an enhanced syntax of the select_list with columns to be selected expressed as <table_name> <column_name>. It is a good practice to put table name prefixes on all columns in the select list on a join, and the use of table aliases (sg instead of student_grade) makes the code easier to read.

There is another way to select information from more than one table worth mentioning here. A "subquery" is similar to a join, and in some cases the two of them can be used interchangeably. Internally, subqueries effectively perform an initial select and then return the results to a second select, whereas joins create matrices of potentially matching rows from which the final selection batch is created. Although they can be somewhat more difficult to read and understand, subqueries are sometimes the only way to achieve a result. See Figure 4.9.

The search_conditions of a **select** command are where SQL shows some of its true power. Using a series of "where" clauses, it is possible to fine-tune the data that is selected to an astonishing degree.

Search conditions can take many forms, as listed in the table on pages 74–75. While the choice of search conditions may seem imposing (there are other less frequently used ones in addition to those in the table), it is actually possible to get by with a reasonably small subset of the conditions, especially if this can help to make the code more clear or efficient. For instance, a between clause can be replaced with a set of greater-than and less-than clauses, and a list clause can be replaced with a series of equal-to clauses.

Because the **select** command has such sweeping power, it is necessary to consider performance implications in applications that require optimal response times. For example, "select * from student" will have two effects in Sybase: (1) select all the data in the student table and (2) perform a table-level lock, keeping other users from accessing the table until the select is finished. A table lock may be avoided if a select using a where clause is used, as follows:

The select command expressed as a join:

```
select  sg.student_id,
        sg.student_name,
        st.address_line1,
        st.address_line2,
        st.city,
        st.state_or_province,
        st.country,
        st.zip_or_postal_code
from student_grade sg, student st
where sg.course     = "Physics"
  and sg.term       = "Summer 94"
  and sg.student_id = st.student_id
```

The select command from Figure 4.8 as a subquery:

```
select  student_id,
        student_name,
        address_line1,
        address_line2,
        city,
        state_or_province,
        country,
        zip_or_postal_code
from student
where student_id in (select student_id
                     from student_grade
                     where student_grade.course = "Physics"
                     and student_grade.term     = "Summer 94")
```

Figure 4.9   Interchangeable use of a table join and a table subquery.

```
select * from student where city="Florida"
```

(with a clustered index on city).

4.3.2 Adding Data: The insert Command

An obvious prerequisite to selecting data from the database is to have data present in the first place. Data is most commonly added to the database using the **insert** command. Multiple rows may be inserted us-

Type of "where" clause	Syntax	Example
Comparison (=, !=, >, <, etc.)	`WHERE expression comparison_operator expression`	Select the students who scored 80 or more in a course: `select student_id from student_grade where grade > 80`
Ranges (between, not between)	`WHERE expression [NOT] BETWEEN expression AND expression`	Select the students who scored a "B" in a course (70% to 80%): `select student_id from student_grade where grade between 70 and 80`
Lists (in, not in)	`WHERE expression [NOT] IN ({value_list | subquery})`	Select the students who took one of the three science courses offered: `select student_id from student_grade where course in ("Physics", "Chemistry", "Biology")`
Character matches (like, not like)	`WHERE expression [NOT] LIKE "match_string"`	Select all students whose names begin with "Sm": `select student_id from student where student_name like "Sm%"`
Unknown values (is null, is not null)	`WHERE column_name is [NOT] NULL`	Select the students without a zip/postal code on the database: `select student_id from student where zip_or_postal_code is NULL`

Type of "where" clause	Syntax	Example
Combinations of these (and, or)	`WHERE` `boolean_expression` `{AND	OR}` `boolean_expression`	Select the students who took a science course, whose names begin with "Sm", and who scored better than 80% on a course: `select student_id from` `student_grade where` `course in ("Physics",` `"Chemistry",` `"Biology") and grade >` `80 and student_name` `like "Sm%"`

ing an **insert-select** command, or single rows using the **insert values** command. Taking advantage of defaults attached to the target tables columns, it is also possible to insert values for only certain columns of the table, with the remaining values either taking their datatype's system or user-defined default, or holding a value of NULL (i.e., having no value[8]).

Insert-Select Sometimes it is useful to load one table based on the contents of another one. For instance, the creation of a telephone_directory table could require the loading of student information from our previous

---

[8]Relational database experts have been debating the place of NULL in SQL for many years. Many of them, including C. J. Date, have proposed eliminating NULL from SQL because of the logical complexities that it introduces into the language. Joe Celko, a current member of the ANSI SQL committee, has argued for more stringent processing rules relating to NULL values. In some ways, the debate over NULL is reminiscent of the way in which mathematicians deal with infinity (∞): Most people agree that it is a useful concept, but what does it mean? For instance, what about these questions?

- How can you have ∞ items?
- Does ∞ equal ∞? Under what circumstances?
- What is the value of ∞ plus one?
- Can you add anything to infinity?

- What does it mean for an item to have a color of NULL?
- Does NULL equal NULL? Under what circumstances?
- What is the value of NULL concatenated with "ABC"?
- Can you concatenate anything to NULL?

```
create table telephone_directory              /* Create the table */
       (name                      char (25),
        telephone_number          char (15)
       )

insert telephone_directory             /* Load the table with student
info */
   select student_name, telephone_number
   from student
   where telephone_number is not NULL      /* Exclude students with
unknown phone numbers */
```

Figure 4.10   Using the **insert-select** command to load one table from another one.

example. Rather than using application logic to select students one at a time and insert them into the telephone directory table, a single **insert-select** command can do the job effectively, as shown in Figure 4.10. Its syntax borrows heavily from that of an ordinary **select** command:

```
insert table_name
select select_list
from table_list
where search_conditions
```

Insert Values Although useful in particular circumstances, the **insert-select** command is usually not adequate for all of an application's needs since it only shuffles data between tables rather than adding new data to the database. For that purpose, the **insert values** command is much more appropriate.

A simplified syntax for the **insert values** command is as follows:

```
insert table_name (column list)
values                 (value list)
```

Since it is not mandatory to supply a column list, the insertion of a single student record could be coded as:

```
insert student
values (526389,         /* student_id */
        "Smith",        /* student_name */
```

```
    "123 Any Street",        /* address_line1 */
    "",                  /* address_line2 */
    "Banff",             /* city */
    "Alberta",           /* state_or_province */
    "Canada",            /* country */
    "",                  /* zip_or_postal_code */
    "",                  /* telephone_number */
    )
```

Note, though, that this example assumes we did not have values for three columns: address_line2, zip_or_postal_code, and telephone_number. If we assume the datatypes for these columns have defaults assigned to them that will come into play if no value is given, the **insert values** command can be more specific as to the column data being provided by using a column list:

```
insert student
        (student_id,
         student_name,
         address_line1,
         city,
         state_or_province,
         country)
values (526389,          /* student_id */
        "Smith",         /* student_name */
        "123 Any Street",    /* address_line1 */
        "Banff",         /* city */
        "Alberta",       /* state_or_province */
        "Canada"         /* country */
        )
```

The column list is useful for specifying only certain columns that will take values. It also allows the value list to be provided in any order, so long as it conforms to the order of columns in the column list.

4.3.3 Changing Data: The update Command

The **update** command is used to change the values of specified columns of table rows in the database. The **update** command is similar to the insert command in that each has two formats: one dealing only with the target table and another that relies on data from other tables.

The regular **update** command changes column values on rows that are specified using a where clause identical to that of the **select** command. Its simplified syntax reads as follows:

```
update table
set column_name = expression
 [,column_name = expression]...
where search_conditions
```

Note that the number of columns updated by a single command may vary, and is limited for practical purposes only to the number of columns in the target table.

As in the **insert** statement, the expression may be a constant value, a local variable from a stored procedure, another column name, a function, or a calculated value, and each set clause can use a different type of expression.

The **update** command can act on zero, one, or more rows at the same time, depending on the size of the table and the search_conditions specified. It is not illegal to issue an **update** command that affects no rows, nor is it a problem to issue an **update** command that affects all rows in a table. In a stored procedure, it is often critical to know how many rows were actually affected, and SQL Server provides a global variable called @@rowcount that always contains the number of rows affected by the previous command. When updating a table, for instance, it is common to check the @@rowcount value after the update and, if it is zero (implying that no rows were found to update), to either issue an error or branch to an **insert** command to create the desired row. See Figure 4.11.

The update from format of the **update** command is less frequently used but can be extremely useful when the rows to be updated need to be determined with reference to other tables. It uses a syntax reminiscent of the joined **select** command:

```
update table
set column_name = expression
 [,column_name = expression]...
from table_list
where search_conditions
```

The table_list can theoretically contain one or more tables, although there is little point in including it unless at least two tables are specified. For instance, an amiable Physics professor could add compliments to the records of every student who passed his course with honors (a grade of 80% or better):

An update affecting no rows: Change the province of all students in "Toronto" and "New York" to "ON":

```
update student
set state_or_province - "ON"
where city = "Toronto"   /* Of course, a student
cannot reside in both */
    and city = "New York"   /* Toronto and New York at
the same time. */
```

An update affecting one row: Change the state of student number 123456 to "NY":

```
update student
set state_or_province = "NY"
where student_id = 123456   /* Assuming student_id
is a unique index */
```

An update affecting some rows: Change the province of all students whose telephone numbers start with 403 to "AB":

```
update student
set state_or_province = "AB"
where telephone_number like "403%"
```

An update affecting all rows in a table: Change all student records to generic values:

```
    update student          /* Without a where clause,
all records */
                            /* in the table are updated */
    set student_name        = "John Doe",
        address_line1       = "123 Any Street",
        address_line2       = ""
        city                = "Anytown",
        state_or_province   = "AN",
        country             = "Erewhon",
        zip_or_postal_code  = "11111"
        telephone_number    = "555-1212"
```

Figure 4.11   **Update** commands affecting various numbers of table rows.

```
update student
set student.student_name  = student. student_name +
" (genius)",
                          /* "+" is a concatenation
operator */
    student.address_line2 = "Genius Gardens"
from student, student_grade
where student.student_id  = student_grade.student_id
/* link the two tables */
  and student_grade.course = "Physics"
/* identify the course */
  and student_grade.term   = "Summer 94"
/* identify the term */
  and student_grade.grade  < 80    /* identify
students who passed with honors */
```

4.3.4   Removing Data: The delete Command

Once data has been inserted into the database, updated in the database, and selected from the database, the time may come when it is no longer needed. In this case, the **delete** command is used to remove rows from a table. As with the **update** command, it can delete rows independently from a table based on search conditions, or delete rows based on data in other tables.

The regular syntax for the **delete** command is

```
delete table
where search_conditions
```

Note that no column names are specified in the **delete** command, since only entire rows can be deleted from a table—it does not make sense to speak of deleting specific columns.[9] However, any number of columns, from zero to all columns in the table[10], can be deleted using a single command, with the @@rowcount available to check the actual number of rows affected after execution.

If the deletion conditions for a given table depend on data in other

---

[9]Although individual columns, depending on their definition in the table, can be set to NULL using an **update** command.

[10]The quickest way to delete all of the rows in a table is the "truncate table *table_name*" command, which uses a more efficient transaction logging method than the **delete** command and can take much less time for large tables.

tables, the *delete from* command is very useful. Its syntax is similar to the update from in the last section:

```
delete table
from table_list
where search_conditions
```

Our amiable professor, not being satisfied with adding compliments to the students who passed Physics with honors, could decide to delete them entirely from the database (under the assumption that they no longer need to go to school!):

```
delete student
from student, student_grade
where student.student_id = student_grade.student_id
/* link the two tables */
and student_grade.course = "Physics"
/* identify the course */
and student_grade.term   = "Summer 94"
/* identify the term */
and student_grade.grade < 80      /* identify
students who passed with honors */
```

4.4   SUMMARY

In this chapter, we have reviewed the major data definition and data manipulation commands in SQL. While not an exhaustive survey, the commands and examples here represent all of the basic building blocks necessary to create and use databases in SQL Server. They also illustrate the beauty and simplicity of the Transact-SQL language, with its common and intuitive syntax to handle a wide variety of reasonably complex transaction requirements.

The freedom from procedural logic represented by SQL not only simplifies application coding, but it also facilitates the client/server separation of presentation and data platforms by establishing a logical rather than physical protocol for accessing data. It is not necessary to know the actual physical location of a given table in order to read it, nor is it necessary to know of the physical layout of fields and indexes, since SQL takes care of those requirements internally.

It is worthwhile to mention here that the power of SQL can also represent a pitfall for the novice (or even experienced!) programmer. For instance, imagine a table called stock_trade that contains details about, say, one million trading transactions. The four-word command "select * from stock_trade" would be enough to bring just about any system to its knees! When coding data manipulation commands, it is crucial to ask the following types of questions:

- How many rows do I expect to be affecting?
- If I am affecting many rows, have I considered the table-locking implications while my command runs?
- Will I be using an index? Which one?
- If I am not using an index, is a slow table scan acceptable?
- Do I need to join tables, or can this requirement be satisfied by a single-table operation?

The increased power of SQL over data manipulation in traditional 3GL languages goes hand in hand with an increased ability to misuse the commands and cause serious performance problems in applications of any significant size.

Built-In Functions

In this chapter a reader will learn about:

- Different classes of built-in functions
- String functions
- Date/time functions
- Mathematical functions
- Converting between datatypes
- General functions

5.1 OVERVIEW OF BUILT-IN FUNCTIONS

Transact-SQL offers a rich set of built-in functions that can be used alongside standard SQL queries (i.e., as part of a select), interactively, or in stored procedures. Built-in functions are also referred to as "system" functions.

Built-in functions are generally used to retrieve information from Sybase tables or to manipulate the format of data. Built-in functions can be divided into five categories: (1) string, (2) date/time, (3) mathematical, (4) convert, and (5) general. This chapter discusses the commonly used functions that fit into each of these categories.

5.2 USING BUILT-IN FUNCTIONS

Functions can be used to enhance the flexibility of ANSI SQL commands. For example, in Figure 5.1 a command selects a telephone number from a database. This command retrieves information similar to

```
select telephone from address
    where customer_id = 123
```

Figure 5.1   Select from a database.

```
- - - - - - - - - - -
915-813-9292

(1 row affected)
```

Figure 5.2   Returned information.

```
select substring (telephone,1,3)
    from address
        where customer_id = 123
```

Figure 5.3   Using **substring** in a select.

```
- - -
915

(1 row affected)
```

Figure 5.4   Returned information.

```
select @area_code = substring(@telephone,  1, 3)
if @region = '915'
    select 'customer lives in discount area'
```

Figure 5.5   Functions and stored procedures.

that shown in Figure 5.2. It is possible to use a built-in function to fine-tune data after it is retrieved from the database but before it is presented to the requester. This is done in Figure 5.3 with a built-in function called **substring**. Given a telephone number of 915-812-9292, the previous command would retrieve the information shown in Figure 5.4. Functions can also be used to manipulate data held in local variables within stored procedures, as shown in Figure 5.5.

Users can use functions alongside Transact-SQL commands that are issued interactively, as shown in Figure 5.6. To test the examples in this figure, the reader should only type the SQL Server command, and not the Sybase prompt (i.e., 1> or 2>, etc.).

5.3   STRING FUNCTIONS

String functions are primarily applied to data that is in char or varchar format. Data in other formats can be converted to either of these datatypes to allow the use of string functions.

Syntax and examples for the commonly used string functions follow. These examples are based on the Video Rental Store management data model described in Chapter 17.

Note: In order to test the examples, they should be embedded inside standard Transact SQL code, as follows:

```
select function
go
```

The user should also be logged into SQL Server with the isql command (i.e., isql -Uuserid -Ppassword -Sservername). Before running

```
C> isql -Usa -P
>
1>use video
2>go
1>select substring (video_name, 1, 10)
   from video
2>go
1>select getdate()
2>go
```

Figure 5.6   Interactive function use.

this command set the SYBASE environment variable to the directory containing sybase (i.e., setenv SYBASE /prod/sybase).

```
i.e. select upper ("sector")
go
result: SECTOR.
```

5.3.1   ascii

Returns the ASCII value of the first character in parameter.

Syntax

```
declare parameter    char(30)
ascii (parameter)
```

Examples

a. ascii ("A")

b. select @char_a = ascii ("A")

c. select ascii ("A")
go

result: 65

5.3.2   charindex

Searches for an occurrence of parameter1 inside parameter2. The function returns the starting position of the occurrence of parameter1 inside parameter2, if it is found.

Syntax

```
declare parameter1    char(30)
declare parameter2    char(30)
charindex (parameter1,  parameter2)
```

Examples

a. select charindex ("of", "Blazing balls of fire
lashed from the planet surface")
go

result: 15

b. select @search_string = "of"
select @story = "Blazing balls of fire lashed from
the planet surface"

select @position = charindex (@search_string,
@story)

result: 15   (incorporate this code in a stored
procedure to test it.)

5.3.3   char_length

Returns the number of characters stored in parameter1.

Syntax

char_length (parameter1)

Examples

a. select char_length ("The Empire Strikes Back")
go

result: 23

b. select @movie_title = "The Empire Strikes Back"
select @count = char_length (@movie_title)

result: 23

5.3.4   Concatenation (+)

Used to concatenate two or more strings.

Syntax

declare parameter1   char(30)

declare parameter2   char(30)

parameter1 + parameter2

Examples

a. select @movie_title =

"Star Wars " + "The Empire Strikes Back"

b. select @movie_title =

```
            "Star Wars " + "The Empire Strikes Back" +
      " Part 2"
c.    select @title1 = "Star Wars"

      select @title2 = "The Empire Strikes Back"

      select @title3 = "Part 2"

      select @space = " "

      select @movie_title =
                    @title1 + @space + @title2 + @space +
      @title3
d.    select "War and" + " " + "Peace"
      go

      result: War and Peace
e.    select '"War and' + " " + 'Peace"'
      go

      result: "War and Peace"
```

5.3.5   lower

All characters within parameter1 will be changed to lowercase.

Syntax

```
declare parameter1     char(30)

lower (parameter1)
```

Examples

a. `lower (@name) /* assume 'name' contains 'RaqaEl' */`

    `result: 'raqael'`

b. `lower ('RaqaEl')`

    `result: raqael`

c. `select lower(name),  lower(address)  from customer`

d. `select lower ("SECTOR")`
    `go`

    `result: sector`

5.3.6   ltrim

Remember that the "l" stands for "leading" or "left." This function, consequently, strips leading blanks.

Syntax

```
declare parameter1    char(30)
ltrim (parameter1)
```

Examples

a.
```
select ltrim ('   RaqaEl   ')
go
```
```
result: 'RaqaEl   '
```

b.
```
select ltrim(lower(name))   from customer
```

5.3.7   replicate

The term "counter" specifies the number of times the string stored in parameter1 is to be replicated, up to a maximum size of 255.

Syntax:

```
declare parameter1    char(30)
declare counter       int
replicate (parameter1, counter)
```

Examples

a.
```
replicate ('-', 5)
go
```
```
result:    '-----'
```

b.
```
select 'The answer is'
select replicate ('-',13)
select @name
```

c.
```
select replicate ('0',10)
go
```
```
result: - - - - - - - - - -
          0 0 0 0 0 0 0 0 0 0
```

5.3.8   right

Similar to **substring**; **right** uses the integer value stored in counter as an offset from the right side of the character string stored in parameter1, and returns that position along with the remainder of the string to the left of that position for the length specified.

Syntax

```
declare parameter1    char(80)
declare counter       int
right (parameter1, counter)
```

Examples

a. `select right ("Blazing balls of fire lashed", 5)`
`go`

`result: "ashed"`

b. `right (@story, 5)`

5.3.9   rtrim

Similar to **ltrim**. The leading "r" in **rtrim** stands for "right." This function removes trailing blanks from the string provided as parameter1.

Syntax

```
declare parameter1 char(30)
rtrim (parameter1)
```

Examples

a. `rtrim ('    RaqaEl   ')`

`result: '    RaqaEl'`

b. `select rtrim(lower(name))    from customer`

c. `select rtrim (' Jack and    ') + '' + ltrim(' Jill ')`
`go`

`result:    Jack and Jill`

5.3.10   space

A string containing blanks is returned. The number of blanks is specified in parameter1.

Syntax

```
declare parameter1    int
space (parameter1)
```

Examples

a. `space (15)`

b. `space (3)`

c. `select @first_name, space(16), @last_name`

d. `select 'Jack' + space(5) + 'Jill'`
`go`

`result:    Jack    Jill`

5.3.11   substring

This invaluable function is used to parse strings into substrings. This function is commonly used to extract specific information of fixed length from a larger pool of information.

Syntax

```
declare parameter1    char(80)
declare begin         int
declare size          int
substring (parameter1, begin, size)
```

Examples

a. `select substring ("Blazing balls of fire", 9, 5)`
`go`

`result: balls`

b. `substring (@story, 9, 5)`

c. `select substring (phone, 1, 3) from customer`
   `result:     416`

5.3.12   upper

All characters within parameter1 will be changed to uppercase.

Syntax
```
declare parameter1    char(30)
upper (parameter1)
```

Examples

a. `upper (@name) /* assume 'name' contains 'RaqaEl' */`
   `result:     returns 'RAQAEL'`

b. `upper ('RaqaEl')`
   `result: RAQAEL`

c. `select upper(name), upper(address) from customer`

Variations These functions can be nested. For example, it is possible to concatenate and capitalize strings as follows:

```
upper(@title1 + @title2)
```

5.4   DATE/TIME FUNCTIONS

Transact SQL extensions offer comprehensive date/time functions. A user makes two choices in order to use a date/time function: (1) the date/time function, and (2) the date/time format. Available date/time functions are organized into three classes.

5.4.1   getdate: Current Date/Time

Returns the current system date/time.

Syntax
```
getdate()
```

Examples

a.
```
select @current_date = getdate()
select @current_date
go
```

```
result:  Mar 4 1992 11:57AM
```

b.
```
select @current_date = upper(getdate())
```

c.
```
select video_name, getdate() from video
```

d.
```
select getdate()
go
```

```
returns: Jan 18 1944  6:02 PM
```

5.4.2   Date/Time Format Manipulation

Two functions allow the retrieval of specific components of a date (e.g., day of the week or year). Using either of these also requires specification of a specific component. Components that can be specified with these functions are: year (yy), quarter (qq), month (mm), dayofyear (dy), day (dd), week (wk), weekday (dw), hour (hh), minute (mi), second (ss), and millisecond (ms). Either the full name or the abbreviation shown in round brackets can be used as the component. This is shown in the examples below.

The two date/time format manipulation functions follow.

datename This function retrieves the part of the full_date that corresponds to the component specified in the command. The result is displayed in ASCII format.

Syntax

```
datename(component,  full_date)
```

Examples

a.
```
select datename (day, "October 2, 1993 12:01")
go
```

```
result:    2
```

b.
```
datename (month, "October 2, 1993 12:01")
```

```
result:    October
```

c. `datename (minute, "October 2, 1993 12:01")`

`result:     01`

datepart Similar to **datename**, except results are returned in integer format.

Syntax

`datepart(component,   full_date)`

Examples

a. `select datepart (month, "October 2, 1993 12:01")`
`go`

`result:     10`

b. `datepart (month, getdate())`

`result:     10 (assume that current date is October 2, 1993)`

c. `declare @current_date    datetime`

`select @current_date = getdate()`

`datepart(month, @current_date)`

`result:     10`

5.4.3   Date/Time Calculations

Two functions allow dates to be added or subtracted from other dates. These functions consider events like leap year.

datediff This function returns the difference between date2 and date1 (i.e., date2 - date1) in the component that is selected.

Syntax

`datediff (component, date1, date2)`

Examples

a. `@years = datediff (year, "Jan 1, 1980 00:00",`
`getdate())`

`result:     13 (assuming it is currently 1993)`

b. `@days = datediff (day, "September 28, 1993 00:00",`
`getdate())`

c. `@days = datediff (day, "September 28, 1993 00:00",`
`        "September 20, 1993 00:00")`

`result:    2`

dateadd Units is added to date in the indicated component.

Syntax

`dateadd (component, units, date)`

Examples

a. `select dateadd (day, 2, "October 2, 1993 00:00")`
`go`

`result:    Oct 4, 1993 00:00AM`

b. `dateadd (year, -1, "October 2, 1993 00:00")`

`result:    Oct 2, 1992 12:00AM`

c. `dateadd (minute, 5, "October 2, 1993 00:00")`

`result:    Oct 2, 1993 12:05AM`

d. `dateadd (minute, 4, "October 2, 1993 4:40PM")`

`result:    Oct 2, 1993 4:44PM`

e. `dateadd (minute, 5, "October 2, 1993 16:40")`

`result:    Oct 2, 1993 4:44AM`

5.5   MATHEMATICAL FUNCTIONS

Transact-SQL supports the mathematical functions that are offered by many commercially available spreadsheets and handheld calculators. The table on pages 96–97 identifies these functions.

5.6   CONVERT

SQL Server implicitly converts some datatypes to others in calculations or comparisons (e.g., tinyint and int in a compute clause). Other datatypes must be explicitly converted to a compatible datatype in these

Function	Description	Example	Result
abs	absolute value	select abs(-5) go	5
acos	cosine	select acos(0) go	1.570796
asin	arc sine	select asin(0) go	0.000000
atan	arc tan	select atan(0) go	0.000000
atn2	arc tan2	select atn2(0,3) go	0.000000
ceiling	rounds to the next nearest integer	select ceiling(3.2122) go	4
cos	cosine	select cos(90) go select cos(45) go	-0.448074 0.525322
cot	cotangent	select cot(45) go	0.617370
degrees	radians to degrees	select degrees(1) go	57
exp	exponential (e)	select exp(2) go	7.389056
floor	rounds to the previous nearest integer	select(3.2122) go	3
log	natural logarithm	select log(10) go	2.302585
log10	base 10 log	select log10(10) go	1.000000
power	variable to the power	select power(2,3) go	8
rand	random floating point value (between 0 and 1)	select rand() go select rand() go select rand() go	0.074955 0.760524 0.126335

Function	Description	Example	Result
sign	determines the sign of a variable	select sign(-9) go	-1
		select sign(9) go	1
sin	sine	select sin(90) go	0.893997
tan	tan	select tan(90) go	-1.995200
sqrt	square root	select sqrt(9) go	3.000000
round	rounds to the specified precision	select round(3.2345,1) go	3.2000
		select round(3.67345,1) go	3.70000
pi	pi	select pi() go	3.141593

operations using the **convert** command. Parameter1 is converted to the specified datatype.

Syntax

```
convert (datatype, parameter1)
```

Examples

a.
```
declare @current_date    datetime
declare @display_date    char(25)
select @display_date = convert (char(20),
@current_date)
```

Result:　　Oct 4 1994 5:00PM

b.
```
declare @age    int
select @age = 22
select "Amanda's age is " + convert(char(5), @age)
```

Result:　　Amanda's Age is 22

5.7   GENERAL FUNCTIONS

Transact SQL offers some general-purpose functions that readers will
find useful.

5.7.1   col_length

Returns the length in bytes of the column within the table of the default
database. This refers to the maximum size of data that can be contained
within the column.

Syntax

```
col_length (table_name, column_name)
```

Examples

a. `col_length ("video", "subject")`

b. `select @length = col_length ("video", "subject")`

c.
```
use pubs2
go
sp_help stores
go
select col_length("stores","stor_id")
go

result:    4
```

d.
```
use master
go
select col_length ("pubs2.dbo.stores","stor_id")
go

result:    4
```

5.7.2   datalength

Returns the length, in bytes, of the data stored in parameter1.

Syntax

```
datalength (parameter1)
```

Examples

a. `datalength (@current_date)`

    b. `datalength (@age)`

    c. `datalength ("Royalty stood before them. Tall,`
       `powerful...");`

5.7.3   db_id

Returns the database ID for the database name provided in parameter1. This information is stored in the sysdatabases table in the **master** database.

Syntax

```
db_id (parameter1)
```

Examples

a. `db_id ("sector_db")`

b. `select db_id ("vms_db")`

c. `select db_id ("pubs2")`
   `go`

5.7.4   db_name

Returns the database name for the database ID provided in parameter1. This information is stored in the sysdatabases table in the **master** database. The command can also be used to display the name of the current (default) database.

Syntax

```
db_name (parameter1)
```

Examples

a. `db_name (4)`

b. `select db_name (5)`
   `go`

c. `/* displays the database name of the current data-`
   `base */`
   `use model`
   `go`
   `select db_name()`
   `go`

```
Result:   - - - - - - - - - - - - - - - - - - - - - - - - - - - - -
          model
```

5.7.5   isnull

Table columns and variables are often initialized with a value of NULL. In Sybase, NULL means that the corresponding field is empty or has no value. Such fields cannot be used in calculations. The **isnull** function specifies that parameter1 is substituted into the variable_name if it has a value of NULL.

Syntax

```
isnull (variable_name, parameter1)
```

Examples

a. `select isnull(@price1, 3.00) + isnull(@price2, 5)`

b. `select abs ( isnull(@tolerance, 2) )`

5.7.6   object_id

Returns the object id corresponding to the object name supplied to the function.

Syntax

```
object_id (parameter1)
```

Examples

a. `object_id ("video")`

b. `object_id ("customer")`

c.
```
use pubs2
go
select object_id ("stores")
go
result:    240003886
```

5.7.7   object_name

Returns the object name corresponding to the object id supplied to the function.

Syntax

```
object_name (parameter1)
```

Example

a. `object_name (1500006799)`

b.
```
use pubs2
go
select object_name (240003886)
go
```
```
result:    stores
```

5.7.8   suser_name

Returns login name of current user.

Syntax

```
suser_name ()
```

Example

```
select suser_name ()
go
```
```
result:    Sa
```

5.7.9   suser_id

Returns id of current user.

Syntax

```
suser_id ()
```

Example

```
select suser_id ()
go
```
```
result:    55
```

5.7.10   user_id

Returns user id corresponding to the name entered as a parameter.

Syntax

```
user_id (parameter1)
```

Example

```
select user_id ("video")
go
```

5.7.11   user_name

Returns user name corresponding to the uid entered as a parameter.

Syntax

```
user_name (parameter1)
```

Example

```
select user_name (500)
go
```

5.8   SUMMARY

This chapter focused on built-in functions in Transact-SQL. Examples of usage were provided for five common categories: string, date/time, mathematical, convert, and general. These functions can be used interactively, inside stored procedures, and be freely nested. To use these functions interactively, the reader should sign on to SQL Server, type the function beside the SQL Server prompt, and type go. This is shown in the following sequence of commands.

Inside the operating system, type the following:

```
> setenv   SYBASE   /path
  /* where path is the location of the sybase SQL
Server directory */
> setenv   DSQUERY   SYBASE_NAME
  /* where SYBASE_NAME is the server name in the
     INTERFACES file */
> isql   -Uuserid   -Ppassword
  /* where isql is a program stored in the SYBASE/bin
     directory where userid and password are accounts
     set up in SQL Server */
SQL Server responds with the Sybase prompt, as follows:
1>
```

Inside SQL Server, type the following.

```
1> select function_name_parameter list
2> go
```

Review results.

To use these functions in a stored procedure, refer to Chapter 6.

6

Stored Procedures

In this chapter a reader will learn about:

- Benefits of using stored procedures
- Creating stored procedures
- Compiling stored procedures
- Invoking stored procedures
- Passing parameters to stored procedures
- Remote procedure calls (RPCs)
- Set command

6.1 OVERVIEW OF STORED PROCEDURES

Sybase, Inc. pioneered stored procedures in the first release of SQL Server in 1987. Stored procedures have grown in popularity since then. Several other vendors have incorporated them into their database server products (e.g., Oracle Version 7). Stored procedures are conceptually similar to traditional programs. They are designed and developed in much the same way as C or Pascal programs. Methods such as modularization and top-down design apply equally to writing well-structured stored procedures as they do to third-generation programming languages.

The programming code inside stored procedures can consist of ANSI SQL commands such as **select**, **update**, **create**, and **delete**. Stored procedures can also contain objects and commands in the Transact-SQL set such as functions for string manipulation, date/time functions, and mathematical functions. SQL Server supports a "control-of-flow" language (commands such as if . . . else, begin . . . end, and while) that allows the development of modular programs with conditional, repeating logic, and the use of local variables. This language is discussed in the following chapter.

A stored procedure can be created by following a sequence of simple steps. A stored procedure is first coded using an ANSI text editor (e.g., Brief, EMACS, QuickC, TurboC, and WordPerfect, so long as the file is saved as DOS output). The stored procedure is then "compiled" into a database data dictionary. This involves several system tables in the current database. Key information about the stored procedure is saved in the sysobjects table. The corresponding source code is saved in the

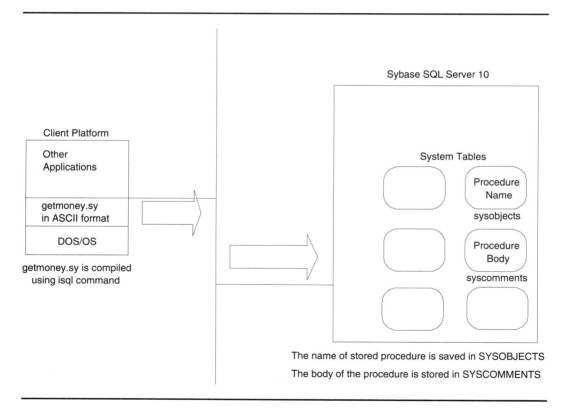

Figure 6.1   Creating stored procedures.

syscomments table. An optimized execution plan (parse tree) is saved in the sysprocedures table.

Following a successful compilation, a stored procedure can be invoked by issuing a single name and an optional parameter list. These steps are shown in Figure 6.1.

A compiled stored procedure can be invoked interactively or in batch mode. As shown in Figure 6.2, a single **exec** command causes many Transact-SQL commands to be executed on the server platform.

6.2 WHY STORED PROCEDURES?

As a prelude to answering this question, consider two alternative strategies for complex manipulation of data within a database server environment.

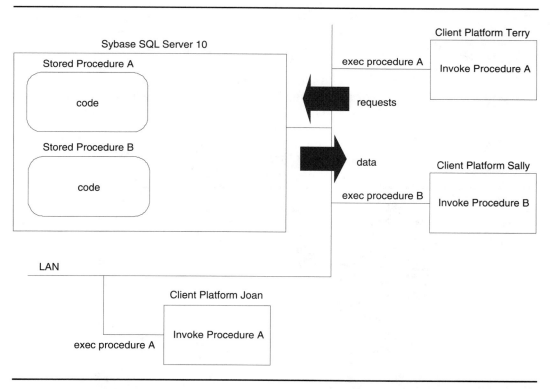

Figure 6.2   Executing stored procedures.

6.2.1 Interactive Transact-SQL Commands

Users can issue **isql** commands to access database tables to initiate inquiries, updates, deletions, and so forth. This could involve accessing multiple tables, and may involve instances where an action is repeated until some condition is reached, or some action is taken depending on a condition. Without stored procedures, a user would be required to re-key a potentially long series of commands every time an activity is desired. Not only is this cumbersome but many types of activities just cannot be done this way (i.e., accept parameters from a program running on a client platform). Readers who have written programs themselves will realize how difficult or frustrating it is to type hundreds of successive keystrokes without making a mistake.

6.2.2 Embedding Transact-SQL Commands

A host language interface (e.g., for C or Pascal) can be used by a client to communicate with SQL Server through embedded SQL calls. Transact-SQL commands can be sent to the SQL Server using this interface. Without stored procedures, this would be done by sending one SQL command at a time to the server across a network. This is shown in Figure 6.3 for an imaginary host language.

The client program sends these commands whenever the function is required, which requires SQL Server to parse and optimize the string of commands with every execution.

```
START BUFFER
 exec send "select 100"
 exec send "select * from customer"
 exec send "where customer_id = '15DOS' and "
  /*D is domestic*/
 exec send "customer_type = 'D'"
 exec send "if @@rowcount = 0"
 exec send "select -10"
 exec send "else"
 exec send "select 10"
 exec send "return"
 exec send "go"
SEND BUFFER
```

Figure 6.3   Example of individual SQL commands.

6.2.3 The Stored Procedure Method

Stored procedures run faster, on average, than the other methods discussed because of a two-part compile and optimization method. A stored procedure is precompiled into a database's data dictionary (syscomments and sysprocedures tables). The first time a stored procedure is invoked, the Sybase Optimizer calculates an optimized query plan based on the contents of the sysprocedures table. The query plan is loaded to cache (if it was not there before) and used on subsequent executions of the stored procedure. The query plan may be flushed from the cache after a period of disuse of the stored procedure or due to contention for cache space.

If multiple users run the same stored procedure at the same time, each may generate their own query plan based on parameters entered with the stored procedure. The two alternatives that were presented earlier do not offer this facility to improve response time. Figure 6.4 illustrates the steps required to build and invoke a stored procedure.

A program running on a client platform can retrieve customers by invoking the **get_customer** stored procedure with a single command.

```
*****************************************
* This code creates a stored procedure*
* called get_customer.               *
*****************************************
create proc get_customer
(
  @cust_id char(6),
  @cust_type char(1)
)
as
  select 100
  select * from customer
    where customer_id = @cust_id and
    customer_type = @cust_type

  if@@rowcount= 0
    select - 10
  else
    select 10
  return
go
```

Figure 6.4   Building a stored procedure.

```
exec get_customer '15DOS', 'D'
go
```

Figure 6.5   Invoking a stored procedure with parameters.

Furthermore, the ability to pass parameters to the stored procedure allows it to be flexible. This is demonstrated in Figure 6.5.

Controlling network traffic is a key factor in building efficient and effective client/server-based solutions. Network traffic affects (1) the cost and capacity of the network hardware; (2) system response time; and (3) reliability.

Stored procedures reduce network traffic in two ways. The first way occurs when queries are initiated by a client platform. Only a single **exec** command needs to travel over a network to cause many Transact-SQL commands to be executed on the server platform. But network traffic does not flow in one direction only. The data volume that is returned by a database server in response to a query should also be optimized. This is the second way that stored procedures reduce network traffic. Since stored procedures support extensive programming constructs such as if, while, and switch, it is possible to include comprehensive validation and referential logic inside a procedure. If designed properly, the stored procedure can act as a funnel or filter—taking in lots of data, massaging it in some way, and returning only the relevant data to the calling client. Since network transfer rates are often a bottleneck in system response time, using a stored procedure as a filter is preferable to having a database server return large volumes of data to the client and subsequently using a third-generation language to do the data manipulation on the client platform.

6.3   COMPONENTS OF A STORED PROCEDURE

A stored procedure has the components shown in Figure 6.6.

A stored procedure has the basic program skeleton shown in Figure 6.7.

There is some flexibility in the syntax shown in Figure 6.7. For example, this stored procedure could also have been written as shown in Figure 6.8 (note the subtlety of the changes).

6.4   COMPILING A STORED PROCEDURE

Stored procedure code is stored in ASCII files. The preceding figures show that the name of the stored procedure is included beside the **create**

→ a name
→ optional parameter list
→ local/global variables
→ Transact-SQL commands (e.g., select, update, functions, convert, if, while, begin..end, et cetera)
→ Calls to other stored procedures
→ return

Figure 6.6   Pieces of a stored procedure.

```
/************************************************
A Stored Procedure has the following basic layout
************************************************/

/* The keywords in the syntax are highlighted */
create proc procedure_name

(
    @parameter_name1        datatype,   /* parameters in */
    @parameter_name2        datatype,
    @parameter_name3        datatype output
)
as
    /* local variable declarations */
    declare @local_variable1    datatype
    declare @local_variable2    datatype
    declare @local_variable3    datatype
    declare @status             int

    /* initializations */
    select @local_variable = 1
    select @local_variable = 'T'

    /* Programming Logic */
        Transact-SQL statements

    /* nested calls to other stored procedures */
    exec @status = other_procedure @parameters_name2

    return @status
go
```

Figure 6.7   Stored procedure skeleton.

```
/***********************************************
A Stored Procedure has the following basic layout
***********************************************/

/* The keywords in the syntax are highlighted */
create proc procedure_name
    @parameter_name1      datatype,  /* parameters in */
    @parameter_name2      datatype,
    @parameter_name3      datatype output
as
    /* local variable declarations */
    declare @local_variable1      datatype,
            @local_variable2      datatype,
            @local_variable3      datatype,
            @status               int

    /* initializations */
    select @local_variable1 = 1,
           @local_variable2 = 'T'

    /* Programming Logic */
      Transact-SQL statements

    /* nested calls to other stored procedures */
    exec @status = other_procedure @parameters_name2


    select @status
go
```

Figure 6.8   Alternative syntax.

proc command. This is generally not the name used for the ASCII file
that contains the stored procedure code. The name of this file is used to
compile a stored procedure into a data dictionary. The name of a stored
procedure is used to execute it. Many stored procedures can be contained
inside a single source file; consequently, a compile of a source file can
result in compiles of more than one stored procedure. See Figure 6.9.

In this figure, the stored procedures contained within filename are
compiled into the default database of the userid/password. Alternatively, add the commands (**use video**, **go**) prior to the **create proc**
command and, assuming the userid has authority to access the video
database, the stored procedure will be compiled into it.

Syntax:

```
isql -Uuserid -Ppassword -ifilename - O optional_output_file
where  -i is followed by the filename containing Sybase commands
       -O is only used to pipe the output display into an ASCII file
```

or

```
isql -Uuserid -Ppassword -Rfilename (on some machines)
where -R is equivalent to -i
```

Figure 6.9   Compiling stored procedures.

6.5   EXECUTING A STORED PROCEDURE

After a stored procedure has been compiled into the data dictionary of a database, it can be executed by using the name of the procedure and supplying an optional parameter list. Four methods for doing this follow.

6.5.1   Interactively

The reader should recall that the following command is used to login to SQL Server and a specific database:

```
isql -Udbname -Pdbname -Sservername
```

Specifically, for the Video Rental Store application used in the tutorial (Chapter 17), the dbname in the sysdatabases table in the **master** database is **video**. The server name is RETAIL[1]. The following syntax allows a user to login to this database:

```
isql -Uvideo -Pvideo -SRETAIL[2]
```

The syntax to execute the stored procedure is shown in Figure 6.10.

---

[1]This is case-sensitive, so the capitals are necessary.

[2]The -Sservername option can also be included in an environment variable for operating systems like MS-DOS, OS/2, and Windows. This option is dropped from the login command in this case, as follows: **isql -Uvideo -Pvideo**

Syntax:

```
execute proc_name [parameter1][,parameter2]...
```

This can be shortened to:

```
exec proc_name [parameter1][,parameter2]...
```

Example:

```
1>exec insert_video  "Toys",   "Robin   Williams",   1993,
                      "Comedy", 15
2>go
```

Figure 6.10   Interactive execution of a stored procedure.

6.5.2   Nested Stored Procedures

Stored procedures can invoke other stored procedures. During such an invocation a stored procedure can pass parameters to the called procedure and specify that some of the parameters will be changed, and the changes will be visible after the called procedure returns. A stored procedure can also receive a "return" value (e.g., status flag) from a called procedure. The basic syntax to call a nested stored procedure is

```
exec return_code = proc_name [@parm1][,@parm2]
                    [,@called_parm1 = @parm3 output]
                    [,@called_parm2 = @parm4 output]
```

- return_code is a value returned by proc_name.
- @parm1 and @parm2 pass values to the called procedure, proc_name. Proc_name can manipulate the passed values without affecting the original variables @parm1 and @parm2.
- @called_parm1 and @called_parm2 are variable names defined in the proc_name stored procedure. Both of these variables will contain the values in @parm3 and @parm4 respectively when the proc_name is invoked. @parm3 and @parm4 will contain the final values that are stored in @called_parm1 and @called_parm2 respectively when proc_name returns.

Examples

1. `exec update_video_inventory "Toys", 1`
2. `exec update_video_inventory "Toys", 1,`
   `    @new_total = @total output`

3. `return_code = exec update_video_inventory, "Toys", 1,`
`    @new_total = @total output`

6.5.3   Invocation through a Client Operating System via Batch Scripts

A particularly useful method of executing stored procedures is by issuing a call via a client platform's operating system. This method allows the commands and parameters that make the invocation to be stored inside an ASCII file created by a text editor.

Example Suppose the operating system of a client platform is MS-DOS. The file in Figure 6.11 could be built using the MS-DOS **copy** command.

The syntax to execute the stored procedure is:

`isql -Uvideo -Pvideo -iinsvideo.txt`

This method offers the advantage of allowing the stored procedure to be executed repeatedly without forcing the user to retype the stored procedure name and the parameter list, which in some applications can get quite long.

The problem with this method is that the parameters are hardcoded. This is resolved by using "embedded" or "library" calls to execute stored procedures.

6.5.4   Embedded and Library Calls

A final method that can be used to execute a stored procedure involves using a host language to issue a request to SQL Server. This allows a parameter list to be passed to SQL Server. This topic is discussed more fully in Chapter 14.

```
copy con insvideo.txt

exec    insert_video    "Toys",    "Robin
Williams",  1993, "Comedy", 3
go
/* go is mandatory
   in the first column */

cntrl-Z
```

Figure 6.11   Building a batch invocation file.

Syntax:

```
drop procedure [DB.owner]proc_name
[,[DB.owner]proc_name   ...
```

Figure 6.12   Dropping a stored procedure.

6.6   DROPPING STORED PROCEDURES

Once a stored procedure is compiled, information about it remains in the database system tables until the procedure is explicitly dropped with the command in Figure 6.12.

Examples

1. `drop procedure get_customer`

2. `drop proc get_customer`

3. `drop proc get_customer, get_video`

It is a good idea to drop a procedure before issuing a **create proc** command. This can be included inside the script file that creates a stored procedure. This is shown in (the **if** command will be discussed in Chapter 7) Figure 6.13.

Creating a procedure with a name that already exists in a database will cause an error message to display, and the new contents of the updated procedure will be ignored. Dropping a stored procedure name before compiling a procedure with that same name avoids this problem altogether. The code in the example has the added benefit of only processing the *drop*, if the stored procedure name exists in the current database.

```
/**********************************************************
The following "if" command checks for the existence of a
stored procedure with a name of "customer" in the data
dictionary. The "customer" stored procedure is dropped, if it
is found.
**********************************************************/
if exists (select * from sysobjects where name = "customers")
   drop procedure customers
go
```

Figure 6.13   Dropping a procedure.

6.7   IMPLICATIONS AND RESTRICTIONS

Size and length restrictions on stored procedures follow.

Maximum Size of a Stored Procedure

Pre-System 10. 4K (code and comments) for most platforms; 8K (code and comments) for some platforms.[3]

System 10. 16 MB.

Maximum Number of Local Variables

Pre-System 10. 125.

System 10. 255 parameters to the stored procedure.
Maximum number of local variables is limited by the amount of main memory that is available to the program.

Maximum Stored Procedure Nesting 12/16.

6.8   RECOMPILING STORED PROCEDURES

A stored procedure should be recompiled if any objects it references are changed. This idea can be expanded to mean that all stored procedures referencing a changed object should be recompiled. This can be an arduous manual task; however, it is easily done with the command shown in Figure 6.14.

This will display the following message: "Each stored procedure and trigger that uses table 'video' will be recompiled the next time it is executed."

6.9   RELATED SYSTEM PROCEDURES

Several system procedures can be used to retrieve information about system procedures from the system tables. These are:

```
sp_help procedure_name
```

---

[3]For example, Stratus platforms. Open Client may only accept 4K, so stored procedures would need to be compiled directly on the Strastas machine.

Syntax

```
sp_recompile    object_name
(where you are the owner of object_name)
```

Examples

```
1. sp_recompile   video
   go

2. sp_recompile   movie
   go
```

Figure 6.14   Stored procedure recompile command.

Displays information about a stored procedure within the current database. Also confirms the existence of a stored procedure in a database's data dictionary. The display includes procedure name, owner, creation date, and a parameter list.

```
e.g.  1>use pubs2
      2>go
      1>sp_help stores
      2>go
```

```
sp_helptext procedure_name
```

Displays the code related to a stored procedure as it was compiled into the data dictionary. This can be piped into an ASCII file to reconstruct a script file for a stored procedure.

```
e.g.  /* create a script file that contains the
      following commands */
      1>sp_helptext  procedure_name
      2>go
      From the operating system type:
      -Usa -Ppassword -iscript -Ooutput_messages
```

```
sp_depends procedure_name
```

Displays a list of all objects that reference the procedure_name in the following format:

```
        object       type      updated      selected
owner.object_name
```

6.10   set COMMAND

The Transact-SQL **set** command allows processing of stored procedures to be customized. The **set** command accepts options and a value for the option. This section identifies some of the commonly used **set** commands.

arithabort This option is used to affect the method of processing when an overflow or a divide by 0 occurs in a stored procedure.

Syntax

```
set arithabort overflow/numeric_truncation on/off
```

Examples

a. `set arithabort overflow on`

b. `set arithabort overflow off`

c. `set numeric_truncation on`

d. `set numeric_truncation off`

cursor rows This option is used to affect the number of cursor rows returned by a cursor fetch.

Syntax

```
set cursor rows number for cursor_name
```

Example

```
set cursor rows 5 for inv_cursor
```

role This option allows specific roles to be turned on or off during a session.

Syntax

```
set role "sa/sso/oper" on/off
```

Examples

a. `set role "sa" on`

b. `set role "sa" off`

rowcount Possibly one of the most commonly used of the set commands, **rowcount** establishes a limit on the number of rows that are returned by a select in the same query.

Syntax

```
set rowcount number
```

Examples

a. `set rowcount 1`

b. `set rowcount 18`

c. `set rowcount 100`

d. `set rowcount 0     /* this turns rowcount off, so`
`                         all rows are returned by the`
`                         next select in the query. */`

statistics This option supports fine-tuning and optimization of table accesses and indexing by displaying assorted statistics. The command should be used to determine the efficiency of various queries in an application.

Syntax

```
set statistics io/time on/off
```

Examples

a. `set statistics io on`

b. `set statistics io off`

c. `set statistics time on`

d. `set statistics time off`

showplan This option displays the path a query takes to process a table (see Appendix C). The command shows whether a table scan is being performed (it is best to avoid these), or whether an index is used to access a table. This option displays a great deal of useful information that will assist in optimizing and fine-tuning an application.

Syntax

```
set showplan on/off
```

Examples

a. `set showplan on`

b. `set showplan off`

6.11   SUMMARY

This chapter introduced the reader to stored procedures. Stored procedures are an innovation introduced by Sybase, Inc. that has been incorporated by other database server vendors in their products.

This chapter demonstrated that stored procedures can be written with any standard text editor, and compiled into a database dictionary using the **isql** command.

Stored procedures can be invoked with the **exec** command interactively (typed by a user in a Sybase session), nested inside other stored procedures, or through an application running on a client platform.

Some of the popular and particularly useful options of the set command from a development perspective were also discussed. These included **rowcount**, **statistics**, and **showplan**. They can accept a variable number of parameters and standard SQL commands as well as Sybase's control-of-flow commands. The control-of-flow language is discussed in the next chapter. The tutorial contains examples of more comprehensive stored procedures.

7

Control-of-Flow Language

In this chapter a reader will learn about:

- Control-of-Flow Language

7.1 PROCEDURAL COMMANDS, OR THE CONTROL-OF-FLOW LANGUAGE

Transact-SQL enhancements offer procedural constructs that are as sophisticated as third-generation programming languages such as C, COBOL, and Pascal. In SQL Server terminology, these procedural constructs are referred to as a control-of-flow language.

The commands discussed in this chapter can be used inside stored procedures and triggers.

7.1.1 if..else

The **if..else** expression is used to execute Transact-SQL commands based on the evaluation of a set of boolean conditions. In Figure 7.1, if the condition interprets to a value of TRUE, the next statement is executed.

Conditional Operators The condition portion of the **if..else** expression is built using standard boolean operators, which are described in the following table.

Syntax:

```
if condition
    statement
else
if condition
    statement
else
    statement
```

Figure 7.1   **if..else** syntax.

The following examples can be constructed with these operators.

Examples. The value in the left variable is the same as the value in the right variable, so the Transact-SQL command represented by the statement is executed.

1.
```
if value1 = value2
    statement
```

2.
```
if value1 = value2
    statement1
else
    statement2
```

3.
```
if value1 = value2
    statement1
else
if value1 = value3
    statement2
else
    statement3
```

4.
```
if value1 != value2
    statement
```

5.
```
if value1 > value2
    statement
```

6.
```
if value 1 > value2 and value2 < value3 and value3
> value5
    statement
```

Boolean Operator	Description
=	Equal. Condition is true if both sides of the expression are equal (e.g., (1) x = y. (2) 3 = 3).
!= or <>	Not Equal. Condition is true if both sides of the expression are not equal (e.g., (1) x != y. (2) 3 != 4).
<	Less than. Condition is true if the left side of the expression is less than the right side of the expression (e.g., (1) x < y. (2) 3 < 4).
>	Greater than. Condition is true if the left side of the expression is greater than the right side of the expression (e.g., (1) x > y. (2) 4 > 3).
<=	Less than or equal to. Condition is true if the left side of the expression is less than or equal to the right side of the expression (e.g., (1) x <= y. (2) 3 <= 4. (3) 4 <= 4).
>=	Greater than or equal to. Condition is true if the left side of the expression is greater than or equal to the right side of the expression (e.g., (1) x >= y. (2) 4 >= 3. (3) 4 >= 4).
!<	Not less than. Condition is true if the left side of the expression is not less than the right side of the expression (e.g., (1) x !< y. (2) 4 !< 3).
!>	Not greater than. Condition is true if the left side of the expression is not greater than the right side of the expression (e.g., (1) x !> y. (2) 3 !> 4).
and	Compound. Condition is true if all parts of an expression are true (e.g., (1) x>y and z<y. (2) 5>4 and 1<4).
or	or. Condition is true if one or more parts of an expression are true (e.g., (1) x>y or z<y. (2) 2>4 or 1<4).

```
7. if value 1 > value2 or value2 < value3 or value3 >
   value5
      statement

8. if value 1 > value2 or value2 < value3 and value3 >
   value5
      statement

9. if value 1 > value 2
   begin
           if value 3 > value 4
           begin
                   if status_flag = 'Y'
                           statements
                   else
                           statements
           end
           else
           if value 3 = value 4
           begin
                   statements
           end
           else
           begin
                   statements
           end
   end      /* outer begin */
   else
      statement
```

The statement portion of the **if..else** command as shown above consists of a single Transact-SQL command[1]. Often it is necessary to perform more than one statement within an **if-else** block. This can be done by surrounding a group of Transact-SQL commands with a **begin..end** construct.

7.1.2   begin..end

In the C programming language, the symbols { and } are used to surround a group of C language commands so that they count as one statement in commands such as **if**, **while**, and **for**. The same idea holds true

---

[1]For example: 1. exec procname
                 2. select * from customers

Syntax:

```
begin
        Transact-SQL commands
end
```

Figure 7.2   **begin..end** syntax.

for Transact-SQL, where the keywords **begin** and **end** are used instead. See Figure 7.2.

Example

```
begin
        select * from customer
        select * from movie
        select * from rentals
end
```

7.1.3   Declaring Variables

Standard SQL commands, though simple in their usage, suffer from their inability to save values that are retrieved into variables. Transact-SQL solves this problem by supporting local and global variables. Before a variable can be used, it must be declared; it is often done immediately after a **create proc** command and the procedure parameters.

Local variables are visible only inside the stored procedure in which they are defined. The syntax in Figure 7.3 is applicable.

Multiple local variables can be defined using either of the following options.

Option 1

```
declare    @variable_name1 datatype
declare    @variable_name2 datatype
declare    @variable_name3 datatype
```

Syntax:

```
declare @variable_name data_type

(the @ is a mandatory prefix of all user defined variables)
```

Figure 7.3   **declare** syntax.

Option 2

```
declare    @variable_name1 datatype,
           @variable_name2 datatype,
           @variable_name3 datatype
```

Global variables are described later in this chapter.

7.1.4   Datatypes

The previous examples show that datatype is part of the syntax used to declare local variables. As mentioned in Chapter 4, SQL Server supports the following datatypes.[2]

Datatypes	Valid Values	Storage Requirements (Bytes)
Numeric		
int	Between $-2^{31}(2,147,483,648)$ and $2^{31}(2,147,483,647)$ inclusive	4
smallint	Between $-2^{15}(-32,768)$ and $2^{15}-1(32,767)$ inclusive	2
tinyint	Between 0 and 255, inclusive	1
numeric(p,s)	Between -10^{38} and $10^{38}-1$	2 to 17
decimal(p,s)	Between -10^{38} and $10^{38}-1$	2 to 17
float	varies	4/8
double precision	varies	8
real	varies	4
money	Money columns store exact values between -922,337,203,685,477.5808 and 922,337,203,685,477.5807 with four places of precision	8
small money	Between -214,718.3648 and 214,748.3647	4
Character		
char(n)	Character columns (letters, numbers, symbols) up to 255 characters in length	n fixed

[2]Source: Sybase SQL Server brochure, printed by Sybase.

varchar(n)	Variable length—up to 255 characters	actual n based on entry string

BLOB (Binary Large Object)

Text	Variable length—up to $2^{31}-1(2,147,483,647)$ bytes in length	0/2K multiples
Image	Variable length—up to $2^{31}-1(2,147,483,647)$ bytes	0/2K multiples
binary(n)	Binary columns up to 255 bytes in length	n fixed
varbinary(n)	Variable-length binary columns up to 255 bytes	actual n based on entry data

Miscellaneous

bit	Bit columns hold either 0 or 1	1
datetime	Date and time of day with a precision of 1/30th of a millisecond (January 1, 1753 to December 31, 9999)	8
smalldatetime	Date and time of day with a precision of 1 minute (January 1, 1900 to June 6, 2079)	4
timestamp	A column of timestamp type is automatically updated when a record is altered	

7.1.5   while

Repeat logic is supported in stored procedures using the **while** command, with the syntax shown in Figure 7.4. Condition and statement are handled like the **if..else** command.

```
while condition
    statement
```

Figure 7.4   **while** syntax.

Example. Suppose we want to continue selecting movies, one year at a time, until the current year is reached. This is done by the following logic:

```
/************************************************************
Recall that datepart and getdate are both date functions.
************************************************************/

declare @until_year     int,
        @current_year   int

select @until_year = datepart (year, getdate())
select @current_year = 1960
while @current_year != @untilyear
begin
    select @current_year
    select * from movies
        where release_year = @current_year

    select @current_year = @current_year + 1
end
```

Nesting Note that **while** commands can be nested, as follows:

```
while (condition)     /*First outer while*/
begin
    select ....

    while (condition)          /*Second while*/
    begin
        select ....
    end                        /*end Second while*/

        while (condition)  /*Third while*/
        begin
            select ....

            while (condition)   /*Fourth while*/
            begin
                select ....
            end                     /*end Fourth while*/
        end                     /*end Third while*/
end                 /* end outer while */
```

while

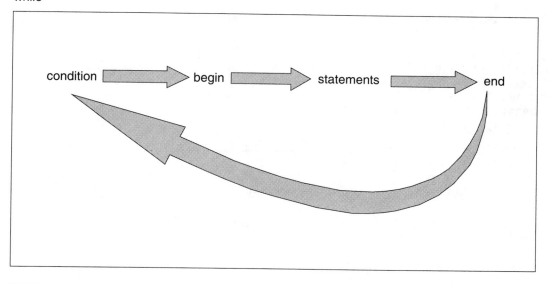

Figure 7.5   Processing path.

7.1.6   continue

For the previous example, processing continues as shown in Figure 7.5.
In some instances it is desirable to alter this path by skipping some logic and branching directly to the start of the loop condition. This is handled through the **continue** command (see Figure 7.6).

Example. Suppose in the preceding example we did not want to select any movies for 1970, for some reason. It could be done in several ways. One way is to use the **continue** command.

Syntax:
continue

Figure 7.6   **continue** syntax.

```
/*************************************************************
Recall that datepart and getdate are date functions.
 Modified to include a continue command.
*************************************************************/

select @until_year = datepart (year, getdate())
select @current_year = 1960

while @current_year != @untilyear    ←──────────────────┐
begin                                                   │
                                                        │
    if @current_year = 1970                             │
       continue ────────────────────────────────────────┘
    select @current_year
    select * from movies
       where release_year = @current_year

    select @current_year = @current_year + 1
end
```

7.1.7   break

Sometimes it is desirable to exit from the normal top-to-bottom processing of a **while** loop, but not by branching to the **while** condition with the **continue** command. The **break** command (Figure 7.7) is used to stop processing of a loop, unconditionally. Control immediately passes to the first command that follows the **while** statement.

Example. In the following example, the **break** command is used to exit from the **while** loop if no records are found for a year. Since this is assumed to be an error condition, a message is returned prior to issuing the **break** command. Notice the use of the @@rowcount variable, a global variable that will be discussed later in this chapter along with the other global variables.

Syntax:

```
break
```

Figure 7.7   **break** syntax.

```
/**********************************************************
   Recall that datepart and getdate are date functions.
   Modified to include a continue command.
   Modified to include a break command.
**********************************************************/
select @until_year = datepart (year, getdate())
select @current_year = 1960
while @current_year != @untilyear    <───────────────┐
begin                                                 │
                                                      │
    if @current_year = 1970                           │
       continue ──────────────────────────────────────┘
    select @current_year
    select * from movies
       where release_year = @current_year
    /* check if any records were found for this year */
    if @@rowcount = 0
    begin
       select 'No records found for year = ', @current_year
         break ─────────────────────────────────────────┐
    end                                                  │
                                                         │
    /* increment to next year */                         │
    select @current_year = @current_year + 1             │
end                                                      │
                                                         │
select @tax_rate = tax_rate    <─────────────────────────┘
    from fiscal_taxes
     where type = "PST" and year = @current_year
if @@rowcount = 0
begin
    select 'major problem'
    select @tax_rate = .07
end
```

7.1.8   Global Variables

SQL Server supports a set of variables that have a global scope and that provide useful information about the Sybase environment or a just-completed operation (i.e., a transaction). These are identified with a @@ (recall that local variables have a @ prefix) prefix. Note that these global variables can be used inside stored procedures, triggers, and so forth. Their contents can be inspected with Transact-SQL commands such as **if**.[3]

---

[3]Source: Sybase SQL Server Release 10.0 Reference Manual.

Variable	Contents
@@char_convert	0 if character set conversion not in effect; else 1.
@@client_csname	Client's character set name.
@@client_csid	Client's character set id.
@@connections	The number of logins or attempted logins.
@@cpu_busy	Measures the time that has passed in CPU ticks since the last time SQL Server was running on the platform.
@@error	If the last transaction succeeded, this variable contains 0; otherwise it will contain the error number that is generated by the system.
@@identity	Updated whenever a row is inserted into a table column created with the IDENT datatype to contain the last sequential number that was used.
@@idle	Measures SQL Server idle time in CPU ticks.
@@io_busy	Measures SQL Server active time (in terms of input and output operations) in CPU ticks.
@@isolation	Updated to contain the isolation level of the current program.
@@langid	Local language id.
@@language	Name of the local language.
@@maxcharlen	Maximum length of multibyte character in default character set.
@@max_connections	Specifies the maximum number of connections that can be supported by SQL Server.
@@ncharsize	Average length (bytes) of a national character.
@@nestlevel	Monitors nesting of current transaction. Will abort the transaction if more than 16 levels[4] of nesting occur for any procedure.
@@pack_received	Number of input packets read by SQL Server.
@@pack_sent	Number of output packets written by SQL Server.
@@packet_errors	Number of packet errors.
@@procid	Stored procedure ID of currently executing procedure. This id is stored in the syscomments table (also contained in other system tables as well).
@@rowcount	This is a commonly used variable. It contains the number of rows affected by the last query. Contains 0 if no rows are affected, or a positive integer reflecting the actual number of rows affected.

@@servername	Contains the name of the SQL Server (who am I?). This information is important in invoking the SQL Server.
@@spid	The server process ID number of the current process.
@@sqlstatus	This variable is used to interpret the results of the **cursor fetch** command.
	if @@sqlstatus = 0 fetch was successful
	if @@sqlstatus = 1 fetch encountered an error
	if @@sqlstatus = 2 end of result set reached
@@textsize	Limit on the number of bytes[5] of text or image data that can be returned by a select.
@@thresh_hysteresis	Specifies free space delta that will trigger a threshold.
@@timeticks	Number of microseconds per CPU tick.
@@total_errors	Sum of errors encountered by SQL Server in reading and writing.
@@total_read	Number of disk reads by SQL Server since it was started.
@@total_write	Number of disk writes by SQL Server since it was started.
@@tranchained	Contains transaction mode of current Transact-SQL program.
	if @@tranchained = 0 transaction mode is unchained
	if @@tranchained = 1 transaction mode is chained
@@trancount	Count of active transactions for current user.
@@transtate	Provides state of a transaction. Valid values range from 0 to 3.
@@version	Date of the current version of SQL Server.

[4]This is the maximum level of nesting for stored procedures.

[5]32K bytes for **isql**.

Users should avoid declaring local variables with these names. Doing so will override the global variable and make the user unable to access the global information.

These variables can be used inside many Transact-SQL commands

Syntax:

```
/* this is a comment */
```

Figure 7.8   comments syntax.

such as **while** and **if**. A system procedure, **sp_monitor**, can also be used to view these variables by an owner of the sybsystemprocs database.

7.1.9   Comments

Comments have been included in many of the examples presented so far. The syntax to do this (Figure 7.8) is similar to the way comments are delimited in the C programming language. Conventional wisdom suggests that internal program documentation should be thorough and be encouraged. This philosophy requires rethinking when using stored procedures because compiled stored procedures have size limitations. For SQL Server versions prior to System 10, this limit is a length of 4K[6]. For SQL Server 10 this limit is dramatically higher, namely 16MB. Comments are included in this limit, so each byte in a comment means one less byte of code in a stored procedure.

Stored procedures that exceed this size do not get compiled into the database system dictionary. In fact, the stored procedure compiler ceases to work after this threshold is reached but does not always provide a warning. The user discovers that the stored procedure was not compiled when trying to execute it. Since there are no other warnings when this happens (except "procedure not found"), a user should first check the size of the stored procedure. This problem required several days to discover and resolve in the author's first client/server development project.

Comments are useful only to someone reading code. The system tables do not use it in any way. For this reason, it is possible to position comments outside the create procedure block in script files. This is shown in Figure 7.9.

Some of the comments are positioned outside the stored procedure body that is compiled into the data dictionary. They are still visible to the programmer, but they do not add to the size of the stored procedure.

---

[6]On some platforms, such as the Stratus, this limit is 8K. However, some versions of Sybase Open Client restrict the size of stored procedures to 4K, making it the effective limit.

```
************************************************
* Filename: videol.sy                         *
* Author:    Neil Sector                       *
* Date:      July 1992                         *
* Description:                                 *
*                                              *
* This file contains the following 3           *
* stored procedures:                           *
* i. The purpose of insert_video is to ... *
* ii. The purpose of get_video is to ...   *
* iii. The purpose of select_customer is...*
************************************************/
/* NOTE: Notice that many of the comments in this file
are positioned outside the body of the stored procedure
that is compiled into the data dictionary */

print ' Processing INSERT_VIDEO'

if exists ( select * from sysobjects where name =
'insert_video')
   drop proc insert_video
   go
/*****************************************
 * The logic of this stored procedure is *
 * divided into three key blocks ....    *
 *****************************************/
create procedure insert_video
(
   video_name        char (30),
   video_price       money
)
as
declare     number_of_units        int
.....
go

/* end of insert_video */
 etc.
```

Figure 7.9   Placement of comments.

Not all comments should be stripped out of a stored procedure. Some are invaluable to programmers for maintenance of a program. Since 4K (pre-System 10 versions of Sybase) is a size limitation on a single stored procedure, it is possible to use modular design techniques to bypass this limit on an application level. An application can be divided into discrete blocks or functions. Each stored procedure is designed to satisfy the requirements of a single function. The stored procedures can then be called when a function is required, consequently allowing more than 4K/16MB of memory for the entire application. When nesting stored procedures, developers should take care to design solutions that do not require nesting levels greater than 16.

7.1.10   goto

The **goto** command causes an unconditional branch to a label in another part of the stored procedure. See Figure 7.10.

Example

```
create proc update_price
(
@old_price       money,
@increase        money,
@tax_increase money
)
as
 declare
 @new_tax money,
 @new_price money

new_movie:

set rowcount = 1
select @new_tax = tax, @newprice = price
  from movie where price = @old_price

/* test conditions */

select @new_tax = @new_tax + @tax_increase
select @new_price = @new_price + @increase

update movie
set tax = @new_tax,
   price = @new_price
```

Syntax:

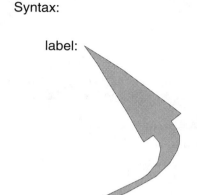

Figure 7.10   **goto** syntax.

```
if @@rowcount = 0
begin
  select "major problem here — "
  select "record just found is gone"

   select "call system administrator"
end

goto new_movie

go
```

The **goto** command is discouraged in many computer languages because of its nonmodular influence. Its use should also be kept to a minimum in stored procedures. The developer should try using the **while**, nested procedure calls, or better-qualified **select** statements before resorting to using the **goto**.

7.1.11   return

The **return** command is an unconditional exit from a stored procedure from any place it is issued. See Figure 7.11.

Syntax:

```
return
```

or

```
return value
        where value is returned to the
        caller and can be used as a
        status flag.
```

Figure 7.11   **return** syntax.

Examples

1. `return`

2. `return 0   /* success */`

3. `return -1  /* program failure */`

4. `return -99 /* database problem */`

5. `return 29  /* customer found */`

7.1.12   print

The **print** command is used to display a message or a variable's contents on the system output. See Figure 7.12.

7.1.13   raiserror

The **raiserror** command can be used by a user to force a system error, which is recorded in the @@error global variable. See Figure 7.13.

Syntax:

```
1. print text
2. print variable
3. print text, variable
```

Figure 7.12   **print** syntax.

Syntax:

```
raiserror error_num [variable | message]
```

Figure 7.13   **raiserror** syntax.

7.1.14   waitfor

The **waitfor** command will stop processing of a stored procedure until a time of day or length of time has elapsed. See Figure 7.14.

7.2   REVISITING NESTED STORED PROCEDURES AND OUTPUT

As discussed previously, nested stored procedures can receive parameters from a calling stored procedure. The nested call can identify which of these parameters can be modified by the called procedure so that the new value is retained when control is returned to the caller. "Output" is the keyword used to signal that this should happen.

Example. Suppose we want to build a stored procedure that retrieves a movie title belonging to a movie number. This requires the stored procedure to accept two parameters, one of which is read only, the other of which is modifiable by the stored procedure being called. The logic to do this, including Transact-SQL commands, is provided in Figures 7.15 and 7.16.

7.3   SUMMARY

Transact-SQL's procedural language was examined in this chapter. This consists of **if..else** and **while** commands that are as powerful as any third-generation language such as C. Other constructs such as comments, **return**, and **raiserror** were also discussed.

These commands are used inside stored procedures and triggers.

Syntax:

```
waitfor {delay "time" | time "time" }
```

Figure 7.14   **waitfor** syntax.

```
/*************************************************
 Filename: video S.sy
 Author:   Neil Sector
 Date:     July 1993
 This file contains 2 stored procs.
 *************************************************/

if exists (select * from sysobjects where
             name = "validate_movie")
   drop procedure validate_movie
go

create proc validate_movie
(
   @movie code     int,
   @release_year int,
   @price        money
)
as
declare @description char(30),
      @return_code int

if @release_year < 1930 or @release_year > 2000
begin
  select -15 /* invalid year */
  return
end

/* get movie description */
@return_code = exec get_movie_description
  @movie_code,
  @temp_description = @description output

if @return_code = -1
begin
  select -5
  return         /* invalid description */
end
select @temp_description /* display movie name */
/* validate price and update database */
select 0
return
```

Figure 7.15   Using output to pass parameters (part A).

```
if exists (select * from sysobjects where
            name = "get_movie_description")
   drop procedure get_movie_description
go

create proc get_movie_description
(
 @movie_code   int,
 @temp_description char(30) output
)
as

declare @description char(30),
      @return_code int

select @temp_description = name from movie
      where movie_id = @movie_code

if @@rowcount = 0
   return -1   /* no movie found */

return0    /* success */

go
```

Figure 7.16   Using output to pass parameters (part B).

This chapter demonstrated extensive use of the Sybase go command. This is used to submit a batch of commands for processing. Commands within the batch are not executed until the go is encountered. This has important implications in that commands that affect other commands should be separated into different batches for them to be successful. This is demonstrated in the following examples:

Example 1: Correct use of the go command

```
1> use master
2> go
1> use pubs2
2> go /* go is important */
1> select * from stores
2> go
```

Example 2: Incorrect use of the go command

```
1> use master
2> go
1> use pubs2
2> select * from stores
3> go        /* will not work. Sybase looks for the
                stores table in the master database—
                not pubs2! */
```

Triggers

In this chapter a reader will learn about:

- Overview of triggers
- Creating triggers
- Dropping triggers
- Temporary trigger tables
- Trigger design
- Characteristics

8.1   OVERVIEW OF TRIGGERS

All triggers are stored procedures, but all stored procedures are not triggers. Having said this, it is still necessary to learn another level of commands and concepts to make effective use of triggers.

Triggers offer an effective method for ensuring referential integrity[1] in a database. They are designed to activate in response to **insert**, **delete**, **update** operations on a table. Just like stored procedures, triggers contain Transact-SQL commands. Likewise, triggers are created using a batch script (with a **create trigger** command) and are com-

---

[1]In a relational database system, this means that key fields should have correct values across related tables, and also that all changes are propagated to related or associated fields in the database (or distributed database).

piled into a data dictionary. Triggers that are no longer required can be dropped, while triggers that require modification can be compiled back into the data dictionary after the batch script is modified.

Developers planning to use triggers are faced with certain considerations. In many cases, either triggers or stored procedures could be used to perform a function. Consider the following example in the Video Rental Store case study (Chapter 17).

> A customer rents a movie video on Friday and returns it on Saturday. An application should insert a record into the invoice_items table. To maintain data integrity, the application should also update the invoice table and the movie_allocation table (on-hand inventory).

Deciding to use a stored procedure or a trigger to change the invoice and movie_allocation table is not an exact science. Some factors that could be used to make a choice are (a) response time, (b) number of different events that require this function, (c) organization standards, and (d) ease of modification.

These issues are discussed in this chapter.

8.2 TRIGGER ARCHITECTURE

Figure 8.1 shows the architecture of triggers in Sybase.

A trigger is tied specifically to a table or a field within a table (Figure 8.2). It is automatically invoked whenever an **insert**, **delete**, or **update** operation is applied to the table or field. At this point, control passes to the trigger. The operation being applied to the table or field is not yet complete, so the trigger can accept, roll back, or modify the results of the operation. The insert and delete tables temporarily contain records being inserted, deleted, or updated in the active table.

Figure 8.3 shows the effect of an **insert** operation.

Figure 8.4 shows the effect of a delete operation.

Each table can have a trigger for each one of these operations. A trigger can be programmed to fire for one, two, or all three of the operations.

8.3 CREATING A TRIGGER

A trigger is created by typing Transact-SQL commands into an ASCII file in the same way as was done for stored procedures.

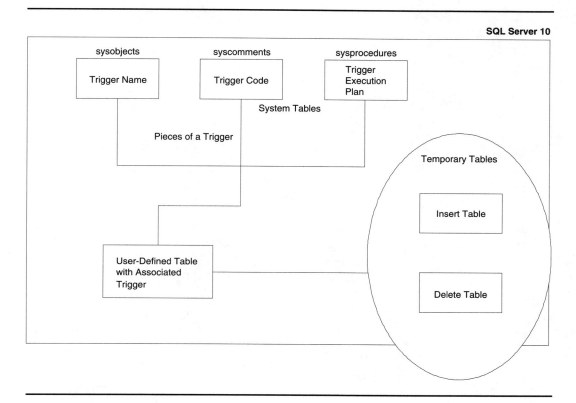

Figure 8.1   Trigger architecture.

Syntax

```
create trigger trigger_name
    on table_name
    for {insert, update, delete}
as
    statements
```

Examples

```
1. create trigger open_items
     on invoice_items
    for update
    as
```

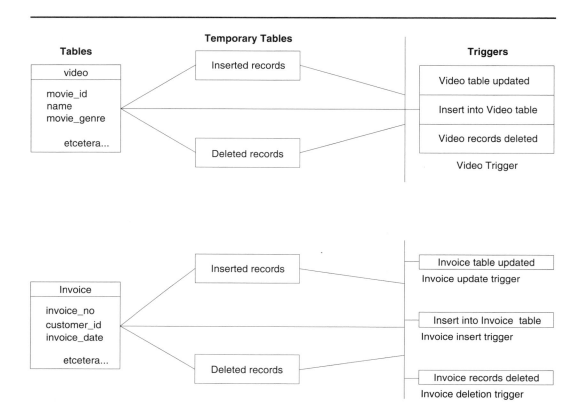

Figure 8.2   Relationship between tables and triggers.

```
/* select firing open_items trigger*/
if update (date_returned)
begin
  update invoice
  set items_open = items_open - 1
  from inserted
    where invoice.invoice_no = inserted.invoice_no
  if @@rowcount = 0
  begin
    print 'impossible condition'
  end
end
go
```

Operation

Intermediate View

Figure 8.3   Insert table used by trigger fired by insert operation.

```
2. create trigger delete_invoice
     on movie
   for delete
   as
     delete invoice
       from  movie, deleted
       where invoice.movie_id = deleted.movie_id
   go

3. create trigger insert_inventory
   on master_file
   for insert
   as
         declare  @movie_id          int
         declare  @name              char(30)
```

Operation

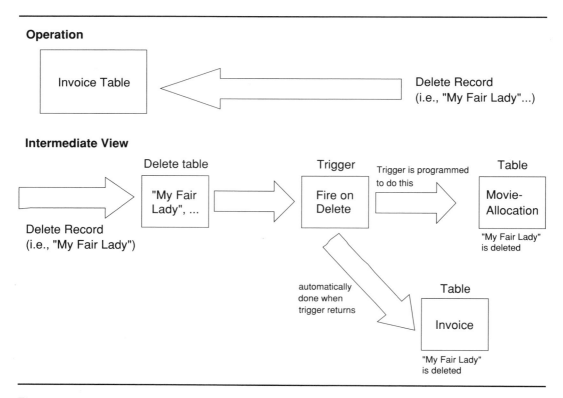

Figure 8.4   Delete table used by trigger fired by delete operation.

```
          declare   @movie_genre_code   int
          declare   @product_code       int
          declare   @release_date       datetime
          declare   @language_code      int
          declare   @cost               money
          declare   @plot1              char(100)
          declare   @plot2              char(100)
    select @movie_id = inserted.movie_id from inserted
    select @name = inserted.name from inserted
    select @movie_genre_code = inserted.movie_genre_
          code from inserted
    select @product_code = inserted.product_code from
          inserted
    select @release_date = inserted.release_data from
          inserted
```

```
select @language_code = inserted.language_code from
        inserted
select @cost = inserted.cost from inserted
select @plot1 = inserted.plot1 form inserted
select @plot2 = inserted.plot2 form inserted
insert movie
(movie_id, name, movie_genre_code, product_code,
release_date, language_code, cost, plot1, plot2)
values
(@movie_id, @name, @movie_genre_code,
 @product_code, @release_date, @language_code,
 @cost, @plot1, @plot2)
go
```

8.4   DROPPING TRIGGERS

Triggers can be dropped by either dropping the trigger table (this will drop all the triggers in the table) or by issuing the following command:

Syntax

```
drop trigger trigger_name
```

8.5   TRIGGER ISSUES

While triggers are useful in maintaining referential integrity, the author has found that their implementation has the potential of having a negative impact on performance. For this reason, they should be used with care, and sparingly. Given a choice between using a stored procedure or a trigger, the author's benchmarks show that it is usually better to use a stored procedure from a performance perspective. A general rule of thumb is to restrict trigger usage to simple functions only.

Another potential pitfall is the trigger self-recursion feature. SQL Server provides the option of turning this on/off with the **set self_recursion on/off** command. If self_recursion is turned on, a trigger can invoke itself repeatedly (i.e., if it fires as a consequence of updating the same table). An example of this is where Table A has an update trigger that fires if any of the fields in the table are updated. The update trigger itself updates Table A, which in turn fires the trigger again, and so on. This situation, although potentially flawed, may be acceptable in some cases—say, in the case where the trigger will stop the recursion when some condition is reached. The reader should be aware of this potential pitfall before modifying the value of the self_recursion variable.

Another situation to avoid is shown in Figure 8.5.

Triggers can be nested for up to 16 levels. Nesting can be disabled by using the **sp_configure** system procedure as follows:

```
sp_configure "nested triggers", 0
reconfigure
go
```

The following examples of methods display information about triggers in a particular database (the user should be logged onto SQL Server and the desired database should be in use):

Examples

```
1. /* to get a list of triggers in a database */
   select name from sysobjects where type = 'TR'
   go
```

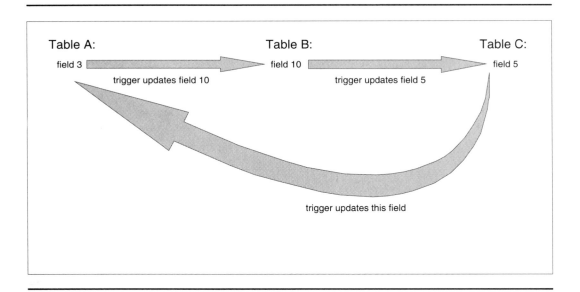

Figure 8.5   This situation results in a loop.

```
/* type = 'U'   /* user table */
         'V'   /* view */
         'L'   /* log */
         'P'   /* procedure */
         'R'   /* rule */
         'D'   /* default */
         'TR'  /* trigger */
         'RI'  /* referential constraints */
*/
```

2. ```
   /* to get basic information about a specific
      trigger */
   1>sp_help trigger_name
   2>go
   ```

3. ```
   /* to display the Transact-SQL code corresponding
      to a trigger */
   1>sp_helptext trigger_name
   2>go
   ```

The example that follows creates 3 tables, each with an update trigger. The reader is taken through an exercise to demonstrate Sybase's ability to enforce a nested limit of 16 on triggers (and stored procedures).

```
/*****************************************************************
 * Type the following script into an ascii file named           *
 * trigger_tables.sql                                           *
 *****************************************************************/

/*****************************************************************
 Filename:  trigger_tables.sql
 Author:  Sanjiv Purba
 Date:  Nov 1993

Purpose:  This batch script will demonstrate Sybase's ability to
detect an infinite loop condition caused by the firing of nested
triggers.

Maintenance Log:


*****************************************************************/
use pubs2
go
```

```
/************************ Create Table ************************/

/* drop tables (ignore error/warning messages on first run */
drop table table1
go

drop table table2
go

drop table table3
go

/* create three simple tables */

print ' '
print ' Creating table1 ———————'
print ' '
go

if exists (select name from sysobjects where name = "table1")
   drop table table1
go

create table table1
(
  id        int
)
go


print ' '
print ' Creating table2 ———————'
print ' '
go

if exists (select name from sysobjects where name = "table2")
   drop table table2
go


create table table2
(
  id        int
)
go
```

```
print ' '
print ' Creating table3 ———'
print ' '
go

if exists (select name from sysobjects where name = "table3")
   drop table table3
go


create table table3
(
  id        int
)
go

/* insert one record into each of the tables */
insert table1
values (0)
go

insert table2
values (0)
go

insert table3
values (0)
go

/* create three triggers to allow cascading effect */
create trigger table1update
   on table1
   for update as
 declare @id int

    select @id = id from table2
    select @id = @id + 1

    update table2
     set id = @id

  print 'updated table2'

go
```

```
create trigger table2update
   on table2
   for update as
 declare @id int

    select @id = id from table3
    select @id = @id + 1

    update table3
     set id = @id

   print 'updated table3'

go

create trigger table3update

   on table3
   for update as
 declare @id int

    select @id = id from table1
    select @id = @id +1

    update table1
     set id = @id

   print 'updated table1'

go


/********************* END OR STORED PROCEDURE *******************/

/* compile the stored procedure into the Pubs2 database */

sentenv SYBASE /appl/sybase        /* path to the directory containing
                                      the Sybase executable code. */
sentenv DSQUERY FIRST    /* FIRST is the name of SQL Server in
                            interfaces file */

isql -Uvideo -Pvideo -itrigger_tables.sql

/* invoke the triggers */
1> use pubs2    /* recall that the 1> is the sybase prompt */
2> go
```

```
1> update table1 set id = 1
2> go
```

Sybase's response (with the sp_configure "nested triggers" variable
set to 1):
(Note: to see the configuration values, type: 'sp_configure' and
'go' on separate lines beside the Sybase prompt)

```
    Msg 217, Level 16, State 1:
    Procedure 'table1update', Line 11:
    Maximum stored procedure nesting level exceeded (limit 16)
```

8.6   SUMMARY

This chapter discussed triggers. Triggers are automatically activated
when **update/delete/insert** operations are completed on a field or a
table.

A trigger is a special type of stored procedure that is written with a
standard text editor and compiled into a database's data dictionary to
guarantee referential integrity between tables.

This chapter provided a number of examples to demonstrates how
triggers are used in applications.

Cursors

In this chapter a reader will learn about:

- Overview of cursors
- Types of cursors
- Declaring cursors
- Opening cursors
- Fetching data
- Changing data through cursors
- Closing cursors
- Deallocating cursors
- General considerations

9.1   OVERVIEW OF CURSORS

Cursors are a powerful addition to SQL Server 10 and have traditionally been available in some versions of Open Client. This enhancement to SQL Server 10 allows processing of the results of an SQL request one record at a time. This is demonstrated as follows:

```
select employee_id, last_name, first_name, phone
    from employee
        where city="New York" and substring(phone, 1, 3)
                != "905"
```

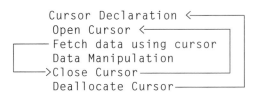

Figure 9.1   Steps to use a cursor.

This query returns all records that are qualified by the where clause. In many cases, however, it is desirable to have the records returned one at a time to local variables. After manipulation of the single record, another qualifying record is desired. Prior to System 10, SQL Server did not offer an easy solution to this requirement. It was possible to write a stored procedure containing fairly complicated and convoluted logic to step through the records in a table, one at a time, but developers have always been asking, "Isn't there a better way?" Cursors are that way. The steps required to use cursors are described in Figure 9.1.

A cursor must be declared before it can be used. After declaration, the cursor must be opened. This action invokes the SQL command (e.g., **select * from invoice**) within the cursor and creates a "cursor result set," which is a buffer or pool of records that meet the conditions of the **select**. Subsequent **fetch** commands retrieve records (one at a time, by default) that can be individually manipulated. Changes to the records in the cursor result set are passed to the original database table.

Unfortunately, the **fetch** command only operates in the forward direction. This means that it is not possible to re-read a record from the dataset by traversing backwards through the records. The way around this is to close the cursor and reopen it again to reposition the **fetch** at the starting of the cursor result set, which is shown by an arrow in the preceding figure. The opposite of declaring a cursor is to deallocate it. This eliminates all memory of the cursor from SQL Server.

9.2   ARCHITECTURE OF CURSORS

Figure 9.2 provides the architecture of cursors.

9.3   TYPES OF CURSORS

Although the name "cursor" evokes the image of another database object, in reality cursors have more in common with a while loop or some other piece of stored procedure code or embedded SQL commands. In

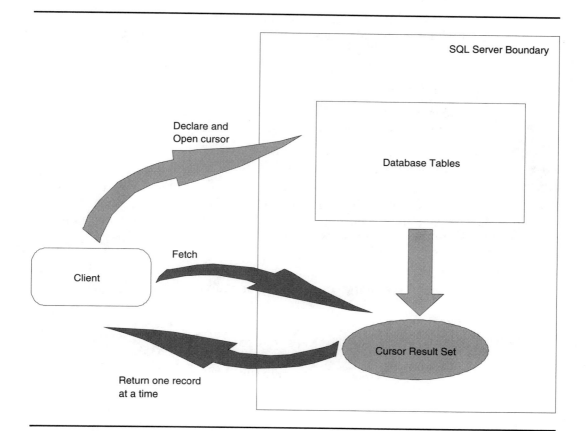

Figure 9.2   Cursor architecture.

fact, cursors behave very much like local variables in regard to their scope of visibility. Code to declare and manipulate cursors is contained inside a stored procedure, or a program on a client platform. There are two categories of cursors.

Category 1: Cursor on Server Cursors belonging to this category are manipulated in SQL or inside stored procedures. The scope of the cursor is the stored procedure that created them, or the SQL command that created them.

Category 2: Cursor on Client Cursors belonging to this category are manipulated by client platforms using Open Client software or embedded SQL calls. Opening a cursor creates the cursor result set that is then manipulated through Open Client calls. This is discussed in Chapter 14 (Open Client 10.0).

9.4 USING CURSORS

Using cursors, regardless of their type, essentially involves using the syntax shown as follows.

9.4.1 Declaring Cursors

A cursor must be declared before it is used. The syntax to declare a cursor can be included in a stored procedure or a third-generation language application. The cursor will be visible within the stored procedure that declares it, or until it is deallocated.

Syntax

```
declare name cursor for request
```

Examples

1. ```
declare inv_details cursor
   for
      select * from invoice_items
         where invoice_no = '123'
go
```

2. ```
declare sub_inv_details cursor
   for
    select movie_title, date_due, price
        from invoice_items
           where invoice_no = '123'
go
```

9.4.2 Opening Cursors

Opening a cursor causes its request statements to execute. The consequential cursor result set is created, and a pointer is positioned before the first record in the set. The pointer is moved forward by the **fetch** command.

Syntax

```
open cursor
```

Examples

1. `open inv_details`

2. `open invoice_headers`

9.4.3 Fetching Data

By default, every execution of a **fetch** command retrieves the next record in the cursor result set and makes it available to the calling routine (stored procedure or client application). This process is shown in Figure 9.3.

Syntax (there are two forms for the fetch)

1. `fetch cursor`

2. `fetch cursor into pool`

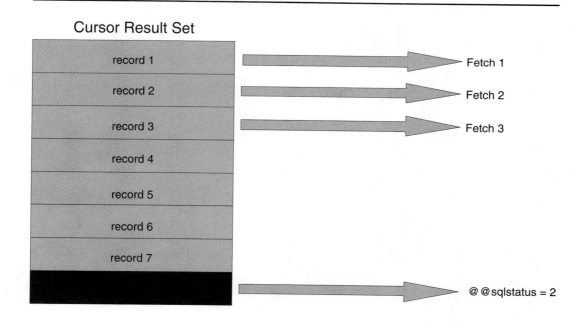

Figure 9.3   Operation of **fetch**.

```
if @@sqlstatus = 0
   'successful completion of fetch'
else
if @@sqlstatus = 1
   'error encountered in previous fetch'
else
if @@sqlstatus = 2
   'end of result set reached'
```

Figure 9.4   @@sqlstatus values.

Examples

1. `fetch inv_details`

2. `fetch sub_inv_details into @title, @due_date, @price`

Every fetch retrieves the next record in the data pool. Readers should examine the @@sqlstatus global variable to determine the success of a **fetch** operation. Figure 9.4 interprets the possible return values. If more than one row needs to be fetched at a time, users can use the **set cursor rows** command as follows:

Syntax

```
set cursor rows number for cursor
```

Examples

1. `set cursor rows 2 for inv_details`

2. `set cursor rows 5 for inv_details`

9.5   CLOSING CURSORS

Cursors should be closed to save resources when no longer needed. Closing and reopening a cursor is the only method of repositioning the pointer to the start of the cursor result set to re-read a record. This is shown in Figure 9.5.

Syntax

```
close cursor
```

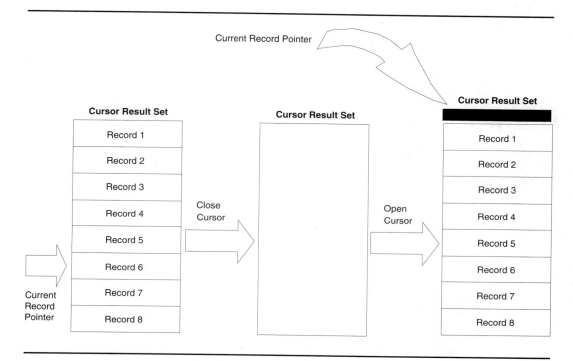

Figure 9.5   Repositioning the pointer.

Examples

1. `close inv_details`

2. `close invoice_cur`

9.6   DEALLOCATING CURSORS

To reuse a cursor name it is necessary to first deallocate the cursor. This will release the cursor entirely from SQL memory.

Syntax

```
deallocate cursor name
```

Examples

1. `deallocate cursor inv_details`

2. `deallocate cursor invoice_cur`

9.7   CURSOR EXAMPLES

Example 1. This section uses a cursor inside a stored procedure to apply an overdue charge for movies that are late in the Video Rental Store used in the tutorial in Chapter 17. Because the Video Rental Store offers personal service, valued customers are offered more leeway in returning late movies than are less frequent customers. Late charges are applied under the following conditions:

1. A movie is more than 5 days late.
2. If a movie is late, but the customer has taken out more than 5 movies in the past month, or more than 15 in the past 4 months, DO NOT apply a late charge.
3. If a movie is late, but the customer has been renting at least 1 movie every year for the past 10 years, DO NOT apply a late charge for 2 days (i.e., 2 day grace period).
4. If a movie is late, but the customer has provided at least 2 credit card numbers AND has been awarded a minimum of a 15% discount, DO NOT apply a late charge for half a day (i.e., 5 day grace period).

It may be possible to construct SQL queries to simultaneously resolve these requirements (but there will be performance penalties if the join/subquery accesses too many tables at one time or if the scope of the **select** is too wide); however, an effective and easy-to-maintain method is to step through all late invoice_items one at a time applying these conditions. This latter method also reduces locking contention on the table being accessed. The author has experience implementing a similar routine that steps through the records of a mission-critical online application one record at a time and applying considerably more complex requirements than those defined above, with no discernable impact on system response time.

The following stored procedure fragment demonstrates how a cursor would be used to solve this problem:

```
/************************************************
* ProcName:    late_charges                     *
* Author:      Sanjiv Purba                      *
* Date:        Nov 1993                          *
*                                                *
* Purpose: This program uses a cursor to step    *
*          through late movies one at a time     *
*          to determine the extent of late        *
```

```
*            charges that should be applied to   *
*            a customer's account.                *
*************************************************/
create proc late_charges
(
    @in_current_date            datetime
)
as
    declare @due_date           datetime,
            @invoice_no         int,
            @movie_code         int,
            @discount           int,
            @forever            int

/* initializations */
select @forever = 1 /* used for infinite while loop */

/* create cursor */
declare late_movies cursor
    for
        select invoice_no, due_date, movie_code, discount
            from invoice_items
                where due_date < @in_current_date and
                        product_code='M' /* 'M' = movies */

open late_movies

while @forever = 1
begin
    fetch late_movies into @invoice_no, @due_date,
                        @movie_code,@discount

/* Examine value of @@sqlstatus flag.
            2 means no more records to fetch
            1 means a fetch error has occurred */

if @@sqlstatus = 2
begin
    select 10 /* no more late movies to fetch */
    break
    end

if @@sqlstatus = 1
begin
```

```
    select -100 /* cursor fetch error */
    break
end


/*******************************
 * Process Invoice_items record *
 *******************************/
exec apply_late_charge @invoice_no, @due_date,
                  @movie_code, @discount

end /* outer while */

close late_movies

deactivate cursor late_movies

return 0
go


create proc apply_late_charge
(
@inv       int,
@due       datetime,
@movie     int,
@disc      int
)
as


        INSERT LOGIC HERE
go
```

Example 2. The following stored procedure uses a cursor to browse a table in the pubs2 database (the reader should type this into an ASCII file and save it under the name cursor.sql in order to test the stored procedure).

```
*******************************************************************

/*********************************************
 * ProcName:    browse_stores               *
 * Author:      Sanjiv Purba                 *
 * Date:        Nov 1993                     *
```

```
* Filename:    cursor.sql                      *
* Purpose: This program uses a cursor to step  *
*          through the stores table in the     *
*          PUBS2 database.                      *
************************************************/

use pubs2
go

drop proc browsestores
go

create procedure browsestores
as
     declare @input        int,
          @store_id        char(10),
          @city            char(20),
          @state           char(20),
          @status_sw       int

     declare browse_stores
               cursor
          for select stor_id, city, state from stores

     open browse_stores

     select @input = 1
     select @status_sw = 1

     while @status_sw = 1
     begin
     fetch browse_stores into @store_id, @city, @state
     if @@sqlstatus = 2
     begin
        select "no more rows to fetch"
        select "@status_sw =", @@sqlstatus
        break
     end
     else
     if @@sqlstatus = 1
     begin
        select "unknown cursor error"
        select "@status_sw =", @@sqlstatus
        break
        end
     else
```

```
        begin
            select "@status_sw =", @@sqlstatus
        end
        select 'selected values are: ',@store_id, @city,
        @state, @status_sw

        if @input > 100 /*only print 100 records for the
        test, max*/
        begin
            select 'breaking'
            break
        end

        select @input = @input + 1
        end

        select 'record read: ', @input

        return
go
**********************************************************************
```

The reader should compile this stored procedure into the **pubs2** database using the following command:

```
    isql -Uvideo -Pvideo -icursor.sql
```

(Assume that video is a valid user/password combination.) If the compile was successful, the cursor can be tested by using the commands in the following list:

```
isql -Uvideo -Pvideo
use pubs2
go
select db_name() /* should show pubs2 database name */
go
sp_help /* display list of objects, look for
browsestores)
go
exec browsestores
go
/* a list of stores and related information will appear
on the screen. */
exit /* quit SQL Server */
```

The folowing example demonstrates use of the "read only" option in declaring a cursor. Output after running the stored procedure is also included.

```
/*************************************************************
Filename:        browse_stores.sql
Author:          Sanjiv Purba
Date:            Nov 1993

Purpose:         The stored procedure in this script file demonstrates
                 a technique for declaring a read-only cursor, that
                 does not exclusively lock tables. Use of the read-
                 only keyword means that the stored procedure cannot
                 update the original table through an update of the
                 cursor result set.
Maintenance Log:

*************************************************************/

use pubs2
go

drop proc browsestores
go

/* READ ONLY example */

create procedure browsestores
as
   declare @input        int,
      @store_id          char(10),
      @city              char(20),
      @state             char(20),
      @status_sw         int,
      @msg               char(70)

   declare browse_stores
    cursor
    for select stor_id, city, state from stores for read only

   open browse_stores

   select @input = 1
   select @status_sw = 1
```

```
  while @status_sw = 1
  begin

    fetch browse_stores into @store_id, @city, @state

    if @@sqlstatus = 2
    begin
     select '@@rowcount =',  @@rowcount
     select "no more rows to fetch"
     break
    end
    else
    if @@sqlstatus = 1
    begin
       select "unknown cursor error"
       break
    end

    select @msg = 'selected values are:  ' + @store_id + ' ' + @city
+ ' ' + @st

    print @msg

    if @input > 100       /* defensive programming */
    begin
       select 'breaking'
       break
    end

    select @input + @input + 1

  end

  select 'record read: ', @input

  return
go

selected values are:  5023 Concord MA
selected values are:  6380 Seattle WA
selected values are:  7066 Tustin Asgirus CA
selected values are:  7131 Remulade WA
selected values are:  7896 Fremont CA
selected values are:  8042 Portland OR
```

```
selected values are:   8888 NYC NY


 _____  _____
 @@rowcount =            0
 (1 row affected)


 _____
 no more rows to fetch
 (1 row affected)


 _____
 record read:            8
 (1 row affected, return status = 0)
```

9.8   SUMMARY

This chapter introduced the reader to cursors, which are a very useful System 10 innovation. Cursors allow traversal of a table one record at a time.

Like the *control-of-flow* commands that have been discussed, cursors can be used within stored procedures. A status flag is returned by SQL Server to allow interpretation of the cursor's status after an invocation.

Many cursors can be declared and processed within a single stored procedure. Because cursors involve overhead, they should be deallocated when they are no longer required by a program.

Cursor performance is affected by the performance of the underlying **select**. Consequently, indexing can be used to allow the **select** to execute faster. Another factor to consider is that an extra step is required to traverse the result set after the **select** is executed. In some cases, traversing the actual records in a table may be faster than using a cursor. Cursors, however, offer the advantage of reducing contention time on a table by generating a result set for an application, which can then access the data without contending with other users.

10

Joins and Subqueries

In this chapter a reader will learn about:

- Overview of joins
- Understanding joins
- Types of joins
- Examples of joins
- Overview of subqueries
- Syntax of subqueries
- Nesting subqueries
- Examples
- General considerations
- Summary

10.1 OVERVIEW OF JOINS AND SUBQUERIES

In relational databases, the reader will recall, information is stored in a collection of tables. This collection is called a database. Relations between the tables allow information to be retrieved in a variety of formats and sequences. Relations are defined on "key" fields that can be composed of one or more attributes in the tables.

Tables having the same key fields can be related in a variety of ways in response to requests. Three common methods follow.

Sequential Search of the Individual Tables Cursors can be used for this (see Chapter 9).

Joins Described later in this chapter.

Subqueries Described later in this chapter.

It is an inexact science to determine which of these is ideal for a given situation. Joins and subqueries have their benefits, but care should be exercised in their use. It is often easy to conceptualize a solution using one of these; however, an implementation under Sybase requires the consideration of such things as indexing and the number of parameters in a where clause required to achieve optimization. At some point, the Sybase Optimizer chooses a table scan as a method of responding to a request, which can be devastating for response time when large tables are being used.

All joins and subqueries should be benchmarked prior to acceptance, but careful use makes them powerful and elegant solutions for many requirements.

10.2   OVERVIEW OF JOINS

Joins, a feature of ANSI SQL, can be used to retrieve information from multiple tables in a single request by joining on the relations between relational tables. Similar results can be achieved by using constructs such as subqueries and multiple individual selects in stored procedures. Joins, however, have the advantage of portability across different flavors of SQL and offer an elegant, intuitive structure.

10.3   UNDERSTANDING JOINS

Joins offer an intuitive way of looking at data in relational tables. The Video Rental Store data model in the tutorial in Chapter 17 has two tables that are natural candidates for a join. The invoice table contains header information about a customer's invoice. The invoice_items table contains detail information that appears on a printed invoice. This includes items such as the movies rented and products purchased by the customer. A join on these tables will retrieve the invoice header information and the related details to allow construction of the printed invoice copy.

Other tables such as customer can also be used in the join. The invoice table contains a relation with the customer table through the customer_id field. These relations are shown in Figure 10.1. A join on

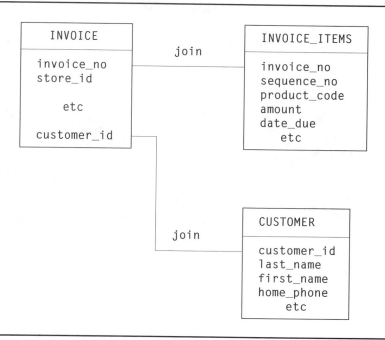

Figure 10.1   Tables participating in a join.

these fields will select an invoice header, the related invoice detail, and the customer detail.

10.4   TYPES OF JOINS

This section discusses two types of joins: (1) natural, and (2) outer.

10.4.1 Natural Joins

The "natural" join (also called the "equi-join") retrieves qualifying records from two or more tables. Only records that have records with matching key values in all the tables are retrieved by the request.

Syntax

```
select list
         from [table1][, table2][, table3][,...]
```

```
        where table1.join-field1 = table2.join-
    field1 and
        table2.join-field8 = table3.join-field8
```

Notes

1. List can be:
   A. If (*) then all fields from the tables participating in the join are selected by the query.
   B. Individual fields are identified and only they are selected by the query.
2. Join fields should have the same datatypes or use the **convert** command to make them so.
3. Inequality operators (i.e., <, >, <=, >= can be used in place of the equality operators) can affect performance when used in the **where** clause of a **select**.

Examples

1. ```
/* select all fields from two tables */

select * from invoice, invoice_items
    where invoice.invoice_no =
invoice_items.invoice_no
```

2. ```
/* select specific fields from two tables */

select invoice.invoice_no, invoice.invoice_date,
        invoice.total_amount,
        invoice_items.movie_id,
invoice_items.due_date
from invoice, invoice_items
    where invoice.invoice_no =
invoice_items.invoice_no
```

3. ```
/* select specific fields from three tables */

select invoice.invoice_no, invoice.customer_id,
        customer.last_name, customer.first_name,
        customer.home_phone,
        invoice.invoice_date,
        invoice.total_amount,
        invoice_items.movie_id,
invoice_items.due_date
```
```

```
    from invoice, invoice_items, customer
      where invoice.invoice_no =
    invoice_items.invoice_no and
          invoice.customer_id = customer.customer_id
```

4. ```
   /* Select specific fields from two tables with a
   specific
     condition. Notice that the unique field names do
   not
     need a table name prefix qualification. */

   select invoice.invoice_no, invoice_date,
       total_amount,
       invoice_items.movie_id, invoice_items.due_date
   from invoice, invoice_items
     where invoice.invoice_no =
   invoice_items.invoice_no and
           invoice.next_due_date < getdate()
   go
   ```

5. ```
   use pubs2
   go
   select * from stores, sales where stores.stor_id =
   sales.stor_id
   go
   ```

6. ```
   use pubs2
   go
   select * from stores st, sales sa where st.stor_id
   = sa.stor_id
   go
   ```

7. ```
   use pubs2
   go

   select stores.stor_id, stores.stor_name,
   sales.ord_num from stores, sales where
   stores.stor_id = sales.stor_id
   ```

8. ```
   select stores.stor_id, stor_name, ord_num,
   sales_date from stores, sales where stores.stor_id
   = sales.stor_id and sales.date < getdate ()
   go
   select distinct (stor_id) from stores
   go
   ```
   ```

```
select distinct (stor_id) from sales
go
/* if all stores in sales are not in the stores
table, some records will not be selected by the
join. */
```

Natural joins can also use inequality operators and other system procedures in the where clause. The reader should notice that only records that have records with matching keys in the tables participating in the join are selected.

10.4.2 Outer Joins

Suppose we want to design a query to select invoice header information and customer names. This can be done by joining the invoice and the customer tables. However, not every invoice will have a matching customer record, which is easily explainable because some customers will walk into the store, choose merchandise, and pay in cash. Such customers may not be added to the database as store members. The inner joins as presented in the previous section will not select these records.

The solution to this business requirement is provided by the outer join. The outer join selects all records from one table (designated in the join request) and any matching records from the other tables.

Syntax

```
select list
   from [table1][, table2][, table3][,...]
      where table1.join-field1 OPERATOR table2.join-
field1
```

Notes

1. List has the same notes as the natural join.
2. OPERATOR can be:
   A. "table1 *= table2" selects all records from table1.
   B. "table1 =* table2" selects all records from table2.

Examples

1. ```
   select invoice_no, invoice_date, total_amount,
   total_discount,
   ```
   ```

```
            customer.last_name, customer.first_name,
            customer.home_phone
        from invoice, customer
            where invoice.customer_id *=
customer.customer_id
```

2.  ```
    select invoice_no, invoice_date, total_amount,
    total_discount,
            customer.last_name, customer.first_name,
            customer.home_phone
        from invoice, customer
            where customer.customer_id =*
    invoice.customer_id
    ```

3.  ```
    select invoice_no, invoice_date, total_amount,
    total_discount,
            customer.last_name, customer.first_name,
            customer.home_phone
        from invoice, customer
            where invoice.customer_id *=
    customer.customer_id and
                credit_card_type != " "
    ```

4.  ```
    use pubs2
    go
    select sales.stor_id, stor_name, ord_num from
    sales, stores
        where stores.stor_id * = sales.stor_id
    ```

5.  ```
    use pubs2
    go
    select sales.stor_id, stor_name, ord_num from
        sales, stores where stores.stor_id = *
    sales.stor_id
    go
    ```

10.5 OTHER ISSUES

Joins can be used interactively or inside stored procedures. In interactive mode, joins can be typed at the Sybase prompt and executed by typing go on a separate line. Joins can be used inside stored procedures as freely as other Transact-SQL commands. Join results can be saved and manipulated inside local variables, as shown in Figure 10.2. Per-

```
/* only return one row from the select */
set rowcount 1

/* select specific fields from two tables */
select @invoice_no    = invoice.invoice_no,
       @invoice_date  = invoice.invoice_date,
       @total_amount  = invoice.total_amount,
       @movie_id      = invoice_items.movie_id,
       @due_date      = invoice_items.due_date
    from invoice, invoice_items
      where invoice.invoice_no =
               invoice_items.invoice_no
```

Figure 10.2   Joins inside stored procedures.

formance using joins can be improved by indexing the columns used in the joins.

10.6   OVERVIEW OF SUBQUERIES

Subqueries can be used instead of joins to extract information from two or more relational tables. Conceptually, subqueries are a series of nested queries, as shown in Figure 10.3.

In the previous segment, Query C is at the lowest level. It executes first and returns results to Query B, which executes and returns results to Query A. Nesting levels can continue indefinitely.

Subqueries offer an intuitive method of extracting qualified information from relational databases and can be used interactively, inside stored procedures, and through remote procedure calls. The author recommends readers consider their use in addition to joins. This knowledge is portable because both of these constructs can be used in other

```
Query A
 where
  Query B
  where
   Query C
    where . . .
```

Figure 10.3   Nested queries.

relational database languages that use ANSI SQL (such as Oracle, Informix, and Ingres).

In many cases, complex queries can be divided into subqueries. Sybase returns results faster for smaller queries on indexed fields than for large queries using the same indexes.

10.7   TYPES OF SUBQUERIES

This section discusses two types of subqueries that are supported by Sybase's Transact SQL.

10.7.1 Mathematical Operator Subqueries

Mathematical operators can be used (e.g., =, !=, >) in subqueries, as shown in Figure 10.4.

Examples

1.
```
select last_name, first_name, home_phone
    from customer
        where customer_id =
            (select customer_id from invoice
                where invoice_no = 123)
    /* useful only if one value is returned by the
    subquery */
```

2.
```
select * from payment_method
    where payment_method_code =
        (select payment_method_code from invoice
            where invoice_no = 123)
```

```
select field_list
  from table1
    where FIELD1 operator
        |
        | 1 value is returned
        |
        |
    (select FIELD1_value
       from table2
         where condition)
```

Figure 10.4   Mathematical operator subqueries.

```
select field_list
    from table1
        where field in
            (select field
                from table2
                where
                    condition)
```

Figure 10.5   Subqueries and **in**.

10.7.2 Subqueries and the In Command

The subquery option discussed in the previous section had the implicit limitation of requiring the lower-level subqueries to retrieve a single value for the outer (higher) level of the subquery. In many cases, this is not possible, or is cumbersome to engineer (e.g., this can be done by using the **set rowcount 1** command). The in keyword allows subqueries to behave like the join option and are not affected by this limitation.

The format of the in keyword is shown in Figure 10.5.

Examples

1. ```
   select * from invoice_items
       where invoice_no in
           (select invoice_no from invoice
                   where items_open > 0)
   ```

2. ```
   select * from credit_card_type
           where credit_card_type in
               (select distinct credit_card_type from
                   customer)
   ```

3. ```
   use pubs2
   go
   select au_lname, phone from authors where au_id in
           (select au_id from titleauthor where
               royaltyper = 100)
   go
   ```


10.8   OTHER CONSIDERATIONS

Several variations are available to tailor the use of these subquery formats and are examined in this section.
   ```

10.8.1 > all

This command is used with mathematical operators to select records that are greater than all values selected by the nested subquery, allowing the query to return more than one value.

Example

```
select * from invoice
    where total_taxes > all
        (select pst+other_taxes from invoice_items)
```

10.8.2 > any

Use of this command is similar to the **> all**. This command means that the highest level of the query will retrieve records that are larger than at least one value returned by the lower-level subquery.

Example

```
select * from customer
    where discount_percent > any
        (select discount from invoice_items where
            due_date <= getdate() )
```

10.8.3 = any

This will retrieve records that have a matching field value with any fields returned by the lower-level subquery.

Example

```
select last_name, first_name, date_joined, phone from
customer where customer_id = any
        (select customer_id from invoice
            where items_open > 0)
```

10.8.4 Using Update in a Subquery

Update, **delete**, and **insert** SQL commands can be used with subqueries.

Example

```
1. update invoice
      set next_due_date = dateadd (day, 2, getdate)
   where invoice_no in
```

```
         (select invoice_no from invoice_items
              where product_code = 18)
2.  update discounts
       set stor_id = 'TTTT'
    where discount = any
     (select price from titles)
    go
```

Note: The presence of NULLS in fields that are used in the qualifying conditions of these examples can make them unsuccessful.

10.9   SUMMARY

This chapter focused on SQL joins. Joins are used to retrieve information from two or more relational tables. Two types of joins were discussed: natural and outer. Joins can be used interactively or inside stored procedures. This chapter also focused on subqueries as they are used in Transact-SQL. Syntax and examples of single value and **in** keywords were discussed.

This chapter also examined variations such as the **= any, > any,** and **> all** commands.

11

SQL Server System Procedures

In this chapter a reader will learn about:

- System procedures
- Catalog procedures
- sp_configure
- sp_dboption

11.1 INTRODUCTION TO SYSTEM PROCEDURES

Sybase SQL Server offers a rich group of system procedures, identifiable by a sp_ preface, to assist users in managing the Sybase environment and system tables. System procedures are essentially stored procedures developed by Sybase, Inc. Users can also utilize system procedures to insert/delete/update information into system tables, instead of using Transact-SQL commands such as **insert/update/delete**.

System procedures are basically used by system administrators, system officers, and system operators to do their jobs. Application developers generally use a small subset of these procedures. This small subset is provided in the next section.

In pre-System 10, system procedures were stored in the **master** database. In SQL Server 10, system procedures have been moved to a separate database called **sybsystemprocs**. This has shrunk the size of the **master** database, thus assisting housekeeping functions on the **master** database (i.e., backup and recovery is faster).

The system procedures stored in **sybsystemprocs** are accessible to users regardless of their current database. Users can also create their own system procedures just as they would any other stored procedure (see Chapter 6 on creating stored procedures), except that the name should be prefixed with an sp_, and preferably stored in **sybsystemprocs** (although system procedures can be stored in a user database just as well).

Users who are curious to find out what is contained in system procedures can use another system procedure to display the contents of any system procedure that is desired. This can be done by using the following commands.

Example

```
/* logon to sybase: isql -Uuserid -Ppassword */
use sybsystemprocs
go
sp_helptext sp_helpuser
go
or
sp_helptext sp_helptext
go
System 10 users can also use a system procedure to
display help about other system procedures, as
follows:
1> sp_syntax sp_helptext
2> go
This will display the following:
Syntax Help
————

System Procedure
sp_helptext - Prints the text of a system procedure,
trigger, view, default, rule, or integrity constraint
  sp_helptext objname
```

The first part of this chapter focuses on a subset of system procedures that are specifically used by programmers and developers during normal day-to-day application development, based on the author's experience. Such system procedures generally provide information about system tables, as opposed to making infrequent changes (e.g., **sp_addlanguage**) to a Sybase environment. The second part of this chapter divides the majority of Sybase's system procedures into categories by the functions they perform.

11.2   SOME COMMONLY USED SYSTEM PROCEDURES

The following commands are usually entered interactively. The user first signs into SQL Server and selects a default database, for example, isql -Uvideo -Pvideo. In this example, video is a user (with password video) that can have a default database identified in the syslogins table. Any of the following commands can then be entered followed by "go" to initiate execution.

11.2.1   sp_depends

Provides a cross-reference of database objects (e.g., stored procedures, view, triggers) that are used by the object specified in parameter, as well as the objects that use it. Shows parent-child relationships.

Syntax

```
sp_depends parameter
```

Examples

a. `sp_depends syskeys`

b. `sp_depends video`

11.2.2   sp_help

Displays information about the object specified in parameter. This can consist of defaults, logs, rules, stored procedures, tables, triggers, and views.

Syntax

```
sp_help parameter (parameter is optional)
```

Examples

a. `sp_help video`

b. `sp_help`
`result: display of sysobjects`

c. `sp_help insert_video`

11.2.3   sp_helpdb

Returns information about databases.

Syntax

```
sp_helpdb parameter
```

Examples

a. sp_helpdb /* lists information about all databases
        */

b. sp_helpdb VMS /* displays specific information
        about
        the specified database i.e. db_size, owner, status,
        device_fragments, size, usage, and free kbytes. */

c. sp_helpdb SECTOR

11.2.4   sp_helpindex

Retrieves information about a table's indexes (clustered and nonclustered). The tablename is specified in the parameter.

Syntax

```
sp_helpindex parameter
```

Examples

a. sp_helpindex video

b. sp_helpindex customer

c. use pubs2
        go
        sp_helpindex stores
        go

11.2.5   sp_helptext

Displays the compiled code corresponding to a stored procedure, trigger, view, default, or rule, as specified in parameter. This code is retrieved from a database syscomments system table.

Syntax

```
sp_helptext parameter
```

Examples

a. `sp_helptext insert_video`

b. `sp_helptext add_insert`

c. `/* create a current copy of a stored procedure by saving the screen output in a file, as follows. */ sp_helptext proc_name > pipe results into a batch file.`

11.2.6   sp_helpuser

Displays information about a user or all users in the default database.

Syntax

```
sp_helpuser parameter (parameter is optional)
```

Examples

a. `sp_helpuser`

b. `sp_helpuser manager`

11.2.7   sp_lock

Provides information about all locked processes. This information is supported by the sysprocesses table.

Syntax

```
sp_lock parameter1, parameter2
     (these parameters are optional)
```

Examples

a. `sp_lock 4`

b. `sp_lock`

c. `sp_lock 2`

11.2.8   sp_primarykey

This function is used to specify which fields in a table record form the primarykey for the table.

Syntax

```
sp_primarykey parameter1, parameter2, parameter3
parameter1          = table_name
parameter2...       = field_names
```

Examples

a. `sp_primarykey video, movie_title`

b. `sp_primarykey customer, last_name, first_name`

c. `sp_primarykey rental, date_due, movie_title, customer_code`

11.2.9   sp_recompile

Flags a table so that each stored procedure and trigger that uses it is automatically recompiled when it is next executed.

Syntax

```
sp_recompile parameter
```

Example

```
sp_recompile video
```

11.2.10   sp_reportstats

Displays information about system usage. Parameter can contain a user name as specified in the sysusers system table (must have sa role).

Syntax

```
sp_reportstats parameter (parameter is optional)
```

Examples

a. `sp_reportstats victoria`

b. `sp_reportstats`

11.2.11 sp_spaceused

Displays space usage for database objects in the default database.

Syntax

```
sp_spaceused parameter (parameter is optional)
```

Examples

a. `sp_spaceused`

b. `sp_spaceused video`

c. `sp_spaceused customer`

11.2.12 sp_who

Displays information about active users in a database. Parameter is used to get information about a single user (by user name) or an active process (by sp_id).

Syntax

```
sp_who parameter (parameter is optional)
```

Examples

a. `sp_who`

b. `sp_who manager`

c. `sp_who "1"`

11.2.13 sp_addlogin

This system procedure is used to add login information for a user into the *master* database. The user must have the privilege to do this.

Syntax

```
sp_addlogin user, password, default database
```

Example

```
use master /* master must be the default database */
go
```

```
sp_addlogin "sector", "sector", "video"
go
```

11.2.14 sp_adduser

This system procedure is used to add a user to a user-defined database.

Syntax

```
sp_adduser user
```

Example

```
use video
go
sp_adduser "sector"
go
```

11.3   sp_configure

The next two sections of this chapter examine two system procedures that allow monitoring and changing the Sybase environment through flags and variables. **sp_configure** is a powerful system procedure that can be used to query and change the Sybase configuration variables that control the Sybase environment. In its simplest form, it displays the Sybase environment variables and their current settings, as follows:

```
sp_configure
go
```

The following list of environment variables is displayed with values filled in. Notice that valid values must fit within the min/max range. Each of these variables is assigned a default value after SQL Server installation. Users should not feel obligated to change any of these anytime soon as they are sufficient to get started.

A user must be signed on as a system administrator in order to change the value of a Sybase environment variable. To modify the value of one of the environment variables, use the following sequence of commands:

```
sp_configure "recovery interval", 2
reconfigure
go
```

run_value	min	maximum	config_value	run_value
recovery interval	1	32767	0	5
allow updates	0	1	0	1
user connections	5	2147483647	0	25
memory	3850	2147483647	0	5120
open databases	5	2147483647	0	10
locks	5000	2147483647	0	5000
open objects	100	2147483647	0	500
procedure cache	1	99	0	20
fill factor	0	100	0	0
time slice	50	1000	0	10
database size	2	10000	0	2
tape retention	0	365	0	50
recovery flags	0	1	0	1
nested triggers	0	1	1	1
devices	4	256	14	20
remote access	0	1	1	1
remote logins	0	2147483647	0	30
remote sites	0	2147483647	0	8
remote connections	0	2147483647	0	25
pre-read packets	0	2147483647	0	4
upgrade version	0	2147483647	1000	1000
default sortorder id	0	255	50	50
default language	0	2147483647	0	0
language in cache	3	100	3	3
max online engines	1	32	1	8
min online engines	1	32	1	6
engine adjust interval	1	32	0	0
cpu flush	1	2147483647	200	200
i/o flush	1	2147483647	1000	999
default character set id	0	255	1	1
stack size	20480	2147483647	0	28672
password expiration interval	0	32767	0	0
audit queue size	1	65535	100	100

run_value	*min*	*maximum*	*config_value*	*run_value*
additional netnum	0	2147483647	0	0
default network packet size	512	524288	0	512
maximum network packet size	512	524288	0	512
extent i/o buffers	0	2147483647	0	0

The reader should notice the range restriction on each of the parameters as well as the default value. The default values tend to be acceptable until a team is well into project development.

11.4   sp_dboption

Like **sp_configure**, this stored procedure can also be used to control the Sybase environment, specifically through database options (hence the name "db" + "option"). This command has several variations, as shown by the following syntax.

Syntax

```
sp_dboption    dbname, optname, true/false
where dbname is the name of the database that
should be affected.
     optname is the name of the database option to
be changed.
     set the optname to true or false.
```

For a list of options, enter the procedure name without parameters:

Examples

```
1. use master /* it is necessary to run this procedure
                 with the master database as
                 default. */
   go
   sp_dboption
   go /* displays a list of database options */
2. use master
   go
```

```
sp_dboption video, "no chkpt on recovery", true
go
```

3. ```
   use master
   go
   sp_dboption video, "trunc log on chkpt", true
   go
   ```

A list of database options and their usage follows.

11.4.1 abort tran on log full

If this option is set to "true," transactions running in a database that write to a transaction log that has had the last_chance threshold stored procedure fired will be aborted. If this option is set to "false," the transactions will be suspended until space becomes available in the transaction log.

11.4.2 allow nulls by default

If true, columns defined as "not null" will be defaulted to "null."
If false, columns defined as "not null" will remain "not null."

11.4.3 dbo use only

If true, access to a database is restricted to its owner.

11.4.4 ddl in tran

If true, wider scope of Transact-SQL commands can be used in user transactions.

11.4.5 no chkpt on recovery

If true, an extra copy of a database is maintained.

11.4.6 no free space acctg

If true, it turns off threshold actions and free space accounting calculations.

11.4.7 read only

If true, it allows users read-only access to the affected database.
   ```

11.4.8   select into/bulkcopy

If true, it allows the execution of functions like fast BCP that do not write modified records to the transaction log.

11.4.9   single user

If true, only a single user is allowed access to a database.

11.4.10   trunc log on chkpt

If true, transaction log is truncated at a checkpoint. This feature should only be used in development environments, as the truncation will cause a database and its transaction log to become slightly out of sync.

11.5   CATALOG STORED PROCEDURES

Sybase SQL Server 10 offers a library of stored procedures intended for use across database gateways. Some of the commonly used stored procedures are **sp_columns**, **sp_databases**, **sp_server_info**, **sp_statistics**, **sp_stored_procedures**, **sp_table_privileges**, and **sp_tables**. They can also be used interactively.

11.6   SUMMARY

This chapter focused on system procedures, which can be found in the **sybsystemprocs** database. System procedures are essentially stored procedures that manage the system tables and the Sybase environment.

This chapter examined some of the commonly used system procedures from a development perspective, such as: **sp_help**, **sp_helptext**, **sp_who**, and **sp_helpdb**.

This chapter also examined two administration system procedures, namely **sp_configure** and **sp_dboptions**.

A SQL Server 10 system procedure, **sp_syntax**, was introduced because it can be used to display help information. The **syntax** database must be installed to access this information.

A complete list of system procedures can be found in Appendix J.

Transaction Logs

In this chapter a reader will learn about:

- Overview of transaction logs
- syslogs table
- Log placement
- Dump commands
- Checkpoints
- Managing logs through dboption
- Thresholds

12.1 OVERVIEW OF TRANSACTION LOGS

SQL Server transaction logs are important from a standpoint of transaction recoverability in a high-performance, online environment. Every Sybase database has a corresponding transaction log, which is stored in the syslogs table. Although it is part of a database, the transaction log can (and should) be stored on a physical device separate from where the corresponding database is positioned. Some reasons for doing this are as follows:

1. Database device corruption will not affect the corresponding transaction log, so full recovery is possible.
2. Transaction log can be backed up separately from the database files (requiring less time, so it can be done more frequently).

3. Additional **dump transaction** commands can be used to manipulate the transaction log.
4. There will be improved performance due to spreading of workload across several physical device controllers.
5. There will be an ability to use thresholds.

Separating a transaction log from its database is done by allocating a separate physical device (i.e., raw partition or operating system file) in the master..sysdevices and master..sysusages tables. This separate device is used as part of the **create database . . . . log on device_name** command that was presented in Chapter 4. These relationships are shown in Figure 12.1.

For a development environment, it is acceptable to use operating system files as devices. For production environments, however, it is

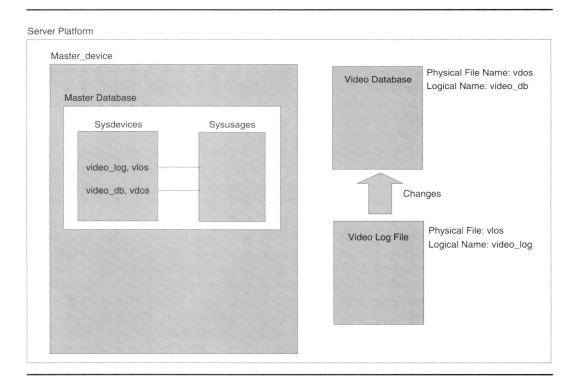

Figure 12.1 Databases and transaction logs.

highly advisable to use raw partitions to allow full recoverability of transactions following a crash. In the latter case (raw partition), SQL Server has full control over when transactions are written to disk. In the former case, SQL Server communicates to the operating system that a write to a disk file is to be done and then steps out of the picture—not knowing if and when the write was actually done. This uncertainty is completely undesirable in production environments.

As changes are made to a database, SQL Server writes information to the end of the transaction log (appends) so that the change can either be committed or backed out if a problem is encountered. The transaction log is clearly the first point of activity and can easily be filled up. SQL Server offers several administrative commands to be discussed in this chapter that allow manipulation of the contents of a log file, shown in Figure 12.2.

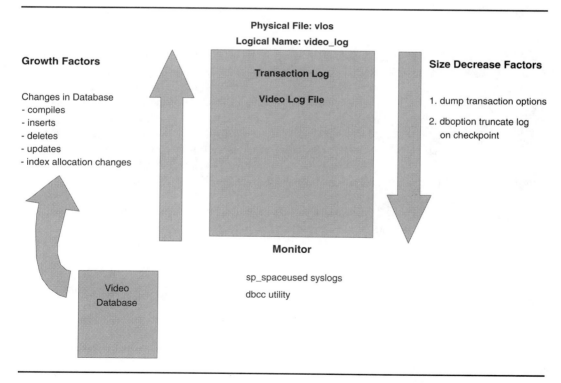

Figure 12.2   Transaction log content changes.

12.2   CHECKPOINT PROCESSING

Committed transactions are made to a portion (data pages) of the database that is stored in a memory data cache. Readers who have used shrinkwrap software such as WordPerfect, Lotus, or Word on a PC should recognize the parallel between having something in memory and having it saved permanently on disk. In the data cache case, a system crash will cause transactions that were recorded in the cache (i.e., "dirty" pages) but not saved on disk to be lost. This is where the parallel between the shrinkwrap software and SQL Server ends. SQL Server can recover completed transactions automatically.

While restarting following a crash, SQL Server accesses the transaction log of each database and reapplies completed transactions to that database if they were not saved to disk prior to the crash. This reverts databases to their precrash status. Of course, it takes time, and depending on the number of transactions that were lost from cache, the recovery time could become quite lengthy. This potential problem is averted by using "checkpoints" to ensure that database recoverability time does not exceed a value (in minutes) specified in the recovery interval configuration parameter.

The **checkpoint** procedure is a background job that accesses every database in SQL Server on a frequent basis (e.g., every minute) to determine if its cache data pages should be written to disk. In making this decision, the checkpoint procedure uses the value stored in the recovery interval configuration parameter (default is 5 minutes) to ensure that if a crash were to occur, complete recovery for the database could be done within this time parameter. In the case when recovery is expected to take longer than the value (say 10 minutes) stored in recovery interval, the checkpoint process writes the contents of the data cache (dirty pages) for the database to disk.

Figure 12.3 shows the background **checkpoint** procedure.

The **checkpoint** command can also be manually issued to write dirty pages to disk. However, this imposes limitations in dumping the transaction log, so it is not equivalent to the background checkpoint process.

The recovery interval can be changed by using the following commands:

```
sp_configure "recovery interval", 2
reconfigure
/* the reader should note that they should have a
system administrator role in order to execute these
commands. */
```

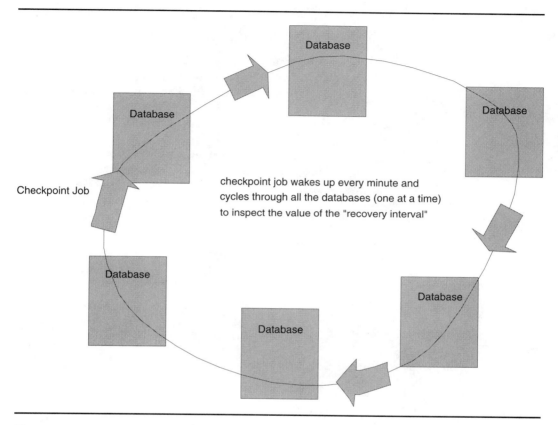

checkpoint job wakes up every minute and
cycles through all the databases (one at a time)
to inspect the value of the "recovery interval"

Figure 12.3   Checkpoint background job.

```
/* ensure that the new value has taken effect */
sp_configure
go
```

12.3   DUMP COMMANDS

Since database changes are appended to the bottom of a transaction log, sooner or later it will get filled up. It is a serious situation that must be avoided. If a transaction log gets filled up, there could be a recovery problem because the log will need to be dumped without saving to disk. It happens because the command to write the transaction file to disk adds change information to the same transaction log—which it is unable to do because the log is full. Before a log gets completely filled up, it can be safely dumped to disk.

In order to back up or dump a transaction log, make a copy of it and remove the "inactive" portion of the log to free up space. In some cases, especially during development projects, it is desirable to remove the inactive portion of the log without making an archive copy of the transaction log. This is shown in Figure 12.4 for a transaction log that is stored on a device separate from its database.

During development projects, the **no_log** option is acceptable. In fact, during periods of heavy compiling and testing, developers should know how to use this command, otherwise (speaking from experience) they will discover that their 2 A.M. work session must be interrupted because they are unable to execute additional compiles into their working database.

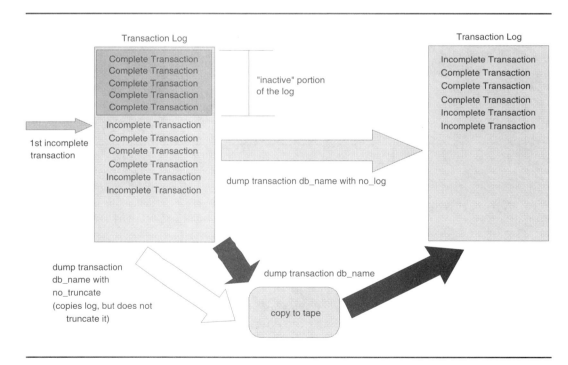

Figure 12.4   Dumping a transaction log on a separate device.

Unless work teammates do not mind calls at that hour, the developer will have to wait until someone with this knowledge comes to work.

Another time to use the **no_log** option is in production environments when the transaction log becomes completely full and hence is unable to accommodate commands that write data to the log file. The **with no_truncate** variation can be used to make backup copies of a transaction log without removing any data from it.

Transaction log processing for logs stored on the same device as their databases is a little more cumbersome and slower. The database should be copied before the transaction log is truncated. The **dump transaction db_name**, **dump transaction db_name with no_log**, and **dump trans db_name with no_truncate** commands cannot be used on logs with this positioning and is shown in Figure 12.5.

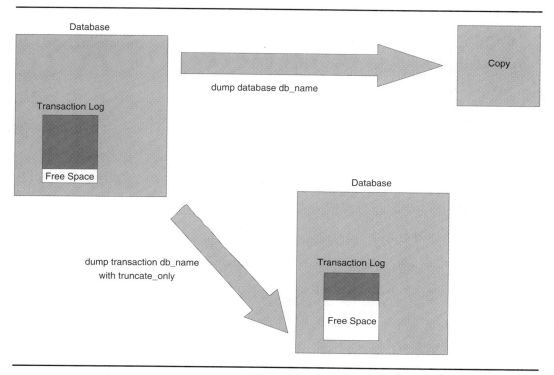

Figure 12.5   Dumping a transaction log that is on the same device as its database.

A common strategy for supporting backup and recovery requirements is to do the following:

1. Separate database and transaction logs on separate physical devices.
2. Do a full database backup (lots of data) once a week (Tape A) to tape.
3. Back up transaction logs at least once a day (Tape B, C, D) to tape.

In the event of a system crash that cannot be recovered automatically (this is attempted automatically when SQL Server starts up), load the database (i.e., load A from device) with the tape copy, then load the transaction logs (i.e., load B from device, load C from device, load D from device) with the individual tape copies.

12.4   DBOPTION VARIATIONS

It is possible to reduce the size of a transaction log by piggybacking on the checkpoint background process. Since this process runs every minute or so, it can be used to remove committed transactions from the inactive portion of the transaction log file.

In order to instruct the checkpoint process to truncate the log corresponding to a database, use the following commands:

```
use master
go
sp_dboption dbname, "trunc log on chkpt", true
go
```

These commands will operate on the database identified in the sp_dboption. This approach is only acceptable during development. It should not be used in production systems because full recovery will not be possible following a system crash because the transaction log is not being backed up.

This option can be turned off using the following commands:

```
use master
go
sp_dboption dbname, "trunc log on chkpt", false
go
```

12.5   THRESHOLDS

Thresholds are a System 10 feature that remove some uncertainty in the management of transaction log space. Quite simply, a threshold is created at the database level for a transaction log (which must have its own device/segment) to specify an amount of free space (defined in pages) that must exist in the log at all times. A stored procedure is triggered when free space falls below this value. Further transactions on the database are not allowed until the amount of free space increases appropriately. These transactions are either aborted (if "abort tran on log full" is TRUE) or suspended until the situation changes.

The stored procedure is intended to clear up transaction log space by issuing a **dump transaction** command on the database. A special system procedure, **sp_thresholdaction**, is executed when a last-chance threshold is crossed. The idea here is that any further usage of the transaction log, with the exception of dumping it to a backup, will make it impossible to use the dump command later on. Up to 256 thresholds can be assigned to a database, but in practice, only a few may be required to effectively manage log space. Figure 12.6 shows the relationship of various thresholds on a log file.

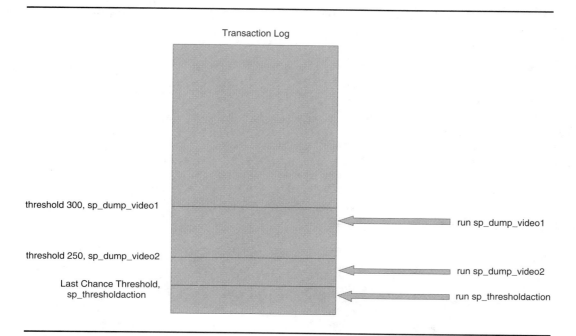

Figure 12.6   Multiple thresholds in a database.

12.5.1 Display Threshold Information

To see information about thresholds in a database, it is necessary to make the desired database the current one. This is shown in the following example:

```
use video
go
sp_helpthreshold        /* this will display all
                           thresholds in the database */
go
```

To retrieve information about a specific threshold, it is necessary to know the name of the threshold, as follows:

```
sp_helpthreshold segment_name
go
```

12.5.2 Adding Thresholds

Thresholds can be added to a database and applied at the segment level, up to the maximum of 256 for a database, using the following command:

Syntax

```
sp_addthreshold db_name, seg_name, free_space, procedure
where
   db_name      = the database name (current database)
   seg_name     = the name of the segment holding the log
   free_space   = the threshold in pages
   procedure    = the name of the procedure to execute if the
                  threshold is crossed
```

By default, two thresholds with the same free_space on the same segment has no meaning.

Examples

1. `sp_addthreshold video, video_seg, 300, sp_dump_vid300`

2. `sp_addthreshold video, video_seg, 200, sp_dump_vid200`

In these examples, the stored procedures that are identified in the previous examples could be similar to the following:

```
/********************************************************************
 * Procedure Name: sp_dump_vid300                                   *
 * Author:         Naveen Parkash                                   *
 * Date:           Jan 1994                                         *
 * File Name:      vid300.sql                                       *
 *                                                                  *
 * The following procedure will be invoked when threshold 300       *
 * is crossed.                                                      *
 ********************************************************************
create procedure sp_dump_vid300
   @database char(50),
as
   select "printing database ", @database
   dump trans @database to "device"
   return
go
```

12.5.3 Modifying Thresholds

To modify any of the parameters of an existing threshold, use the following command:

Syntax

```
sp_modifythreshold db_name, seg_name, freespace,
               new_proc, new_free, new_segname
where
   db_name      = name of current database which
should be the name of the database to affect
   seg_name     = original segment name
   freespace    = original freespace
   new_proc     = name of stored procedure
   new_free     = new amount of free space
   new_segname  = new name of segment
```

Example. To change the first threshold above, use the following format:

```
sp_modifythreshold, video, "video_seg", 300, NULL,
250, "video_seg2"
```

This will change the free space threshold from 300 to 250 pages. The command will also change the segment name.

12.5.4 Dropping Thresholds

Thresholds on a segment can be dropped with the following command:

Syntax

```
sp_dropthreshold db_name, seg_name, freespace
where
   db_name    = name of current database
   seg_name   = name of segment
   freespace  = used to select the threshold that is
to be dropped
```

Example

```
sp_dropthreshold video, "video_seg", 250
```

12.6   OTHER CONSIDERATIONS

Based on the discussion in this chapter, it is clear that the size of a transaction log will affect the amount of attention required to manage

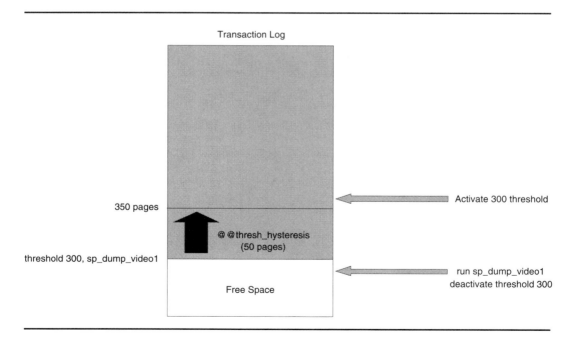

Figure 12.7   Use of @ @thresh_hysteresis and thresholds.

the log space. How large should a transaction log be? The *Sybase System Administration Guide* suggests a value of 20 percent as a good place to start; this is a reasonable approach. A caveat is that databases requiring few operations can start with a log size that is less, perhaps 10 to 15 percent of the size of the database. Log files with anticipated heavy activity and online usage can start as high as 25 percent.

Developers should monitor their log size utilization and change its size as required. Developers should also be aware of Transact-SQL commands that write data to the log files, and how much they write to the log files, relative to other commands (i.e., use of NULL, truncate table writes less information to the log than the **drop table** command; volatile portions of a record should be normalized into a separate table so that the nonvolatile record data is not repeatedly written to the transaction log).

Once a threshold is crossed and its corresponding stored procedure is triggered, that threshold becomes inactive until another event, dic-

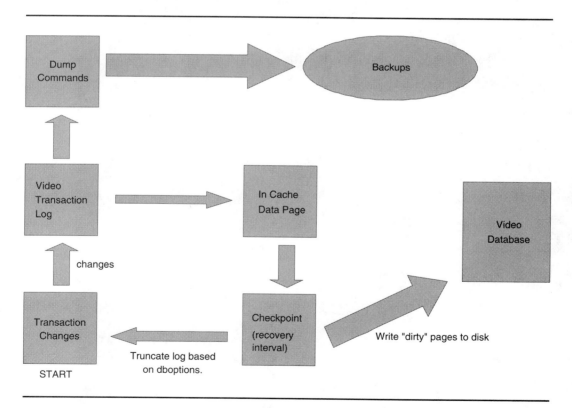

Figure 12.8   Summary of transaction log management.

tated by the environment variable @@thresh_hysteresis, occurs. @@thres_hysteresis contains a value in pages that is added to the threshold. When the freespace rises above this sum, the threshold is reactivated, shown in Figure 12.7.

12.7 SUMMARY

While there are relatively few commands that affect transaction logs, it is important for developers and system administrators to be aware of how transaction logs operate in SQL Server. It is important to understand which commands cause heavy log activity and which do it. Some relatively simple choices (i.e., use **truncate** instead of **delete**) can improve response time significantly.

This chapter includes general considerations in transaction log management, log placement, checkpoints, backup/recovery of transaction logs, and thresholds. Figure 12.8 summarizes some of the relationships in the management of transaction log files.

User-Defined Datatypes, Defaults, and Rules

In this chapter a reader will learn about:

- User-defined datatypes
- Defaults
- Rules
- NULL

13.1 OVERVIEW OF USER-DEFINED DATATYPES, DEFAULTS, AND RULES

This chapter provides further detail and examples for the concepts introduced in Chapter 4 for user-defined datatypes, defaults, and rules. User-defined datatypes are useful for customizing table columns and local variables by providing defaults and rules for them. The process for doing this is sequential and is shown in Figure 13.1.

These objects are created into a database. They can be created into the **model** database to automatically copy them to subsequently created user-created databases. They are usually created directly into an appropriate user database.

13.2 USER-DEFINED DATATYPES

User-defined datatypes can be created for commonly used datatypes that require standardization, standard default values, or domain rules.

1.   Create User-defined datatype
2.   Create default
3.   Bind default to field or datatype
4.   Create rule
5.   Bind rule to field or datatype
6.   Unbind default
7.   Drop default
8.   Unbind rule
9.   Drop rule

Figure 13.1   Steps to follow.

By changing the definition of the User-defined datatype, all occurrences of it will be affected. User datatypes should be created with a database in use.

sp_addtype, a system procedure, is used to create a user-defined datatype according to the following:

Syntax

```
sp_addtype  name, datatype, NULL/"not null"
```

Examples

1. `sp_addtype char_5, "char(5)", "not null"`

    `go`

    `sp_help sp_addtype`

    `go`

2. `sp_addtype int_0, "int", "not null"`

3. `sp_addtype char_10, "char(10)"`

4. `sp_addtype phone, "char(12)", NULL`

Use the following syntax to drop a user-defined datatype:

Syntax

```
sp_droptype name
```

Examples

1. `sp_droptype int_0`

2. `sp_droptype char_10`

It is helpful to include all user-defined datatype creation commands in a script file that first drops the name, then creates it. This allows a database environment to be reestablished to the same point of reference at any time. This script file should be separate from a table creation script, and it should be executed first.

13.3   ASSIGNING DEFAULTS

Part of the decision in designing relational database tables is to consider the following four issues:

1. A field must have a unique (key) value entered in it.
Use "not null" with no default value; For example,

`credit_card_id int not null`

2. A field must have a value. A predefined value (default) is acceptable.
Use "not null" with a bound default value.

3. There may be a future requirement to change the default value for a group of fields with the same datatype.
Use a user-defined datatype with "not null" with a bound default value.

4. A field can accept a NULL value; For Example,

`credit_card_id int null`

Allowing NULL into a field has side effects that the author favors avoiding by using default values instead. A NULL actually means: "This field contains some unknown value." Because the value is not known, fields containing NULL cannot be used in joins or numeric functions. Conversely, using default values gives total predictability to the contents of a field by inserting a predefined value (e.g., blank or 0) if no value is specified during a record insert.

Creating and dropping defaults is straightforward. The following syntax shows how default variables are created:

Syntax

`create default default_name as "value"`

Examples

1. `create default vid_5spaces as "   "`

2. `create default phone_no as "111 111 1111"`

The syntax to drop a default is as follows:

Syntax

```
drop default default_name
```

Examples

1. `drop default vid_5spaces`

2. `drop default phone_no`

The default must not be bound to table fields or user-defined datatypes if it is being dropped.

13.4   BINDING DEFAULTS

Defaults can be bound to a field or a user-defined datatype according the following syntax:

Syntax

```
sp_bindefault default_name, "table_name.field_name"

sp_bindefault default_name, datatype
```

Examples

1. `sp_bindefault phone_no, "customer.hphone"`

2. `sp_bindefault phone_no, phone`

3. `sp_bindefault "video.vid_5spaces", "authors.city"`
   `/* use this format if you are not the object owner`
   `and if you have the permission. */`

Defaults are unbound by specifying an object name to a system procedure. The following syntax is used to unbind defaults:

Syntax

```
sp_unbindefault "table_name.field_name"

sp_unbindefault datatype
```

Examples

1. `sp_unbindefault "customer.hphone"`

2. `sp_unbindefault phone`

Drop a previous default before binding a new default to a field or user datatype.

13.5   RULES

Rules are created and bound to table fields or user-defined databases. They offer another level of data validation to ensure that only acceptable data is entered into a database.

Syntax

```
create rule rule_name
        as
@variable_name expression
```

Examples

1.  ```
    create rule sex
        as @sex in ("M", "F")
    go
    sp_help sex
    go
    ```

2.  ```
    create rule num_code
        as @store_id between 1 and 4
    go
    ```

13.6   BINDING RULES

Bind rules to table fields or user-defined databases by using the following syntax:

Syntax

```
sp_bindrule rulename, object_name
```

Examples

1.  ```
    sp_bindrule sex, "customer.sex" /* table field
    name */
    ```
    ```

    2. `sp_bindrule num_code, "int_0" /* user defined`
    `datatype */`

13.7   UNBINDING RULES

Unbind a rule by specifying the field name or the user-defined datatype:

Syntax

```
sp_unbindrule object_name
```

Examples

1. `sp_unbindrule "customer.sex"`

2. `sp_unbindrule "int_0"`

13.8   DROPPING RULES

Drop a rule if it is not bound to any objects in the database by using the following syntax:

Syntax

```
drop rule rule_name
```

Examples

1. `drop rule sex`

2. `drop rule num_code`

13.9   BATCH SCRIPT

There is value in combining all the defaults and types into a single batch script for an application. The script should also contain commands to unbind and drop the defaults and types. This allows a system environment to be reestablished consistently and easily. An example of a simplified batch script to create an environment for the Video Store application described in the Chapter 17 tutorial is included in this section.

The following commands should be entered into a file called environ.bat, using a standard text editor that saves files in ASCII format:

```
- Create environ.dat
use video
```

```
go
sp_unbindefault alpha5
go
sp_unbindefault name5
go
sp_unbindefault error15
go
sp_unbindefault int_max
go
/* Alpha Example: drop default and user defined
datatype */
if exists (select name from sysobjects where name =
"space5")
drop default space5
go
create default space5 as "   "
go
sp_droptype alpha5
go
sp_addtype alpha5, "char(5)"
go
sp_bindefault spaceS, alpha5
go
/* create another alpha datatype and bind to the
default */
sp_droptype name5
go
sp_addtype name5, "char(5)"
go
sp_bindefault space5, name5
go
/* create another alpha datatype and another default
and bind to the default */
if exists (select * from sysobjects where name =
"xs")
drop default xs
go
create default xs as "XXXXXXXXXXXXXXX"
go
sp_droptype error15
go
sp_addtype error15, "char(5)"
go
sp_bindefault xs, error15
go
```

```
/* Numeric Example: drop default and user defined
datatype */
if exists (select * from sysobjects where name =
"ninetynine" )
drop default ninetynine
go
create default ninetynine as 99
go
sp_droptype int_max
go
sp_addtype int_max, smallint
go
sp_bindefault ninetynine, int_max
go
```

This script should be compiled into the SQL Server data dictionary using a command similar to the following:

```
isql -Uvideo -Pvideo -SSYBASE -ienviron.dat
```

Notice that the commands in the environ.bat will be stored in the video database because of the **use video** command at the top of the program. This can be confirmed by logging into SQL Server, making "video" the default database and using "sp_help object" to look for these objects.

13.10 RULES BATCH SCRIPT

The following script creates a simple table, a rule, binds the rule, inserts data, and shows how to test rules:

```
/* Type the following script into an ascii file named test_rules.sql */

/******************************************************************
Filename:    test_rules.sql
Author:      Sanjiv Purba
Date:        Nov 1993
Purpose:     This batch script is intended to demonstrate the use of
             rules in validating input into a table. This is done by
             creating a simple table, rule, binding the rule, and
             inserting data into the table. The output from
             execution of this script is attached to show the reader
             that an inappropriate data value is not allowed to be
             inserted into the table - automatically by Sybase.
Maintenance Log:
******************************************************************/
```

```
use pubs2
go
/********************* Create Table *****************************/
print ' '
print ' Creating test_rules table -------------'
print ' '
go
if exists (select name from sysobjects where name = "test_rules")
drop table test_rules
go

create table test_rules
(
name char(20),
sex char (1)
)
go

/***************** Rule *****************/
print ' '
print ' Creating a rule --------------'
print ' '
go
sp_unbindrule "test_rules.sex"
go
drop rule sex_code
go
create rule sex code
as @sex in ("M", "F")
go
sp_bindrule sex_code, "test_rules.sex"
go

/****************** insert data ***********/

/* valid data */
print ' '
print ' Inserting VALID Data -------------'
print ' '
go
insert test_rules
values ("Sector", "M")
go
insert test_rules
values ("Marsha", "F")
go
```

```
/* invalid data - should not be inserted into the table */
print ' '
print ' Inserting Invalid Data ------------'
print ' '
go
insert test_rules
values ("Amanda", "T")
go
insert test_rules
values ("Bob", "U")
go

/***************** Display table contents ****************/
print ' selecting table contents ------------'
print ' '
go
select * from test_rules
go

print ' '
print 'That is all!'
go

/**************************************************************/
/* Compile the script: eg, isql -Uvideo -Pvideo -itest_rules.sql -o
test_rules.d */
Creating test_rules table ------------

Creating a rule ------------
The specified column has no rule.
(return status = 1)
Rule bound to table column.
(return status = 0)
Inserting VALID Data ------------
(1 row affected)
(1 row affected)
Inserting INVALID Data ------------
Msg 552, Level 16, State 1:
Line 2:
A column insert or update conflicts with a rule bound to the column.
The command is aborted. The conflict occurred in database 'pubs2',
table 'test_rules', rule 'sex_code', column 'sex'.
Msg 3621, Level 16, State 0:
Line 2:
Command has been aborted.
```

```
Msg 552, Level 16, State 1:
Line 2:
A column insert or update conflicts with a rule bound to the column.
The command is aborted. The conflict occurred in database 'pubs2',
table 'test_rules', rule 'sex_code', column 'sex'.
Msg 3621, Level 16, State 0:
Line 2:
Command has been aborted.
selecting table contents -----------
name                      sex
--------------------      ---
Sector                    M
Marsha                    F
(2 rows affected)
```

13.11 SUMMARY

This chapter discussed methods of inserting data into fields and applying various layers of validation to data before it is inserted or updated into a table. This chapter also showed how to manage user-defined datatypes, defaults, and rules. Defaults and rules must be bound to objects (table fields and user-defined datatypes) to become effective. A batch script was developed to create defaults and user-defined datatypes for an application. The script also contained **unbind** and **drop** commands to allow the script to be executed repeatedly without display misleading error messages. Another script that created a simple table and tested rules was also provided in this chapter.

Open Client

In this chapter a reader will learn about:

- Overview of Open Client
- Net-Library
- DB-Library

14.1   OVERVIEW OF OPEN CLIENT

Open Client is a Sybase software product that is packaged separately from SQL Server. Open Client allows PCs to act as clients of Sybase by using library functions to communicate service requests across a network. Open Client consists of two modular components, Net-Library and DB-Library, that are discussed in this chapter. Open Client software must be installed on every intelligent client platform that requires a connection to Sybase SQL Server. In configurations that use dumb terminals, a single copy will service all the terminals.

This textbook focuses on Sybase SQL Server internals. Other components, such as Navigation Server, Open Server, and Replication Server, would require a separate book in themselves. Open Client also falls into this category; however, enough information is presented in this book to allow readers to understand Open Client basics and put together an application with this software. Open Client for C language is one of the most popular flavors on the market and is consequently used in the examples in this chapter. Detailed Open Client considerations covering

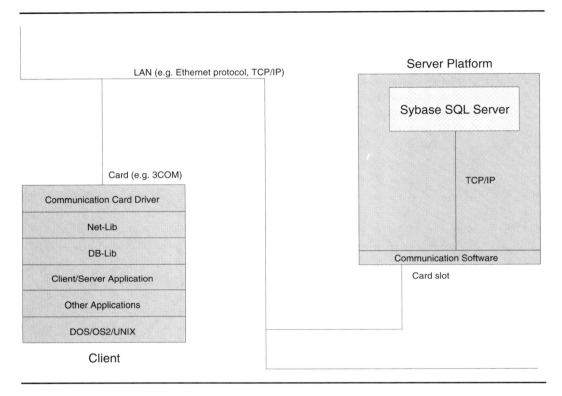

Figure 14.1 Open Client architecture.

issues such as application design and optimization can fill an entire book in themselves.

Figure 14.1 shows the relationship of Open Client to SQL Server and Client platforms:

14.2 Net-Library

The Net-Lib (i.e., Network-Library) component is installed on the PC client and serves as a low-level software layer for service requests originating on the PC to be communicated with SQL Server. Use of this component is seamless to the application and it does not affect design considerations of the application.

Different versions of this component are available for different network software, protocols, and the client platform's operating system.

This allows an application to be easily ported across combinations of these software products. For example, an application running under MS-DOS in an Ethernet TCP/IP environment can be ported to another environment by replacing this component with no application changes or recompiles being necessary. A network component also resides on the server platform to support communication calls across the network.

A utility program called ping is often used to test that a connection exists with a server platform. The syntax to do this is straightforward, as shown in the following:

Syntax

```
ping network_address
```

This test verifies the existence of a link between a client and the specified server platform only. As mentioned in Chapter 3, to verify that a link exists between the client platform and Sybase SQL Server on the server platform use dbping, as shown in the following syntax.

Syntax

```
dbping server_address
```

The server_address is contained in an interfaces file on the client platform. Readers who do not know where this file is can use the DOS **file search** command. **GREP** under UNIX, or the Norton **ff** (file find) utility (or similar command depending on the operating system). Examine the contents of this file by using any standard text editor or a file display command.

14.3   DB-Library

DB-Lib (DB-Library) consists of an application programming interface (API) that contains functions that are compiled with an application on a client platform. These APIs are available for many popular languages such as C, Pascal, FORTRAN, and COBOL. A version compatible with the programming language being used to build an application should be selected.

The DB-Library functions are responsible for setting up an environment on a client platform to send and receive data from SQL Server and also to support calls to other database servers.

To create a link with SQL Server, the **ping** and **dbping** commands should be used to verify that a network link to the database server indeed exists. On large projects many physical things can go wrong. The author has experience on projects where network cabling was unplugged on a distant floor in the building by cleaning staff who forgot to reconnect it. Other events, such as missing Ethernet cards, bad hard disks, incomplete cabling, and missing software on any one of several platforms have also occurred. It is helpful to isolate these possibilities before trying to build an application and then trying to track down a multitude of possibilities, from the physical to the syntactical, when a problem inevitably occurs in the course of a development project.

DB-Library functions on the client platform are issued to connect to the database server, provide login information, and create a communication channel. Multiple channels can be created to enable parallel service request processing. DB-Library also offers functions that can manipulate data that is returned by Sybase. Error handlers are installed to process error messages (at the severity level) returned by Sybase. These are shown in Figure 14.2.

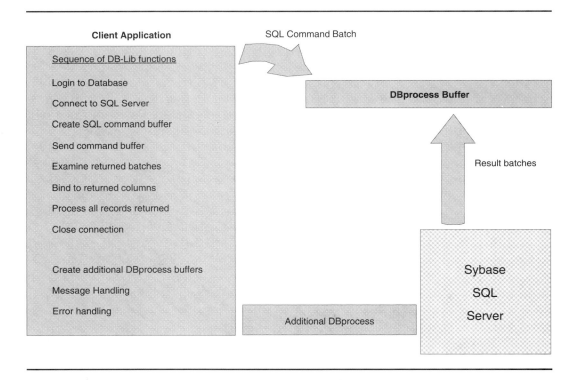

Figure 14.2   DB-Lib activities.

The functional requirements identified in the previous figure are cross-referenced with DB-Library functions in the following table.

Functional Requirement	DB-Lib Function Name
Establish login structure	dblogin()
Connect to SQL Server	dbopen()
Create SQL command buffer	dbcmd()
Send command buffer	dbsqlexec()
Examine returned batches	dbresults(dbproc)
Bind to returned columns	dbbind
Process returned records	dbnextrow(dbproc)
Close referenced DBPROCESS and process between the client and the database server	dbclose(dbproc)
Close all connections and processes	dbexit()
Create additional DBprocess buffers	additional executions of dbopen()
Message handling	dbmsghandle(msg_han)
Error handling	dberrhandle(err_han)

A program skeleton and examples of using these functions is given in the next chapter.

14.4 dblogin()

This function is used to establish a pointer to a login record structure. The user's login information is inserted into the login record using additional library functions, shown in Figure 14.3.

14.5 dbopen()

This function creates a DPPROCESS structure for a process. Multiple processes can be supported in parallel by repeated use of this function. See Figure 14.4.

14.6 dbcmd()

This command is used to fill the DBPROCESS command buffer with SQL commands (including calls to stored procedures). Each invocation

```
                /* allocate pointer to login structure */
                login = dblogin();

                /* establish user id */
                DBSETLUSER (login, "video");

                /*save password in login structure */
                DBSETLPWD (login, "super");

                /* identify application name for sysprocess table */
                DBSETLAPP(login, "videoadm");
```

Figure 14.3   **dblogin** program segment.

```
/************************************************************
dbopen establishes a connection between the client application and
Sybase SQL Server through a DBPROCESS buffer to facilitate the exchange
of information between the client and Sybase SQL Server.

login points to a structure that was populated by the dblogin() function.

Use dbproc in subsequent library functions to refer to this buffer.
************************************************************/
dbproc = dbopen (login, "vid_server")
```

Figure 14.4   **dbopen** segment.

```
                /* the dbproc points to the DBPROCESS structure */

                dbcmd (dbproc, "select * from movie");
                dbcmd (dbproc, " where subject = 'COMEDY' ");
```

Figure 14.5   **dbcmd** segment.

of this command adds to the string that is already saved in the buffer. This is useful in allowing a C program to dynamically build an SQL command string. The DBPROCESS buffer does not validate the contained string in any meaningful way so the user can pass non-SQL or garbage commands into the buffer without receiving a warning. In this event, the Sybase SQL parser will return an error message via the error handler when trying to execute the request. See Figure 14.5.

A C language variation (i.e., **sprintf**) on the format shown in the preceding figure allows improved formatting of the SQL code.

Examples

1.
```
/* define working buffer area */
char cmmd[1000];
strcpy (cmmd, "");
/* clean out the buffer */
sprintf (cmmd, "select * from movie where subject =
'COMEDY' ");
/* move temporary buffer to DBPROCESS structure */
dbcmd (dbproc, cmmd);
```

2.
```
/******** Generalize the search condition ********/
/* define working buffer area */
char cmmd[1000];
char tmp_subject[35];
strcpy (cmmd, "");
/* Get the movie subject from the user to
   generalize the search condition. */
printf ("\n\nEnter subject search titles:\n\n");
scanf ("%s", tmp_subject);
/* clean out the buffer */
sprintf (cmmd, "select * from movie where subject =
            '%s'",tmp_subject);
/* move temporary buffer to DBPROCESS structure */
dbcmd (dbproc, cmmd);
```

3.
```
/* exec a stored procedure with a general search
     condition */
/* define working buffer area */
char cmmd[1000];
char tmp_subject[35];
strcpy (cmmd, "");
```

```
/* Get the movie subject from the user to
   generalize the search condition. */
printf ("\n\nEnter subject search titles:\n\n");
scanf ("%s", tmp_subject);
/* clean out the buffer */
sprintf (cmmd, "exec search_subject '%s'",
tmp_subject);
/* move temporary buffer to DBPROCESS structure */
dbcmd (dbproc, cmmd);
```

4.
```
/* exec a stored procedure with a general search
   condition using dbfcmd version */
/* define working buffer area */
char cmmd[1000];
char tmp_subject[35]
/* Get the movie subject from the user to
   generalize the search condition. */
printf ("\n\nEnter subject search titles:\n\n");
scanf ("%s", tmp_subject);
dbfcmd (cmmd, "exec search_subject '%s'",
tmp_subject);
```

14.7   dbsqlexec()

This simple command is used to send the contents of DBPROCESS to
Sybase SQL Server for parsing and execution. See Figure 14.6.

The next **dbcmd** used after the **dbsqlexec** will clear the contents
of the DBPROCESS buffer before building the new contents.

14.8   dbresults()

The previous commands manage the process of sending serving requests
to SQL Server. The next few commands that are reviewed are con-

---

```
/* dbproc is a pointer to the desired DBPROCESS. This
pointer can be changed to accommodate multiple DBPROCESSs */

dbsqlexec(dbproc);
```

Figure 14.6   **dbsqlexec** segment.

cerned with manipulating information returned by SQL Server in response to the service request.

SQL Server returns information in a batch. A batch can have many headers followed by the associated records. A single service request can cause many headers to be returned in a batch, depending on factors such as the number of **select** commands that were processed as a result of the service request **(dbsqlexec).** This is shown in Figure 14.7.

These three batches could have been generated from a stored procedure as a result of three different **select** statements. Consider the following code fragment:

```
set rowcount 3
/* batch A: returns up to 3 records with 5 columns
    each */
select column1, column2, column3, column4, column5
from tablea
set rowcount 1
```

```
A Batch:

Batch header A              dbresults
                              dbbind
     record (5 columns) ───┐
     record (5 columns)    ├── dbnextrow
     record (5 columns) ───┘

Batch header B              dbresults
                              dbbind
     record (2 columns) ──────── dbnextrow

Batch header C              dbresults
                              dbbind
     record (15 columns) ──┐
     record (15 columns)   │
     record (15 columns)   │
     record (15 columns)   ├── dbnextrow
     record (15 columns)   │
     record (15 columns)   │
     record (15 columns) ──┘
```

Figure 14.7   Batch format.

```
/* following condition is TRUE if batches remain in the
DBPROCESS structure to process */
if ( dbresults (dbproc) == SUCCEED )
{
     /* process records */
}
```

Figure 14.8 **dbresults** segment.

```
/* batch B: returns up to 1 record with 2 columns
    each */
select column1, column2 from tableb
set rowcount 0
/* batch C: returns all records in the table with
    all columns per record */
select * from tablec /*assume this table contains 20
records with 15 columns*/
go
```

The application must be designed to identify the contents of a batch and process the records appropriately.

The syntax that is commonly used to process each of the batches is shown in Figure 14.8.

The previous command can be used with a while loop so that all returned batches are processed. The code can be written as follows:

Example

```
while (dbresults(dbproc) == SUCCEED)
{
        /* process records */
}
```

14.9   dbbind()

An examination of the previous figure shows that each batch can contain a different number of columns than other batches in the same set. The **dbbind()** command is used to bind to each of the desired columns in a returned batch, and is necessary before the records can be processed. The program must be designed so that it knows the number of

---

```
dbbind (dbproc, 1, STRINGBIND, (DBINT) 0, movie_name)
dbbind (dbproc, 3, STRINGBIND, (DBINT) 0, year)
```

Figure 14.9   **dbbind** segment.

columns that are contained in a batch. While it is permissible to skip binding to columns that are not needed, an attempt to bind to a column that is nonexistent (e.g., column 9 when only 3 were returned) will result in a runtime error. See Figure 14.9.

14.10   dbnextrow()

After binding to the columns in a batch, the **dbnextrow** command is used to process the individual records. See Figure 14.10.

14.11   dbclose(dbproc)

This command closes both the DBPROCESS that is referenced as well as the matching process that feeds the DBPROCESS buffer.

Example

```
dbclose(dbproc);
```

14.12   dbexit()

This command closes all connections to Sybase SQL Server.

Example

```
dbexit();
```

```
while (dbnextrow(dbproc) != NO_MORE_ROWS)
{
  /* process individual records */
}
```

Figure 14.10   **dbnextrow** segment.

14.13 dberrhandler()

This function installs a user-supplied error-handling routine to handle errors returned by SQL Server in response to requests for service. Errors have a numeric severity level with the following interpretations:

Severity Level 0:	Information message (nonfatal).
Severity Level 10-16:	User syntax errors (nonfatal).
Severity Level 17:	Environment errors (nonfatal).
Severity Level 18:	Internal errors (nonfatal).
Severity Level 19-23:	Server errors (fatal).
Severity Level 24:	Hardware errors (fatal).

14.14 dbmsghandler()

This function installs a user-supplied message-handling routine to handle messages and errors returned by SQL Server.

14.15 SUMMARY

This chapter provided an overview of Open Client, which consists of two components, Net-Library and DB-Library. Net-Library is a set of routines that provide network compatibility to an application running on a client platform. Developers are not required to change any of its components. DB-Library is an API that offers functions to establish connections with SQL Server, send service requests, and manipulate responses. This chapter provided a sequence of functions that are required in most client applications. The DB-Lib functions were discussed with examples.

15

DB-Library Programming

In this chapter a reader will learn about:

- DB-Library program skeleton
- Function syntax
- Program samples

15.1 DB-LIBRARY PROGRAMMING OVERVIEW

A client application uses the DB-Lib API to access Sybase SQL Server. The application can consist of one or more programs. Some of the DB-Lib functions discussed in the previous chapter should be used only once per process in the application. The functions **dblogin**, **dbopen**, and **dbexit** fall into this category.

The **dbcmd** and **dbsqlexec** functions are used whenever a service request is sent to SQL Server. It is good programming practice to interpret a response from SQL Server, even if it is only an acknowledgment. This is done by using the **dbresults**, **dbbind**, and **dbnextrow** functions.

This chapter develops examples to demonstrate the use of these commands inside application programs.

15.2 SKELETON DB-LIBRARY PROGRAM

A general program skeleton provided with Open Client can be copied and modified appropriately for new applications. The author has used variations of the following skeleton.

```
/*************************************************************
The following example develops a program skeleton for use with DB-
Library for 'C' language.
*************************************************************
/
#include <stdio.h>
/* Include DB-Lib Header files */
#include <sqlfront.h>
#include <sqldb.h>
#include <syberror.h>
#include <sybtokens.h>
#include <sybloginrec.h>
int err_handler();
int msg_handler();
#define VID_PROBLEM = 0;
#define VID_SUCCESS = 1;
main()
{
     LOGINREC   *login;
     DBPROCESS *dbproc;
     RETCODE        ret_code;
     /* define local variables to bind to returned columns */
     /* WARNING: The sizes in the following declarations must be
                 large enough to hold the information returned by
                 the Data Server. Failure to do this will result in
                 a difficult to debug Run Time error (that has taken
                 the author several days to discover the first time
                 it happened). It is safer to make the following
                 arrays much larger than necessary, rather than to
                 take a chance and count strings down to the single
                 byte level. If in doubt, sign onto Sybase and
                 verify the maximum size of each field being
                 returned. */
     DBCHAR   re_title[35];
     DBCHAR   re_date[20];
     DBCHAR   re_actor1[30];
     DBCHAR   re_actor2[30];
     /* create buffer for temporary command development */
     char cmmd[1000];
     int  flag = 0;
     /* Install asynchronous error and message handlers. */
     dberrhandle(err_handler);
     dbmsghandle(msg_handler);
     /* Create login structure and change the defaults */
```

```
login = dblogin();
DBSETLUSER(login, "video");
DBSETLPWD(login, "owner");
DBSETLAPP(login, "videoadm");
/* Create DBPROCESS structure. Note that 'vid_server' is
    the optionally supplied server name.          */
dbproc = dbopen (login, "vid_server");
          /* subsequent dbopen commands will open
              additional processes on the Data Server */
/*********************
 * Build SQL command *
 *******************/
dbcmd(dbproc, "select title, date, actor1, actor2, director");
dbcmd(dbproc, " from movie ");
dbcmd(dbproc, " where subject = 'DRAMA'");
/* send request to SQL Server */
if (dbsqlexec(dbproc) == FAIL)
{
    dbexit();
    return -1;  /* error sending command to Server */
}
/* Examine returned BATCH headers */
while ((ret_code = dbresults(dbproc)) != NO_MORE_RESULTS)
{
    if (ret_code == FAIL)
    {
        flag= VID_NO;
        break;
    }
    /*****************************************
     * there are results remaining to process *
     *****************************************/
    /* as a safety precaution, verify that the number of
    columns returned is equal to what was expected. */
    if (dbnumcols(dbproc) != 5)
    {
        flag = INCONSISTENT_COLUMNS;
        break;
    }
    /* The '1' in the following command refers to the first
    column in the batch, '2' the second, '3' the third, etc. */
    /* Columns are numbered in the order of their return in
    the batch */
    dbbind(dbproc, 1, STRINGBIND, (DBINT) 0, re_title)
    dbbind(dbproc, 2, STRINGBIND, (DBINT) 0, re_date)
```

```
dbbind(dbproc, 3, STRINGBIND, (DBINT) 0, re_actor1)
dbbind(dbproc, 4, STRINGBIND, (DBINT) 0, re_actor2)
/* notice that there was no bind to the director column
because this information was not going to be used. */
/* Use dbnextrow to process the individual records in the
batch. Each execution of dbnextrow retrieves the next
record in the buffer. NO_MORE_RECORDS is returned when
there are no more records in the current batch header. The
outer dbresults then searches for additional batch
headers. */
while (dbnextrow(dbproc) != NO_MORE_ROWS)
{
     printf ("\ntitle = %s\n", re_title);
     printf ("\ndate = %s\n", re_date);
     /* reformat date into mmddyyyy format */
     parse_date(re_date);
     /* extract time in dd:mm format */
     parse_time(re_date);
     printf ("\nActor1 = %s", re_actor1);
     printf ("\nActor2 = %s", re_actor2);
}   /* dbnextrow while */
}     /* dbresults while */
return 0;
}      /* main */
```

15.3   UNDERSTANDING THE BIND ORDER

The format of the **dbbind** command is affected by the order of the columns in the **select** command. In the previous example, the **select** command was coded in the C program and it was relatively easy to match the column number in the **dbbind** command to the columns that were returned in the batch. This is shown in Figure 15.1.

In most applications, especially those of a large magnitude, stored procedures will be executed using DB-Lib functions. This requires the developer to ensure that the correct column numbers are assigned in the dbbind section of the C program. Furthermore, changes made to the stored procedure that affects the bind order need to be repeated in the C application program. This is one reason not to use the **select * from table** command, because any changes to the fields in a table will automatically force programs to be updated. Using a format like **select name**, **address**, **phone from customer** allows changes to be made to the customer table without requiring changes to application programs so long as these fields are not changed.

Select title, date, actor1, actor2, director from titles ...

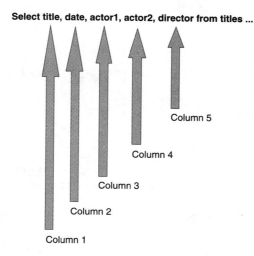

Column 5

Column 4

Column 3

Column 2

Column 1

Figure 15.1   Assigning column numbers.

15.4   USER-DEFINED ERROR HANDLER

Custom-written error handlers can use the following program skeleton.

```
#include <stdio.h>
#include <sybfront.h>
#include <sybdb.h>
#include <syberror.h>
int err_handler (dbproc, severity, errno, oserr)
DBPROCESS *dbproc;
int severity, errno, oserr;
{
        printf ("ERROR\n%s\n", dberrstr(errno));
        /* Other customization */
        return (0);
}
```

15.5   USER-DEFINED MESSAGE HANDLER

Custom-written message handlers can use the following program skeleton.

```
#include <stdio.h>
#include <sybfront.h>
#include <sybdb.h>
#include <syberror.h>
int msg_handler (dbproc, msgno, msgstate, severity, msgtext)
DBPROCESS        *dbproc;
int              msgno, msgstate, severity;
char             *msgtext;
{
     /* skip desired message numbers */
     /* i.e.     if (msgno != xxxxx) */
     printf ("\nSybase Message |%d|: %s", msgno, msgtext);
     /* build messages for other items of interest such as
        severity and msgstate.        */
     /* other customization   */
     return (0);
}
```

15.6 CREATING MULTIPLE DBPROCESS BUFFERS

Creating multiple DBPROCESS buffers allows an application to process records from several different batches at the same time (this is useful in performing a poly phase merge sort, for example). Each DBPROCESS buffer services a process. A program segment to create more than one DBPROCESS is provided in Figure 15.2.

15.7 SUMMARY

This chapter provided a skeleton program that uses DB-Library functions to communicate with Sybase SQL Server. Skeleton programs for user-defined message and error handlers were also provided.

The essential steps required to build a client application that communicates with SQL Server are as follows:

1. Login to SQL Server.
2. Create a buffer for data storage.
3. Build a Transact-SQL command string.
4. Send the command string to SQL Server.
5. Determine if results were sent back by SQL Server via the data buffer.
6. Set up a loop to process result batches and their data.

```
#include<....>
         .
         .
         .
main()
{
        LOGINREC      *login;
        DBPROCESS     *parent;
        DBPROCESS     *child1;
        DBPROCESS     *child2;

        login = dblogin();

        parent = dbopen(login,NULL);
        if (parent == NULL)
        {
          printf("Could not open parent
                            process\n");
          return-1;
        }

        child1 = dbopen(login,NULL);
                .....
        child2 = dbopen(login,NULL);
                .....


     .
     .
     .
  return0;
}
```

Figure 15.2   Creating multiple DBPROCESS buffers.

7. Bind to each column in a result.
8. Process returned data.

It is the developer's responsibility to ensure that the number of columns returned by SQL Server can be interpreted correctly by a client application program.

User Interface Development

In this chapter a reader will learn about:

- User interface development tools
- Overview of JAM from JYACC Corporation
- Rapid prototyping methodology
- Pseudo code

16.1   OVERVIEW OF A USER INTERFACE DEVELOPMENT TOOL

One of the advantages offered by client/server architecture is its support of different types of user interfaces for applications. For example, applications that use intelligent PCs as clients can employ full GUI interfaces or text-based screens.

Dozens of contemporary tools in the marketplace are effectively supporting large, multimillion-dollar applications worldwide. For this reason, there is no "right" tool, but rather a suite of choices that include products such as Powerbuilder, Visual Basic, Visual C++, DataEase for Windows, Microsoft Access and JAM from JYACC Corporation. There is also an increasing trend toward the use of traditional shrinkwrap software such as WordPerfect and Excel in Client/Server applications. Since these word processing packages and spreadsheets offer powerful text formatting and number-crunching features, many organizations are increasingly choosing to include them in client/server applications instead of creating their own custom solutions, thus avoid reinventing the wheel.

Trying to examine all of these ideas in detail is another book in itself. For the purpose of this book the author wants to draw on personal development experience and concentrate on one tool, JAM from JYACC, that has been successfully used in many client/server-based applications ranging from small installations with a few clients to large installations involving hundreds of client platforms supporting mission-critical applications involving tens of millions of transactions per year.

This chapter discusses some of the features of the JAM product, designs a few screens that could be used to support the Video Rental Store application (elaborated in the next chapter), and discusses the issues involved in tying Sybase logic to events occurring on these screens.

16.2   OVERVIEW OF JAM

The JYACC Application Manager (JAM) consists of screens, windows, a data dictionary, hook functions, JAM/DBi, and an application executable. This product is available from JYACC, Inc. based in New York City.

JAM allows character-based or GUI interfaces to be designed with an easy-to-use utility called jxform. After screens are designed through jxform, hook functions can be tied to specific events on the screens, such as the selection of a menu item, pressing of a function key, or the clicking of a button. These functions can be coded in many languages, including C language, and can invoke the DB-Library functions defined in the previous chapter. With the installation of the JAM/DBi component on the client platform, pressing a function key can invoke a call to Sybase SQL Server. Figure 16.1 shows a client platform configured with a client/server application using JAM.

The application can be ported to different technical environments by replacing the Net-Lib, DB-Lib, and JAM/DBi components. Since the JAM screens are in binary mode, they can also be ported to different environments (e.g., DOS to Unix). The application itself can also be lifted and merged with another user interface tool with much of the programming logic and Transact-SQL code intact.

Since C language and JAM are popular combinations, this chapter uses C to build examples.

16.3   DESIGNING USER SCREENS

Although there are numerous development methodologies in the IS world, the author has used a "rapid prototyping" methodology with great success on many projects in the past. This success has also been confirmed by other professionals on small and large development projects.

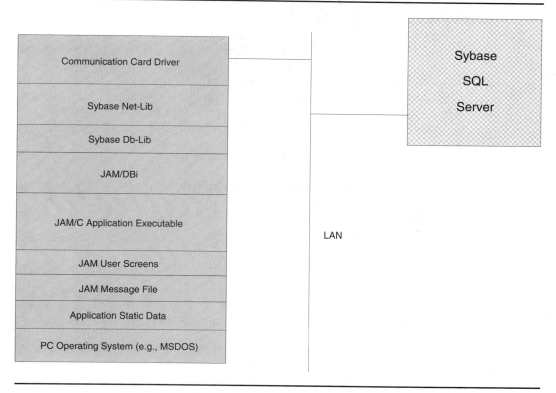

Figure 16.1   Client platform configuration.

The first important phase of the rapid application prototyping (RAD) methodology is to involve key users in the design of the user screens early in the development process. This is a departure from traditional approaches whereby analysts do most of the design work, then try to sell their design to experts in the user community. The traditional method tends to be a slower process, and more prone to errors, than RAD which involves getting the user experts to do much of the design work in cooperation with the analyst/architect. It also gets more users to buy into an application early in the development cycle.

The next important phase in this methodology is to iteratively refine a prototype. A prototype is an early working model of a system developed with minimal effort and cost. Prototypes, in this context, do very little real work, but allow an accurate "look and feel" of the final system. This is called a working prototype. Users should be encouraged to make changes and help refine the working prototype until it accurately captures the business requirements.

Once the prototype is accepted, development of the final system can begin, which involves writing the Sybase SQL Server components, establishing the network interfaces, and building the client environment and application. Establishing network interfaces is a technical task that should be completed by network experts. Different components are selected and implemented according to the following categories.

- Communication vehicle (direct line, datapac)
- Choice of LAN/WAN
- Communication protocol (Ethernet/Token Ring)
- Communication cards (Ethernet/Token Ring), hubs, gateways
- Network operating system
- Network software
- Cables, wiring

The network environment should be installed as soon as possible in a client/server project to allow access to full system functionality early in the development cycle. This will uncover bottlenecks in the system and allow the project team enough time to search for solutions.

16.4　SAMPLE SCREENS

Some sample screens for a Video Rental Store management application (and see the next chapter) are presented in this section to serve as examples of user screens that interact with Sybase SQL Server. Due to space limitations, no attempt has been made to make this list exhaustive. Note that there is no limit on the number of screens that JAM will support for an application (except due to space limitations imposed by the size of the hard disk).

The screens presented in this section were designed (i.e., painted) using JAM. Functions coded in C and DB-Lib can be connected to events on these screens (e.g., selecting a menu item).

16.5　MANAGING SCREEN ACTIVITIES

JAM allows many activities to be incorporated into an application directly from *ixform* without wiring programming code. In the screens provided, foreground, background, and text colors can be specified on a field-by-field basis. Each field can be given a name and added to a

```
 -------------------------------------------------------------------
|--------------------------------------------------------------------|
| san200              Video Rental Store              27/Dec/93 |
| Store: 1                                             05:25AM   |
|--------------------------------------------------------------------|
|                                                                |
|                     Logon                                      |
|                     Employee History                           |
|                                                                |
|                     Logoff                                     |
|                                                                |
|--------------------------------------------------------------------|
| Previous Statistics                                            |
|                                                                |
|                                                                |
|                                                                |
|                                                                |
|                                                                |
|                                                                |
|                                                                |
|                                                                |
|--------------------------------------------------------------------|
 -------------------------------------------------------------------
```

```
-------------------------------------------------------------

|--------------------------------------------------------|
|                                                        |
|  san100              Video Rental Store     27/Dec/93  |
|  Store: 1                 Main Menu            05:25AM  |
|--------------------------------------------------------|
|                                                        |
|                                                        |
|                                                        |
|                      Invoice                           |
|                      Customer                          |
|                      Movie                             |
|                      Products                          |
|                      Inventory                         |
|                      Search                            |
|                      Reports                           |
|                      Reprint                           |
|                      Late Movies                       |
|                      Admin Menu                        |
|                                                        |
|                                                        |
|                                                        |
|                                                        |
|--------------------------------------------------------|

-------------------------------------------------------------
```

```
---------------------------------------------------------------------------
|--------------------------------------------------------------------------|
|  san200                Video Rental Store               27/Dec/93  |
|  Store: 1                    Invoice                      05:25AM   |
|--------------------------------------------------------------------------|
|                                                  Salesperson:            |
|    Customer No:                                  Invoice#:               |
|  Customer Name:                                                          |
|        Address:                                                          |
|          Phone: (    )            (home)                                 |
|                 (    )            (work)         Late Charges            |
|--------------------------------------------------------------------------|
| Code  Description  Action  Quantity  Price  Amount  Date Due  Sts |
|                                                                          |
|                                                                          |
|                                                                          |
|                                                                          |
| Subtotal:        Sales Tax:       Other Tax:       Total:          |
|--------------------------------------------------------------------------|
| Customer Search    Employee Search   Price Search   Movie Search  |
|--------------------------------------------------------------------------|
---------------------------------------------------------------------------
```

```
------------------------------------------------------------

|--------------------------------------------------------|
|                                                        |
| san250           Video Rental Store         01/Jan/94  |
| Store: 1               Movie                  06:38PM   |
|--------------------------------------------------------|
|     Movie#:                        Rating:             |
|      Title:                      Language:             |
|    Subject:                 Date Released:             |
|                                                        |
|     Actors:                                            |
|                                                        |
|   Director:                                            |
|   Producer:                                            |
|      Other:                                            |
|                                                        |
|       Plot:                                            |
|                                                        |
|------------------------------| -----------------------|
|    Distribution by Store     |                        |
| Store  Copies  Store  Copies |     Purchase Price:    |
|   1             3            |   Copies Purchased:    |
|   2             4            |         Total Paid:    |
|          Total Copies:       |                        |
|------------------------------|------------------------|

------------------------------------------------------------
```

252

shared data dictionary. As a real time-saver, a field can appear on more than one screen and retain the same data. JAM can be used to apply edits such as date/time, uppercase, lowercase, and numeric on data that is entered into a field. Field edits such as protection, right/left justification, and clear on input are also available.

Item selection lists and help screens can be tied at the field or the screen level. An item selection list is very useful in assisting users working with fields that have finite domains. An example of this is a movie subject field that can have one of a small number of choices (e.g., science fiction, drama, comedy, musical, and romance). Instead of forcing a user to type an entire subject name into a field, it is friendlier to tie an item selection window to a field that is displayed by the user by pressing the <HOME> key (any key can be designated to do this). This is shown in the following series of screens. The first screen is used to search, add, delete, and update movies for the franchise inventory.

The following screen shows a Movie Subjects item selection screen (with the name "san251.jam") appearing as a popup window on the movie screen when <HOME> was pressed with the cursor beside the Subject field. Users move a highlighted bar over the desired Movie Subject and press <ENTER> to select it, or they can also type the first letter of the desired subject. This will insert the subject on the "movie" screen. Users can accept the entry or key over it.

The item selection list was tied to the subject field by entering the name of its screen in one spot in the ixform utility. This is shown in the following example. In particular, readers should notice the placement of san251.jam beside the item selection prompt. This is all that is required to create an item selection list. Putting the name beside the help screen prompt, one line above, would have turned the san251.jam into a <help> window—with no item selection capability. As a <help> window, the subject list could be used to remind users about the list of subjects but would not allow automatic selection of one.

Movement between screens is done through menus or by pressing function keys. From the main menu, selecting one of the options branches to that option. This is made possible by simply designating the desired screen name beside the option name, as shown on the following screen.

16.6   DEVELOPING FUNCTIONS

Functions coded in third/fourth-generation languages are tied to function keys by following these steps:

```
---------------------------------------------------------------

|--------------------------------------------------------------|
|                                                              |
|  san250            Video Rental Store          01/Jan/94  |
|  Store: 1              Movie                    06:37PM    |
|                                                              |
|--------------------------------------------------------------|
|   Movie#:                                                    |
|    Title:                              Language:            |
|  Subject: |-----------------------|   Date Released:       |
|           |    Movie Subjects     |                        |
|   Actors: |-----------------------|                        |
|           | Science Fiction       |                        |
| Director: | Drama                 |                        |
| Producer: | Comedy                |                        |
|    Other: | Action                |                        |
|           | Musical               |                        |
|     Plot: | Documentary           |                        |
|           | Horror                |                        |
|-----------| Sports                ||------------------------|
|    Distr  | Porn                  ||                        |
| Store  Co | Romance               ||   Purchase Price:      |
|    1      |                       ||   Copies Purchased:    |
|    2      |                       ||      Total Paid:       |
|           | PRESS ENTER TO SELECT ||                        |
|-----------|---------------san251 -||------------------------|

---------------------------------------------------------------
```

```
---------------------------------------------------------------------

|----------------------------------------------------------------|
|                                                          4     |
| Store: 1  |----------------------------------|               |
|----------------| field name                  |           --|
|    Movie#: | previous field                  |   or          |
|    Title:  | next field                      |   or          |
|   Subject: | help screen                     |   automatic (y/n) |
|            | item selection san251.jam       |   automatic (y/n) |
|    Actors: | table lookup                    |               |
|            | status text                     |               |
| Director:  | memo text 1                     |               |
| Producer:  |            2                    |               |
|    Other:  |                                 |               |
|     Plot:  | attachments                     |               |
|            | misc. edits                     |               |
|----------------| size                        |----------------------|
|     Distr  | type                            |               |
| Store   Co |                                 |   Purchase Price:  |
|    1       | field 7                         |   Copies Purchased: |
|    2       |    of 28                         |     Total Paid:    |
|            |--------------------------|--|               |
|                              ies:  |               |
|--------------------------|------------------------|

---------------------------------------------------------------------
```

255

```
------------------------------------------------------------

|------------------------------------------------------------|
|                                                            |
|               Video Rental Store          01/Jan/94  |
|                                                            |
| Store: 1                 Main Menu             06:28PM    |
|                                                            |
|------------------------------------------------------------|
|                                                            |
|                                                            |
|                                                            |
|                                                            |
|              Invoice            &san200.jam               |
|                                                            |
|              Customer                                      |
|                                                            |
|              Movie              &san250.jam               |
|                                                            |
|              Products                                      |
|                                                            |
|              Inventory                                     |
|                                                            |
|              Search                                        |
|                                                            |
|              Reports                                       |
|                                                            |
|              Reprint                                       |
|                                                            |
|              Late Movies                                   |
|                                                            |
|              Admin Menu                                    |
|                                                            |
|                                                            |
|                                                            |
|                                                            |
|                                                            |
|                                                            |
|                                                            |
|------------------------------------------------------------|

------------------------------------------------------------
```

1. Insert the name of the function beside the desired function key (shown in the following figure).
2. Identify the function name to JAM.
3. Build a script file with the function code and function name.
4. Compile and link all functions into an executable.

The following screen shows that pressing the <XMIT> function key will invoke a function called **validate_screen** (probably coded in C with JAM and DB-LIB commands) whenever the <XMIT>/<ENTER> key is pressed by a user. Similarly, a function called **invoice_process** is invoked when the function key <PF2> is pressed.

Program skeletons for these two functions are provided as follows.

16.6.1 validate_screen

```
/***********************************************************
Filename: invvalid.c
Author: Sanjiv Purba
Date: Jan 1994
Function: validate_screen
Purpose:
This is a 'C' program that is invoked when the user presses <ENTER>
on the invoice screen.

The program reads all the screen fields (shown in capitals), applies
validation routines, and invokes an SQL stored procedure to validate
against the database.

Successful validation returns SUCCESS. Unsuccessful validation
returns FAIL and displays a meaningful message.
Change History:
DateWho Description
***********************************************************/
/* include 'C' *.h files */
int validate_screen ()
{
/* declarations */
/* read all screen fields into local variables */
/* validate all fields */
/* build buffer string - assume DBPROCESS already exists */
;* examine results returned by the server */
if (return_code != SUCCESS )
return FAIL;
```

```
----------------------------------------------------------------
|-------------------------------------------------------------|
| san200              Video Rental Store          27/Dec/93 |
| Store: 1                 Invoice                   05:25AM  |
|-------------------------------------------------------------|
|                                          Salesperson:       |
|  Customer No:                       SET JAM CONTROL STRINGS |
| Customer Name:                      |---------------------| |
|       Address:                      | XMIT  ^validate_screen | |
|        Phone: (   )       (home) |  PF1                   | |
|               (   )       (work) |  PF2   ^invoice_process | |
|-----------------------------------|  PF3                  | |
| Code  Description  Action  Quantity |  PF4                | |
|                                     |  PF5                | |
|                                     |  PF6                | |
|                                     |  PF7                | |
|                                     |  PF8                | |
|                                     |  PF9                | |
|                                     |--------------------| |
| Subtotal:     Sales Tax:     Other Tax:        Total:       |
|-------------------------------------------------------------|
| Customer Search   Employee Search   Price Search   Movie Search |
|-------------------------------------------------------------|
----------------------------------------------------------------
```

```
return SUCCESS;
} /* validate_screen */
```

16.6.2 invoice_process

```
/*********************************************************
Filename: invproc.c
Author: Sanjiv Purba
Date: Jan 1994
Function: invoice_process
Purpose:
This is a 'C' program that is invoked when the user presses <ENTER>
on the invoice screen.

The program calls the validate_screen function. If SUCCESS is
returned, the program builds a buffer to send to a stored procedure
that inserts/deletes/updates the Sybase database.
Change History:
Date Who Description
*********************************************************/
/* include 'C' *.h files */
int invoice_process ()
{
/* declarations */
/* validate */
if (validate_screen != SUCCESS)
return FAIL;
/* build buffer string - assume DBPROCESS already exists */
dbsqlexec(dbproc);
/* examine results returned by the server */
if (return_code != SUCCESS)
return FAIL;
return SUCCESS;
}
```

16.7   SUMMARY

This chapter examined JAM, a popular third-party tool for designing application user interfaces, in an overview fashion. This product is available in character, GUI, and object-oriented formats. Some user screens for the Video Rental Store management system were offered as examples along with program skeletons to manage common activities on these screens. While this information is specific to JAM, it is similar to other products used for client/server interface development.

The JYACC Application Manager (JAM) allows functions to be written in a third-generation language like C and tied to specific events on a user screen (such as clicking on a button or pressing a function key). JAM supports Sybase SQL Server through an API that allows C functions to handle events like signing onto SQL Server, connecting a process, issuing requests, and receiving data from SQL Server in a client/ server architecture.

This chapter also briefly examined the rapid prototyping methodology as an effective method of designing user screens and conducting application development.

Video Rental Store: Business Problem

In this chapter a reader will learn about:

- Overview of the tutorial
- Business requirements of the Video Rental Store
- Data model of the Video Rental Store
- Physical database layout

17.1 OVERVIEW OF THE TUTORIAL

This part of the book contains a tutorial that spans several chapters and is designed to get readers started in using Sybase SQL Server. At the end of this tutorial, the reader should be able to begin developing applications using Sybase SQL Server 10. It is a practical, easy-to-follow tutorial based on the author's experience using Sybase on client/server development projects.

This tutorial is based on designing a client/server application to manage a Video Rental Store franchise, and will show the reader how to do the following:

- Install SQL Server on a Sun SPARCstation 2 running Sun OS
- Start Sybase SQL Server as a process
- Sign on (connect) to SQL Server
- Recognize the SQL Server prompt
- Initialize disk space

- Build the database
- Add users
- Navigate inside SQL Server
- Create tables and indexes
- Create initialization scripts
- Create stored procedures
- Create triggers
- Create views

The business requirements of the typical video rental store are derived from the author's personal experience in building such a system in the mid-1980s. This system has been presented as a case study in courses for PC Focus, C programming language, data modeling, and dBASE. Many people relate to renting movies and buying items such as popcorn, so this example appears to be more interesting to students than systems designed to manage widgets and screws.

This chapter states the business problem faced by the franchise and proceeds to provide an overview of the business requirements. A data model is developed as part of this exercise. The data model is subsequently used to design a relational database schema. Chapter 18 takes the reader through a first look of SQL Server. Chapter 19 uses the database schema developed in this chapter to build Transact-SQL code that will create the relational database tables for the Video Rental Store application. Chapter 20 builds Sybase programs based on a refined set of application requirements. The reader is encouraged to complete the additional exercises that are described in the tutorial.

17.2 THE BUSINESS PROBLEM

Video rental stores are in the business of renting movie videos to the public for one or more days at a time. Many stores get involved in parallel activities such as selling videos, posters, blank cassettes, popcorn, candies, potato chips, soft drinks, video games, compact disks, and music tapes. Some video stores may also rent sound and viewing equipment.

The video rental store business is driven by intense competition with slim profit margins. Stores lacking streamlined operations rarely survive, and most video rental stores have been forced to computerize their operations.

The 1980s saw the emergence of many video store management packages. Some of these are standalone systems designed to run on 8088/286/386 MS-DOS platforms with applications developed using database management systems such as dBASE3 or Paradox. These systems are generally inexpensive, often have slow response time, a character-based user interface, lack of function upgradeability, and limited data storage capacity. Most of these systems also have little or no security protection for application data (security measures that are programmed into these systems are generally easily circumvented).

On the other end of the spectrum are multiuser systems with significantly higher price tags. Most of these systems are built on a file server-based architecture. This architecture is different from client/server-based architecture that database servers such as Sybase SQL Server support. Applications in file-based systems tend to share computing devices (e.g., printers, modems, and databases) through Local Area Networks (LANs). These systems suffer from the same problems that plague the single-user DOS-based systems mentioned earlier. System response time is slow, there is little or no LAN security, the application generally offers a difficult to learn character-based interface, and a problem anywhere on the LAN can bring the whole system crashing down.

17.3   BUSINESS REQUIREMENTS

For the purpose of this tutorial, the reader should assume the following requirements.

The Video Rental Store is part of a three-store franchise. Management has made the strategic decision to integrate the computer operations of this franchise. A single, secure database server should support the business requirements of all the stores in the franchise. Furthermore, future video store acquisitions should be readily supported by this system.

A typical transaction in any one of the stores occurs when a customer has selected one or more movies to rent for an evening. Sometimes the customer also chooses products such as potato chips or soda pop. These are brought to a checkout counter. Customers are asked to present a magnetically coded card that is swiped (passed) through a card reader to automatically display the customer's information in a blank invoice on the computer screen. The customers who refuse to carry these cards or forget them at home are asked for their phone numbers. This number is used to find the customer record so that the invoice can be populated on the screen.

An invoice is the primary contract between the store and a customer. An invoice is divided into three main sections. The first section contains an invoice number and a customer's personal information (e.g., member number, name, address). The second section of the invoice contains a list of movie titles rented, due dates, and rental fees. The third section contains a description of purchased items and prices. All applicable taxes, subtotal, and total amount are included on the invoice. There is space for a member's signature at the bottom of the invoice, shown in Figure 17.1.

The system must be designed with a user-friendly interface. Checkout counter employee turnover is high, so the system must be easy to learn (preferably intuitive). All the stores in the franchise are doing well and are very busy several times each day, especially on weekends. System response time is critical in alleviating long customer lines.

Many members are in the habit of asking opinions on movies they

---

Video Rental Store Franchise

1 Main Street
Baco Raton, Florida 33287
Store: 1
Tel: (407) 919-3933   Fax: (407) 919-3945

Invoice Number: _____

Date: Time:

Sales Person:

Sold To:

Member No:
Member Name:
Address:

Phone Number:

Payment Method:
Movies rented this month:

Rentals:

Product Code	Description	Qty	Unit Cost	Disc	Price	Due Date
_____	_____	___	_____	____	_____	
_____	_____	___	_____	____	_____	
_____	_____	___	_____	____	_____	
_____	_____	___	_____	____	_____	

Purchases:

Product Code	Description	Qty	Unit Cost	Disc	Price
_____	_____	___	_____	____	_____
_____	_____	___	_____	____	_____

Rental Total: Subtotal: Taxes: Federal: Discount:
Purchase Total: Local:

Please Pay: ▓▓▓▓▓▓▓▓

Signature: _____

Rental Items returned after Due Date will be charged a late fee.

Thank You for Your Patronage.
(Please rewind)

Figure 17.1   Sample invoice.

are about to rent at the checkout counter. Employees should be able to access help screens and information windows from the invoice screen. Members will occasionally be willing to drive to one of the other stores for a specific movie. The system should have the functionality to determine if a movie is available at the other locations. Ultimately, the system will be built to have the functionality to reserve movies, although this is not a current requirement.

The system should also have the ability to return purchased merchandise. Late fee charges are automatically calculated and allocated for movies that are returned past the due date.

The system must also be able to produce a set of reports. Among these is a list of movies in stock (with associated actors, directors, purchase price, etc.), a customer list, movies rented, outstanding invoices, late movies, and members owing money. Management is especially interested in purchasing a shrinkwrap report generator tool such as Microsoft Access or DataEase Express for Windows.

17.4   BUSINESS DATA MODEL

The data model represented in Figure 17.2 can be designed using the information gathered in the business requirements analysis phase.

17.5   DETAILED PHYSICAL SCHEMA

The following physical schema is designed using the preceding data model.

```
1. store
     store_id                    int
     address1                    char(30)
     address2                    char(30)
     city                        char(15)
     state                       char(20)
     zip_code                    char(11)
     phone                       char(11)
     fax                         char(11)
     contact                     char(30)
     Index 1:                    store_id

2. work_force
     store_id                    int
     employee_id                 int
     Index 1:                    store_id + employee_id
```

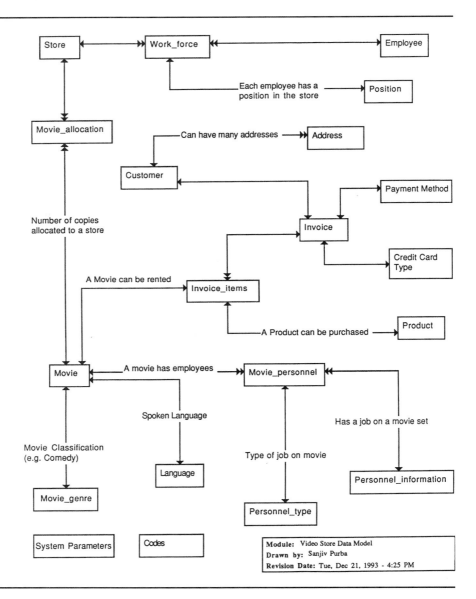

Figure 17.2 Video Store data model.

```
3. employee
     employee_id                    int
     last_name                      char(30)
     first_name                     char(30)
     middle                         char(10)
     address1                       char(30)
     address2                       char(30)
     city                           char(15)
     state                          char(20)
     zip_code                       char(11)
     phone                          char(11)
     fax                            char(11)
     position_code                  int
     Index 1:                       employee_id
     Index 2:                       last_name + first_name

4. position
     position_code                  int
     description                    char(25)

5. customer
     customer_id                    int
     last_name                      char(30)
     first_name                     char(30)
     middle                         char(10)
     address1                       char(30)
     address2                       char(30)
     city                           char(15)
     state                          char(20)
     zip_code                       char(11)
     home_phone                     char(11)
     office_phone                   char(11)
     credit_card_type               int
     credit_card_no                 char(15)
     drivers_licence                char(20)
     discount_percent               float
     Index 1:                       customer_id
     Index 2:                       last_name + first_name
     Index 3:                       home_phone

6. invoice
     invoice_no                     int
     customer_id                    int
     invoice_date                   char(15)
     total_amount                   money
```

```
        total_taxes                money
        total_discount             money
        payment_method_code        int
        credit_card_type           int
        credit_card_no             char(20)
        next_due_date              char(15)
        items_open                 int
        store_id                   int
        employee_id                int
        Index 1:                   invoice_no
        Index 2:                   customer_id +
        invoice_date

    7.  invoice_items
        invoice_no                 int
        sequence_no                int
        product_code               int
        movie_id                   int
        amount                     money
        pst                        money
        other_tax                  money
        discount                   money
        due_date                   datetime
        date_returned              datetime
        Index 1:                   invoice_no + sequence_no
        + product_code

    8.  payment_method
        payment_method_code        int
        description                char(20)

    9.  credit_card_type
        credit_card_type           int
        description                char(20)

    10. movie_allocation
        store_id                   int
        movie_id                   int
        allocated_amt              int
        available                  int
        Index 1:                   store_id + movie_id

    11. movie
        movie_id                   int
        name                       char(30)
```

```
    movie_genre_code          int
    product_code              int
    release_date              datetime
    language_code             int
    cost                      money
    plot1                     char(100)
    plot2                     char(100)
    Index 1:                  movie_id
    Index 2:                  name
    Index 3:                  movie_genre_code
    Index 4:                  language_code

12. movie_genre
    movie_genre_code          int
    description               char(15)

13. language
    language_code             int
    description               char(15)

14. movie_personel
    movie_id                  int
    personel_id               int
    personel_type             int
    movie_id                  int
    last_name                 char(30)
    first_name                char(30)
    middle_name               char(20)
    Index 1:                  movie_id + personel_id +
    personel_type

15. personel_type
    personel_type             int
    description               char(20)

16. product
    product_code              int
    part_type                 char(10)
    description               char(30)
    price                     money
    Index 1:                  product_code + part_type

17. system_parameters
    name                      char(20)
    date_effective            char(15)
```

```
        parameter_type              int
        value1_from                 int
        value1_to                   int
        value2_from                 float
        value2_to                   float
        value3_from                 char(30)
        value3_to                   char(30)
        date_from                   datetime
        date_to                     datetime
        last_update                 datetime

    18. codes
        code_type                   char(5),
        code_value                  int,
        description                 char(20)
```

17.6   SUMMARY

This chapter introduced the reader to the business requirements of a Video Rental Store. This is the first chapter of a tutorial designed to teach the reader about the basic Sybase SQL Server commands required by a developer of client/server applications to get started. Physical installation and configuration of SQL Server are described in the next chapter.

18

Installation, Configuration, and Connecting to SQL Server

In this chapter a reader will learn about:

- Sybase SQL Server installation
- Server startup and shutdown
- Server connection and navigation (a first look)
- Database creation
- Adding users and setting permissions

Readers should note that commands prefaced with a ♦ are to be entered by them at the console.

While the examples in this tutorial have been tested for completeness and accuracy, readers should examine all commands with the original syntax if results do not conform to their expectations. Readers should not necessarily duplicate every command in this tutorial. Instead, they should read the examples and understand them first, and then feel free to experiment with or change any of the exercises.

18.1   INSTALLATION

Installing Sybase SQL Server is a specialized task that is usually best done by technical staff. Sybase, Inc. has a technical department that assists licenced users of this product with general issues, and is specifically helpful when installing SQL Server. Organizations that are new to SQL Server should involve Sybase technical staff or external consultants (perhaps the hardware vendor) in this operation.

Installation procedures for Sybase SQL Server 10 are dependent on the server platform and the operating system. There are some variations in these procedures across platforms. Readers should refer to the *Sybase SQL Server Installation* manual for instructions on their specific configuration. This documentation is complete for several configurations with which the author has worked.

Generic Installation A generic installation of SQL Server requires the following steps:

1. create a Sybase user account and establish a $sybase home directory (as discussed below);
2. load tape/disk/optical disk;
3. load **sybload** utility to server platform hard disk;
4. run **sybload** to load renaming Sybase files to server platform;
5. build kernal file;
6. build shared memory;
7. calculate Sybase space requirements (e.g., 35 MB)
8. run **sybconfig** utility (found in $sybase/install, shown in directory listing that follows) to complete Sybase installation script; and
9. load system procedures.

The reader should modify these to match the specific configuration that is being used in his or her organization. The interfaces file, which is in ASCII (readable) format, contains the name and network address of the Sybase SQL Server. This information will also be included in this file for additional SQL Servers and the backup server.

SQL Server can be installed on a platform that can also serve as a client platform. An overview of the directory structure of Sybase SQL on a generic platform is as follows.

```
$sybase1/bin
        bcp
        buildmaster
        charset
        console
```

---

[1]$sybase is the root path aplicable to the reader's environment. For example, on the author's test machine, this path was /export/home/sybase.

```
        dataserver
        defncopy
        diagserver
        isql
        langinstall
        probe
        syman
$sybase/charsets
        ascii_8
        cp437
        cp850
        iso_1
        mac
        roman8
$sybase/diag
        bin
        custom
        formdefs
        locales
        termdef
$sybase/doc /* following ASCII files are contained in
this directory. man=manual */
        addalias.man
        addgroup.man
        addlanguage.man
        addlogin.man
        addmessage.man
        addremotelogin.man
        addsegment.man
        addserver.man
        addtype.man
        addumpdevice.man
        adduser.man
        bcp.man
        bindefault.man
        bindrule.man
        buildmaster.man
        changedbowner.man
        changegroup.man
        commonkey.man
        configure.man
        console.man
        dataserver.man
        dboption.man
        defaultdb.man
```

```
defaultlanguage.man
defncopy.man
depends.man
diskdefault.man
dropalias.man
dropdevice.man
dropgroup.man
dropkey.man
droplanguage.man
droplogin.man
dropmessage.man
dropremotelogin.man
dropsegment.man
dropserver.man
droptype.man
dropuser.man
extendsegment.man
foreignkey.man
getmessage.man
help.man
helpdb.man
helpdevice.man
helpgroup.man
helpindex.man
helpjoins.man
helpkey.man
helplanguage.man
helplog.man
helpremotelogin.man
helpprotect.man
helpsegment.man
helpserver.man
helpsort.man
helptext.man
helpuser.man
indsuspect.man
isql.man
langinstall.man
lock.man
logdevice.man
monitor.man
password.man
placeobject.man
primarykey.man
recompile.man
remoteoption.man
```

```
        rename.man
        renamedb.man
        serveroption.man
        setlangalias.man
        showserver.man
        spaceused.man
        startserver.man
        syman.man
        unbindefault.man
        unbindrule.man
        who.man
$sybase/install
        runserver
        spr
        addl_char.hlp
        addl_lang.hlp
        coll_seq.hlp
        def_char.hlp
        def_lang.hlp
        ds.hlp
        ds_upgr.hlp
        errorlog
        ins_ssrv
        loadschema
        setperm_all
        showserver
        startserver
        sybconfig ———— sybase installation script
$sybase/interfaces ———— user file that is used to
access SQL Server
$sybase/bin/locales
$sybase/master_dev
        master.dat
$sybase/msgs
        serno_ds
$sybase/scripts
        ins_syn_dblib
        ins_syn_sql
        inscsproc
        installmaster
        installmodel
        installpix2
        installpubs2
        iso_1
        installintpubs
$sybase/upgrade
```

Syntax:

RUNSERVER

or

startserver

It is helpful to run the process in the background. In UNIX, this is done by using the '&' to run the process in the background.
(ie. startserver &)

Figure 18.1   Starting SQL Server.

18.2   STARTING SQL SERVER

SQL Server runs as a task under a multiprocessing operating system. The process is initiated by typing a startup command beside the OS prompt, as shown in Figure 18.1. The reader should change to the directory containing these scripts and enter these commands. For example, the following sequence of commands can be used in a Unix-based system:

* `cd /$sybase/install`
* `startserver &`

The runserver will bring up the server under the name SYBASE. This can be verified, as discussed in the next section. The & is a Unix option to run Sybase in the background.

18.3   SEEING SQL SERVER RUNNING AS A PROCESS

Operating system commands can be used to verify that SQL Server is currently running as a process. This command is dependent on the operating system being used. In Unix (or Unix-based systems), the following command displays active processes:

* `ps -aux`

The reader should use this command to verify that the **startserver/runserver** command was successful.

After installation of SQL Server, it is necessary to install system procedures in the **master** database. This is done by following these steps:

* `cd $SYBASE/install`
* `startserver & /* start the SQL Server */`

```
♦   cd $sybase/scripts
♦   /* set up environment variable to point to the
    name of SQL Server */
    setenv DSQUERY SYBASE (or type set DSQUERY SYBASE
    in DOS systems)
    setenv SYBASE /export/home/sybase
♦   isql -Usa -P -iinstallmaster -SSYBASE
    /* the -SSYBASE is not required if the DSQUERY
    environment variable is set up properly, otherwise
    it is required. */
♦   /* install permissions in the model database */
    isql -Usa -P -iinstallmodel -SSYBASE
```

An ASCII errorlog file, contained in the install directory, contains useful system information (e.g., about logons, state of the transaction log).

18.4   CONNECTING TO SQL SERVER

Once SQL Server is running, configured client platforms can connect to SQL Server (the platform running SQL Server can also serve as a client without requiring Open Client or additional software).

Readers should connect to SQL Server by using the following command, on the platform that has SQL Server installed and running. Alternatively, a client platform can also be used to connect to SQL Server with this command, if a network connection exists and Open Client (or other Sybase Software such as Embedded SQL) is installed:

```
♦   isql -Usa -P -SSYBASE     /* -Uusername
                                  -Ppassword require a
                                  valid combination */
```

This will connect the reader to SQL Server with the permission of a system administrator. The reader may need to find a valid supported userid/password combination for his or her system. Sybase responds by displaying the system prompt shown in Figure 18.2.

SQL Server commands are typed beside this prompt. The enter key is pressed to submit the command to Sybase (e.g., select getdate()). The number (1>) will increment to (2>) and (3>), etc., until go is entered to cause the batch of commands to be compiled, optimized, and executed.

```
1>
```

Figure 18.2   Sybase system prompt.

18.5   NAVIGATION

Congratulations, welcome to Sybase SQL Server! From the prompt 1>, the reader can do many things. Some things to try initially are the following.

- ```
  sp_who
  go
  /* This shows the running tasks. There are a
  minimum of four. */
  ```
- ```
  use master /* in case this was not the default for
  the login id */
  go
  select name, crdate from sysdatabases
  go
  /* If SQL Server was just installed, this command
  should show at least three databases (i.e. master,
  model, tempdb, sybsystemprocs), and optionally the
  pubs2 database. */
  ```
- ```
  /* use a system procedure to get similar
  information */
  sp_helpdb
  go
  ```
- ```
  select * from sysusages
  go
  /* Notice that the dbid field is the relational
  key between these tables. */
  ```
- ```
  select * from sysprocesses
  go
  /* This table contains a list of sleeping or
  duplicate processes. Sleeping processes from the
  same client should not be allowed to accumulate
  because they will ultimately halt the system and
  require a system reboot for resolution. */
  ```
- ```
  sphelp syslogins   /* display field names from
  table */
  go
  ```
- ```
  select suid, accdate, dbname, name from syslogins
  go
  /* Immediately after installation, this will
  display the account information for the 'sa'
  (system administrator) account. */
  ```

To see the system error messages that Sybase can display, the reader can issue the following command (be forewarned that there are well over a thousand rows, so be prepared to wait for a few minutes).
  ```

♦ set rowcount 80
  select * from sysmessages
  go
  set rowcount 0
  go
♦ use model
  go
  /* This will give access to the system tables in
  the model database. Recall that this database
  serves as a template for creating user databases.
  */
♦ sp_help sysobjects
  go
♦ select name, id, type, crdate from sysobjects
  go
♦ /* select any fields that are displayed as a
  consequence of the sp_help sysobjects command */
♦ /* display the name of the current database */
  select db_name()
  go
♦ use master   /* make master the default database
  */
  go
♦ select * from syscomments
  go
♦ use sybsystemprocs
  go
  /* see names of objects in this database,
  especially the names of the system procedures */
  select name, type from sysobjects
  go
  (or sp_help
     go)
     (or: 1>select name from sysobjects where
                 type = 'S'
          2>go
          /* will display all system tables in the
             master database */
)
     (or: /* find different values type can contain
             in this database */
          1>select distinct(type) from sysobjects
          2>go
♦ quit
  /* This will quit from SQL Server and display the
  operating system prompt. */

Before quitting from SQL Server, the reader may want to refer to Chapter 3 and select information from other system tables as well.

18.6   STOPPING SQL SERVER

SQL Server should be manually shut down before a server machine is rebooted or switched off. This is done by issuing the following sequence of commands:

- ◆   `isql -Usa -P /* logon to Sybase with administrator`
  `authority */`
- ◆   `shutdown`
  `go`

The shutdown command is entered at the Sybase prompt 1>, which will cause the message shown in Figure 18.3 to be displayed.

Although the wording may be alarming, it is normal. The operating system prompt should be displayed within a few moments. Normal computer shutdown procedures can now be followed for the specific platform running the database server.

18.7   CREATING A DATABASE

It is desirable to create a region for the physical storage of the user databases. An alternative is to use the region used by one of the two permanent databases, but this is not recommended as a long-term strategy. In fact, it is best to keep the **master** database on its own device for backup efficiency and other performance reasons.

The easiest way to start using SQL Server is to use an operating system file to store user databases. For readers learning Sybase (in test mode), this solution will suffice. Production databases should be stored on "raw partitions." The author recommends that Sybase Technical Support be consulted in the process of creating a production version of a

---

```
Server SHUTDOWN by request.
The SQL Server is terminating this process.
DB-LIBRARY error:
        Unexpected EOF from SQL Server.
```

Figure 18.3   Shutdown message.

system running under Sybase SQL Server in order to optimize backup, recovery, and response time. Consultation with the hardware vendor will also provide value, as Sybase implementation on different platforms has some unique components in each flavor.

Readers can create the test database using the following commands:

- ```
  mkdir /dev/databases
  /* This will create the directory where the
  database will ultimately be stored. */
  ```
- ```
  isql -Usa -P /* signon to Sybase */
  ```
- ```
  select * from sysdevices
  go
  /* The reader should make a note of the entries in
  this table so that they can make a comparison with
  the entry about to be inserted with the "disk
  init" command. */
  ```
- ```
  disk init
     name = "space512", physname="/dev/databases/
  space512",
     vdevno=4, size=512
  go
  (Note: 512 is the minimum number of blocks)
  /* This will create a physical region called
  space512 in the operating system file indicated in
  physname. This region can be allocated to one or
  more databases, but for simplicity, it will be
  allocated to one database in this tutorial. */
  ```
- ```
  select * from sysdevices
  go
  /* A device with the "space512" name should now
  exist in this table. */
  ```
- ```
  create database video on space512=15
  go
  (Note: 15 refers to 15 megabytes. This is the size
  of the database and it can be modified by the
  reader)
  (Note: multiple databases can be defined in the
  same device region)
  ```
- ```
  select * from sysdatabases /* check the names */
  go
  ```
- ```
  /* The video database should now exist */
  use video
  go
  ```
- ```
  sp_spaceused /* examine the space statistics */
  go
  ```
  ```

- ```
  select name, type from sysobjects
  go
  /* This displays the objects stored in this
  database. These should be equivalent to the
  objects stored in the model database because it
  served as a template to create the video database.
  Changes to the model database are only passed to
  databases created after the change was made. */
  ```
- ```
  /* add user */
  use master
  go
  /* sector is user, sector is password, video is
  default database */
  sp_addlogin "sector", "sector", "video"
  /* okiet is user, victoria is password, video is
  default database */
  sp_addlogin "okiet", "victoria", "video"
  go
  ```
- ```
  use video
  go
  ```
- ```
  sp_adduser "sector"
  go
  ```
- ```
  sp_adduser "okiet"
  go
  ```
- ```
  select * from sysusers
  go
  ```
- ```
  /* attach permissions */
  grant all on store to sector
  grant all on work_force to sector
  grant all on employee to sector
  grant all on position to sector
  grant all on customer to sector
  grant all on invoice to sector
  grant all on invoice_items to sector
  grant all on payment_method to sector
  grant all on credit_card_type to sector
  grant all on movie_allocation to sector
  grant all on movie to sector
  grant all on movie_genre to sector
  grant all on language to sector
  grant all on movie_personel to sector
  grant all on personel_type to sector
  grant all on product to sector
  grant all on system_parameters to sector
  grant all on codes to sector
  grant select on codes to okiet
  ```
  ```

```
                /* Whoops, we do not want to give any permissions
                to the user okiet, who has not started work yet.
                This situation is corrected by using the 'revoke'
                command. */
         ♦      /* remove the select permission */
                revoke select on codes to okiet
                go
         ♦      quit
         ♦      /* sign on as user sector. The current database
                will be sector's default database, namely 'video'.
                */
                isql -Usector -Psector
                go
                select db_name()   /* to confirm that the default
                database is video. */
                go
         ♦      quit
         ♦      /* shut down the server */
                isql -Usa -P
                shutdown
                go
         ♦      quit
         ♦      /* restart the server */
                cd $sybase\install
                startserver &
```

18.8   SUMMARY

This chapter contained a tutorial that gave readers a first look at Sybase
SQL Server by going through the basic configuration process of SQL
Server. A database called "video" was created for the tutorial. Readers
were shown how to start SQL Server as a process in a multiprocessor
environment, and how to connect as a client to the running process. Other
issues such as navigating between databases and performing simple system query functions were also addressed in this chapter.Readers were
also shown how to shut down the SQL Server prior to a hardware shutdown. The **shutdown** command can be used with a nowait option to
unconditionally stop SQL Server (i.e., 1> shutdown with nowait).

Table Creation and Initialization

In this chapter a reader will learn about:

- Table creation
- Indexing
- Initialization

19.1   TABLE CREATION OVERVIEW

In this chapter, the reader will use the relational schema designed in Chapter 17 to build relational Sybase tables to support the Video Rental Store application.

The author used a text editor (i.e., textedit &) in Sun/OS under the OpenWindows interface for the production of an ASCII script file (i.e., tables.v1) to contain the Transact-SQL commands required to build tables. The reader can create the tables.v1 script using any text editor that is able to save a file in ASCII format (e.g., textedit tables.v1 &). The reader should examine the descriptive comments included in the script file. This level of documentation is a good practice for the reader to follow, at a minimum.

The second portion of this chapter provides another script (i.e., inittab.v1) to initialize the tables created by running tables.v1. The inittab.v1 script contains commands to insert data into the Video Rental Store database so that the system can be implemented in production.

Similar script files can also be built to insert test data into the

```
              inittab.v1 -initialize database for production

              inittab.t1 -test data for Developer A

              inittab.t2 -test data for Developer B

              inittab.t3 -test data for Developer C

              inittab.bach -large volume of test data for
                            benchmarking
```

Figure 19.1   Layers of script files.

database. Developers can build a series of script files for different purposes, as shown in Figure 19.1.

The **video** database must exist for the exercises in this chapter to work, otherwise the reader can use the pubs2 database instead. Do this by replacing occurrences of "video" with "pubs2" throughout the tutorial.

19.2   SCRIPT TO CREATE TABLES

```
♦  create tables.v1
/*****************************************************************
* Filename: tables.v1                                           *
* Date:     Nov 1, 1993                                         *
* Author:   Sanjiv Purba                                        *
*                                                               *
* This script creates the tables for the Video Rental Store     *
* Database.                                                     *
*****************************************************************/
/* Change to the default database of the Video application */
use video /* open database (note: the name is alphabetically case
[upper/lower] sensitive) */
go
/* go should be typed starting in the first column of the file */
/*****************************************************************
The following command drops the table only if it exists.
The code suppresses an error message in the event that the
table does not exist. Not using this code results in the
appearance  of error messages that clutter the screen, the first
time this script is executed.
```

The reader should recall that sysobjects is a database system table
that contains the name of all objects contained within a database.
This means that there is one record in this table for every table
(and object) in the database.
```
************************************************************      */
/* drop tables if they exist */
if exists (select name from sysobjects where name="store")
   drop table store
/* go invokes the commands entered since the previous go */
go
if exists (select name from sysobjects where name="work_force")
   drop table work_force
go
if exists (select name from sysobjects where name="employee")
   drop table employee
go
if exists (select name from sysobjects where name="position")
   drop table position
go
if exists (select name from sysobjects where name="customer")
   drop table customer
go
if exists (select name from sysobjects where name="invoice")
   drop table invoice
go
if exists (select name from sysobjects where name="invoice_items")
   drop table invoice_items
go
if exists (select name from sysobjects where name="payment_method")
   drop table payment_method
go
if exists (select name from sysobjects where
name="credit_card_type")
   drop table credit_card_type
go
if exists (select name from sysobjects where
name="movie_allocation")
   drop table movie_allocation
go
if exists (select name from sysobjects where name="movie")
   drop table movie
go
if exists (select name from sysobjects where name="movie_genre")
   drop table movie_genre
go
```

```
if exists (select name from sysobjects where name="language")
   drop table language
go
if exists (select name from sysobjects where name="movie_personel")
   drop table movie_personel
go
if exists (select name from sysobjects where name="personel_type")
   drop table personel_type
go
if exists (select name from sysobjects where name="product")
   drop table product
go
if exists (select name from sysobjects where name="sys_parameters")
   drop table sys_parameters
go
if exists (select name from sysobjects where name="codes")
   drop table codes
go
select 'finished dropping tables'
/****************************************************************
 * It is acceptable to include comments or commands in this space *
 ****************************************************************/

/*********
 * store *
 *********/
create table store
(
  store_id            int,
  address1            char(30),
  address2            char(30),
  city                char(15),
  state               char(20),
  zip_code            char(11),
  phone               char(15),
  fax                 char(15),
  contact             char(30)
)
go
/*   Build one cluster index on the store table. This is the
     form of access required for this table.
*/
create clustered index storeid on store (store_id)
                        index    table   field list
                        name     name
go
```

```
/*************
 * work_force *
 *************/
create table work_force
(
   store_id                int,
   employee_id             int,
   last_update             timestamp
)
go
/*  Note: timestamp will automatically be updated by the system,
    and should not be done so by an application program. */
    create clustered index work_force1
                          on work_force (store_id, employee_id).
/************
 * employee *
 ************/
create table employee
(
   employee_id             int,
   last_name               char(30),
   first_name              char(30),
   middle                  char(10),
   address1                char(30),
   address2                char(30),
   city                    char(15),
   state                   char(20),
   zip_code                char(11),
   phone                   char(15),
   fax                     char(15),
   position_code           int
)
go
create clustered index employee_c on employee (employee_id)
go
create nonclustered index employee_n1    /*Create nonclustered
                                           index*/
         on employee(last_name, first_name)
go
/************
 * position *
 ************/
create table position
(
   position_code           int,
   description             char(25)
```

```
)
go
/* no index is necessary because the table will have too
   few records to benefit significantly through use of an index */
/************
 * customer *
 ************/
create table customer
(
  customer_id          int,
  last_name            char(30),
  first_name           char(30),
  middle               char(10),
  address1             char(30),
  address2             char(30),
  city                 char(15),
  state                char(20),
  zip_code             char(11),
  home_phone           char(15),
  office_phone         char(15),
  credit_card_type     int,
  credit_card_no       char(15),
  drivers_licence      char(20),
  discount_percent     float
)
go
create clustered index customer_c on customer (customer_id)
go
create nonclustered index customer_n1   /*Create nonclustered
                                          index*/
        on customer(home_phone)
go

create nonclustered index customer_n2 /*Create nonclustered
                                        index*/
        on customer(last_name, first_name)
go
/***********
 * invoice *
 ***********/
create table invoice
(
  invoice_no           int,
  customer_id          int,
  invoice_date         char(20),
```

```
      total_amount              money,
      total_taxes               money,
      total_discount            money,
      payment_method_code       int,
      credit_card_type          int,
      credit_card_no            char(20),
      next_due_date             char(20),
      items_open                int,
      store_id                  int,
      employee_id               int
)
go
create clustered index invoice on invoice (invoice_no)
go
create nonclustered index invoice_n1      /*Create nonclustered
                                             index*/
         on invoice(next_due_date)
go
/*****************
 * invoice_items *
 *****************/
create table invoice_items
(
   invoice_no                 int,
   sequence_no                int,
   product_code               int,
   movie_id                   int,
   amount                     money,
   pst                        money,
   other_taxes                money,
   discount                   money,
   due_date                   datetime,
   date_returned              datetime
)
go
create clustered index invoice_items on invoice_items
(invoice_no, sequence_no)
go
create nonclustered index invoice_items_n1   /*Create nonclustered
                                                index*/
         on invoice_items(due_date, date_returned)
go
/*****************
 * payment_method *
 *****************/
```

```
create table payment_method
(
  payment_method_code        int,
  description                char(25)
)
go
/********************
 * credit_card_type *
 ********************/
create table credit_card_type
(
  credit_card_type           int,
  description                char(25)
)
go
/*******************
 * movie_allocation *
 ********************/
create table movie_allocation
(
  store_id                   int,
  movie_id                   int,
  allocated_amt              int,
  available                  int
)
go
create clustered index movie_allocation on movie_allocation
(store_id, movie_id)
go
/*********
 * movie *
 *********/
create table movie
(
  movie_id                   int,
  name                       char(30),
  movie_genre_code           int,
  product_code               int,
  release_date               datetime,
  language_code              int,
  cost                       money,
  plot1                      char(100),
  plot2                      char(100)
)
go
```

```
create clustered index movie_c on movie (movie_id)
go
create nonclustered index movie_n1   /*Create nonclustered index*/
         on movie(name)
go

create nonclustered index movie_n2    /*Create nonclustered index*/
         on movie(language_code)
go
create nonclustered index movie_n3    /*Create nonclustered index*/
         on movie(movie_genre_code)
go
/**************
 * movie_genre *
 ***************/
create table movie_genre
(
  movie_genre_code            int,
  description                 char(25)
)
go
/***********
 * language *
 ************/
create table language
(
  language_code               int,
  description                 char(25)
)
go
/*****************
 * movie_personel *
 ******************/
create table movie_personel
(
  movie_id                    int,
  personel_id                 int,
  personel_type               int,
  last_name                   char(30),
  first_name                  char(30),
  middle_name                 char(20)
)
go
create clustered index movie_personel_c on movie_personel
(movie_id, personel_id, personel_type)
```

```
go
create nonclustered index movie_personel_n1   /*Create nonclustered
                                                 index*/
        on movie_personel(last_name, first_name)
go
/*****************
 * personel_type *
 *****************/
create table personel_type
(
  personel_type             int,
  description               char(25)
)
go
/***********
 * product *
 ***********/
create table product
(
  product_code              int,
  part_type                 char(10),
  description               char(30),
  price                     money
)
go
/* The reader may want to build an index on
   product_code, part_type in the future when more records
   are present in the table */
/******************
 * sys_parameters *
 ******************/
create table sys_parameters
(
  name                      char(20),
  date_effective            char(15),
  parameter_type            int,
  value1_from               int,
  value1_to                 int,
  value2_from               float,
  value2_to                 float,
  value3_from               char(30),
  value3_to                 char(30),
  date_from                 datetime,
  date_to                   datetime,
```

```
   last_update                 datetime,
   description                 char(25)
)
go
create clustered index sysparms_c on sys_parameters (name)
go
/*********
 * codes *
 *********/
/* General purpose table to hold system codes not contained in the
    other tables. */
create table codes
(
   code_type                   char(20),
   code_value                  int,
   description                 char(25)
)
go
create clustered index codes_c on codes (code_type, code_value)
go
```

19.3   RUN THE SCRIPT

The tables.v1 script must be compiled into the data dictionary of the
video database used by the Video Rental Store application. Notice the
syntax of the commands that are shown below. Because the tables.v1
script is being compiled with a system administrator userid, the table
creation script must include a command to establish a current database. This is done in the tables.v1 script as the first step.

- ```
  /* compile the table creation script */
  /* SYBASE & DSQUERY environment variables have been
  set previously */
  isql -Usa -P -itables.v1
  ```
- ```
  /* sign on with an appropriate user id. The
  sector user will establish video as the default
  database. */
  isql -Usector -Psector
  ```
- ```
  /* Verify that the tables were created
  successfully. */
  select name from sysobjects
  go
  ```
  ```

19.4   SCRIPT TO INITIALIZE TABLES

```
♦ create initab.v1
/**************************************************************
 * Filename: initab.v1                                       *
 * Date:     Nov 1, 1993                                     *
 * Author:   Sanjiv Purba                                    *
 *                                                           *
 * This script initializes the tables in the Video Rental   *
 * Store Database.                                           *
 **************************************************************/
use video  /* open database */
go
/**************************************************************
 * Initialize store : insert records for the three stores in *
 * the franchise                                             *
 **************************************************************/
/* remove old records from tables */
truncate table store
go
truncate table movie
go
insert store
(
  store_id,
  address1,
  address2,
  city,
  state,
  zip_code,
  phone,
  fax,
  contact
)
values
(
  1,
  "3335 Asgirus Road",
  "Asgirus/Yonge Street",
  "Washington D.C.",
  "Washington",
  "90215",
  "416-858-1111",
  "416-858-1119",
  "Neil Sector"
```

```
)
go
insert store
(
  store_id,
  address1,
  address2,
  city,
  state,
  zip_code,
  phone,
  fax,
  contact
)
values
(
  2,
  "4629 Tobos Lane",
  "Tobos/Bay Street",
  "Washington D.C.",
  "Washington",
  "90215",
  "416-858-2911",
  "416-858-2919",
  "Victoria Tan"
)
go
insert store
(
  store_id,
  address1,
  address2,
  city,
  state,
  zip_code,
  phone,
  fax,
  contact
)
values
(
  3,
  "11 University Road",
  "University/College Street",
  "Washington D.C.",
```

```
  "Washington",
  "90215",
  "416-858-7844",
  "416-858-7899",
  "Steve Ryder"
)
go
/* insert movies */
insert movie
(
  movie_id,
  name,
  movie_genre_code,
  product_code,
  release_date,
  language_code,
  cost,
  plot1,
  plot2
)
values
(
  000001,
  "Star Wars",
  1,
  1,
  "Jan 01 1977 00:00",
  1,
  20.00,
  "An Evil Empire is overthrown by the forces of",
  "good and light"
)
go
insert movie
(
  movie_id,
  name,
  movie_genre_code,
  product_code,
  release_date,
  language_code,
  cost,
  plot1,
  plot2
)
```

```
values
(
  000002,
  "My Fair Lady",
  3,
  1,
  "Jan 01 1965 00:00",
  1,
  20.00,
  "A flower girl is befriended by a travelled English Colonel",
  "and a Professor"
)
go
```

The reader should feel free to insert more records into the movie table.

19.5   EXERCISES FOR READERS

Readers should build similar scripts to populate the other tables in the database. The following list can be used as a cross-reference. Sample data for a record is provided for each table. Readers should build insert statements with this information and similar data (make it up) and insert them into the initab.v1 script:

- ◆ *work_force table*
  ```
  store_id     = 1
  employee_id  = 1000
  last_update  = declared as timestamp datatype, so
  system supplied
  ```

- ◆ *employee table*
  ```
  employee_id   = 1000
  last_name     = "Ryder"
  first_name    = "Steve"
  middle        = "Parkash"
  address1      = "123 Asgirus Blvd"
  address2      = " "
  city          = "New York"
  state         = "New York"
  zip_code      = "12345"
  phone         = "123-345-3433"
  fax           = "123-345-2444"
  position_code = 1
  ```

- *position table*
  ```
  position_code        = 1
  description          = "Clerk"
  ```

- *customer table*
  ```
  customer_id          = 1000
  last_name            = "Flanders"
  first_name           = "Marsha"
  middle               =
  address1             = "11 Main Street"
  address2             =
  city                 = "New York"
  state                = "New York"
  zip_code             = "12345"
  home_phone           = "222 222 2222"
  office_phone         =
  credit_card_type     = 1
  credit_card_no       = "1111111111"
  drivers_licence      = "12341234"
  discount_percent     = .03
  ```

- *payment_method table*
  ```
  payment_method_code  = 1
  description          = "Cash"
  ```

- *credit_card_type table*
  ```
  credit_card_type     = 1
  description          = "VISA GOLD"
  ```

- *movie_allocation table*
  ```
  store_id             = 1
  movie_id             = 000002
  allocated_amt        = 3
  available            = 3
  ```

- *movie_genre table*
  ```
  movie_genre_code     = 1
  description          = "Science Fiction"
  ```

- *language table*
  ```
  language_code        = 1
  description          = "English"
  ```

- *movie_personel table*
  ```
  movie_id             = 000002
  ```

```
        personel_id                  = 1000
        personel_type                = 1
        last_name                    = "Hepburn"
        first_name                   = "Audrey"
        middle_name                  =
```

- ◆ *personel_type table*
```
        personel_type                = 1
        description                  = "Actress"
```

- ◆ *product table*
```
        product_code                 = 1
        part_type                    = 1
        description                  = "Acme Potato Chips"
        price                        = 1.69
```

Readers can add more records, but care should be taken to match key fields as the previous examples have done.

19.6   SUMMARY

This chapter developed two scripts. The first script contains creation commands for the tables and indexes required by the Video Rental Store application. The second script contains commands to initialize some of the tables. This chapter also provided a cross-reference to assist readers in adding more information to the initialization script to populate the tables. Readers should also create insert scripts to populate the tables with additional made-up data.

Application Functionality Description

In this chapter a reader will learn about:

- Discussion of functions required to manage the database server side of the Video Rental Store application
- Sample stored procedures
- Sample triggers
- Sample objects

20.1 DESCRIPTION OF APPLICATION FUNCTIONALITY

The objective of this chapter is to build a few of the Sybase Transact - SQL programs that are required by the Video Rental Store application. Readers can use these as examples to build the remaining functions required by the system.

20.2 INSERT SCRIPTS

Stored procedures to insert data into the tables in the *video* database are developed in this section. The programs are stored in ASCII files.

- ```
  create insstore.syb  (i.e., textedit insstore.syb &)
  /* syb extension is used to denote files containing
  sybase code, as opposed to 'C' code, for example. */
  ```
  ```

```
use video
go
create proc insstore
(
      @store_id      int,
      @address1      char(30),
      @address2      char(30),
      @city          char(15),
      @state         char(20),
      @zip_code      char(11),
      @phone         char(15),
      @fax           char(15),
      @contact       char(30)
)
as
insert store
(
      store_id,
      address1,
      address2,
      city,
      state,
      zip_code,
      phone,
      fax,
      contact
)
values
(
      @store_id,
      @address1,
      @address2,
      @city,
      @state,
      @zip_code,
      @phone,
      @fax,
      @contact
)
if @@rowcount = 0
begin
    select -100    /* store not inserted */
    select 'attempt to insert store_id=', @store_id, '
not successful'
```

```
      return -1
end
return 0
go
```

- save ASCII file
- isql -Usector -Psector -iinsstore.syb /* compile
  stored procedure */
  /* correct any errors, and recompile */
- isql -Usector -Psector
  select db_name() /* confirm default database */
  go
- select name from sysobjects where type = 'P'
  /* confirm that the stored procedure was compiled
  into the database */
  go
- sp_helptext insstore
        /* verify that the stored procedure text is
           stored in the data dictionary */
  go
- /* test this stored procedure */

Method 1:
/* from the 'video' database in Sybase type the
   following commands */
  1> exec insstore 150, '3335 Wonder Rd', '','New York
            City', 'New York', '12345', '416-893-
            9292', '416-212-3234', 'Joe Bradshaw'
  2> go

Method 2:
/* create a text file in the host operating system
and execute it with a batch script. This method has
the advantage of allowing the script to be re-run at
anytime, without requiring the developer to retype
it */
- quit
- create insstore.txt
        exec insstore 150, '3335 Wonder Rd', '','New
            York City', 'New York', '12345',
            '416-893-9292', '416-212-3234', 'Joe
            Bradshaw'
    go
```
```

```
/* save the file */
♦   isql -Usector -Psector -iinsstore.txt
♦   /* verify that the record is added to the store
    table */
    select * from store where store_id = 150
```

The reader should repeat these steps to develop batch insertion scripts for the other tables in the tutorial (created in Chapter 19). The following table headers should be filled in as these scripts are completed. Photocopy the table if additional space is required.

Table Name	Stored Procedure Name	Compile Procedure (Yes/No)	Test Script Name	Run Test Script (Yes/No)
work_force				
employee				
position				
customer				
invoice				
invoice_items				
payment_method				
credit_card_type				
movie_allocation				
movie				
movie_genre				
language				
movie_personel				
personel_type				
product				
codes				
sys_parameters				

Table Name	Stored Procedure Name	Compile Procedure (Yes/No)	Test Script Name	Run Test Script (Yes/No)
work_force				
employee				
position				
customer				
invoice				
invoice_items				
payment_method				
credit_card_type				
movie_allocation				
movie				
movie_genre				
language				
movie_personel				
personel_type				
product				
codes				
sys_parameters				

20.3   DELETE SCRIPTS

♦   create delstore.syb (i.e., vi delstore.syb &)

```
use video
go
drop proc delstore
go
create proc delstore
(
     @store_id      int
)
as
```

```
delete store
   where store_id = @store_id
if @@rowcount = 0
begin
   select -200
   select 'store_id =', @store_id, ' not on file'
   return -1
end
select 200
return 0
go
```

- save ASCII file
- isql -Usector -Psector -idelstore.syb
- isql -Usector -Psector
- select name from sysobjects where type = 'P'
  go
- sp_helptext delstore
  go
- /* test this stored procedure */

  Method 1:
  ```
   /* from the 'video' database in Sybase */
    1> select * from store where store_id = 150
    2> go
    1> exec delstore 150
    2> go
   /* record should be gone */
    1> select * from
       store_id = 150
    2> go
  ```

  Method 2:
  ```
  /* create a text file in the host operating system
  and execute it with a batch script */
  ```
  - quit
  - create delstore.txt
    ```
          exec delstore 150
        go
    ```
  - isql -Usector -Psector -idelstore.txt
- /* verify that record is deleted from the store
  table */
  ```
  isql -Usector -Psector
  select * from store where
  ```

```
      store_id = 150
      go
♦     /* try to delete the same record again */
      isql -Usector -Psector -idelstore.txt
```

The reader should develop batch deletion scripts for the other tables in the tutorial. The following table headers should be filled in as these scripts are completed. Photocopy the table if additional space is required.

20.4   UPDATE SCRIPTS

An update script is used to update an existing record in a table based on the values in some key fields. This section develops such a script to update the store table.

♦   create updstore.syb

```
use video
go
drop proc updstore
go
create proc updstore
(
      @store_id         int,
      @address1         char(30),
      @address2         char(30),
      @city             char(15),
      @state            char(20),
      @zip_code         char(11),
      @phone            char(15),
      @fax              char(15),
      @contact          char(30)
)
as
      update store
      set address1 = @address1,
          address2 = @address2,
          city     = @city,
          state    = @state,
          zip_code = @zip_code,
          phone    = @phone,
          fax      = @fax,
          contact  = @contact
```

```
      where store_id = @store_id
if @@rowcount = 0
begin
   select -300
   select 'store_id =', @store_id,
          ' not updated because it is not on file'
   return 0
end
select 300
return 0
go
```

- ◆ save ASCII file
- ◆ isql -Usector -Psector -iupdstore.syb
- ◆ isql -Usector -Psector
- ◆ select name from sysobjects where type = 'P'
  go
- ◆ sp_helptext updstore
  go
- ◆ /* test this stored procedure */

  Method 1:
  ```
  /* from the 'video' database in Sybase */
  /* Note: store 150 was deleted in the previous
   script, so the following update attempt will return
   an error message */
  1> exec updstore
          150, '3335 Wonderful Rd', '',
          'New York City', 'New York',
          '12121', '613-893-9292',
          '613-212-3234', 'Jackie Davidson'
  2> go
  /* re-insert store 150, and run this script again */
  ```

  Method 2:
  ```
  /* create a text file in the host operating system
  and execute it with a batch script */
  ```
  - ◆ quit
  - ◆ create updstore.txt
    ```
        exec updstore
            150, '3335 Wonderful Rd', '',
            'New York City', 'New York',
            '12121', '613-893-9292',
            '613-212-3234', 'Jackie Davidson'
    ```

```
              go
   ◆  isql -Usector -Psector -iupdstore.txt
◆  /* verify that record is updated in the store table
   */
   isql -Usector -Psector
   select * from store where store_id
   150
   go
◆  /* try to update another store that is not on file */
        1> exec updstore
              998, '3335 Wonderful Rd', '',
              'New York City', 'New York',
              '12121', '613-893-9292',
              '613-212-3234', 'Jackie Davidson'
        2> go
```

The reader should develop batch update scripts for the other tables in the tutorial. The following table headers should be filled in as these scripts are completed. Photocopy the table if additional space is required.

20.5   DROPPING OBJECTS

In the event that a message similar to the one shown in Figure 20.1 appears on the screen when trying to compile a stored procedure, create a table, and so forth; it is necessary to drop the object before trying to recompile it.

Message (Note: the wording may be altered depending on the version of Sybase that is being used) See Figure 20.1.

Solution

```
   ◆  drop procedure insstore
      go
```

A script can be created to drop a group of stored procedures and/or tables.

```
Procedure 'insstore' group number 1 already exists in
the database. Choose another procedure name or
procedure number.
```

Figure 20.1   Error message.

Table Name	Stored Procedure Name	Compile Procedure (Yes/No)	Test Script Name	Run Test Script (Yes/No)
work_force				
employee				
position				
customer				
invoice				
invoice_items				
payment_method				
credit_card_type				
movie_allocation				
movie				
movie_genre				
language				
movie_personel				
personel_type				
product				
codes				
sys_parameters				

20.6   SELECTING INFORMATION

A front-end application frequently issues a request for information from a database. The format of a stored procedure that can respond to this information is as follows:

- Accept a search key from an application program
- Issue a select on the key
- Return a flag if no records were found

Example 1

♦   create retrstore.syb

```
use video
go
create proc retrieve_store
(
     @store_id              int
)
as
    /*
     While the syntax "select * from store" could be used
     in place of the following statement, this can cause
     problems in the life of a system. A front-end
     application will need to bind to the record fields
     returned by this command. Since the * returns all
     the fields in a table record, the addition of new
     fields into a table, after the creation of this
     script, will put the front-end application out of
     sync with the fields being returned by the server.
     This will result in online runtime application
     errors.

     The following code returns records in a specific
     order. Furthermore, new fields added to the table
     record will not automatically be returned to the
     calling application.
    */
    select 200
    select store_id, address1, city, state, contact
        from store
                where store_id = @store_id
    if @@rowcount = 0
    begin
      select -200 /* store_id not on file */
      return -1
    end
return 0
go
```

- save ASCII file
- isql -Usector -Psector -iretrstore.syb
- /* Test this stored procedure */
  /* from the 'video' database in Sybase */
  1> exec retrieve_store 150
  2> go

Example 2

```
/* The previous example returned just one or zero rows
   (records) of information. This example will respond
   to a request with zero to many rows (records) of
   information. Assume that the client application can
   only display one screen (or 10 rows) of information,
   so the stored procedure will limit the rows selected
   by a query to this number.                         */
```
♦   create retrmovie.syb

```
use video
go
create proc retrieve_movie
(
    @release_date        datetime
)
as
    select 200
    set rowcount 10 /* set maximum rows returned to
    10 */
    select movie_id, name, release_date, plot1,
    plot2
        from movie
                where release_date > @release_date
    if @@rowcount = 0
    begin
      select -200      /* no movies on file */
      return 0
    end
    set rowcount 0 /* reset the variable so that the
    next select will display all qualifying records */
return 0
go
```

♦   save ASCII file
♦   isql -Usector -Psector -iretrmovie.syb
♦   /* Test this stored procedure */
```
    /* from the 'video' database in Sybase */
    1> exec retrieve_movie "Jan 01 1985 00:00"
    2> go
```

Similar stored procedures can be written to select information to answer queries such as the following:

- Which movies does "Robin Williams" star in?
- Which movies have "science fiction" themes?
- What is the total amount of money outstanding for late movies?
- Which customers have overdue movies?
- Which movies are currently rented?
- What is the movie inventory list by store?

20.7   MANAGING INVOICES

A more complex stored procedure is required to manage invoices in this application. The procedure will be designed to perform four types of functions for invoices: (1) insert new invoices; (2) update invoices; (3) return information about an invoice to a requester; and (4) delete all parts of an invoice. These functions are requested by a code/flag which is passed to the stored procedure as a parameter.

An invoice is generated at a specific store for a specific customer. Header information is stored in the invoice table, while details are stored in the invoice_items table. Invoice number is automatically generated and stored in the system_parameters table.

◆   create invoice.syb

```
use video
go
drop proc invoice_function
go
create proc invoice_function
(
    @function              char(5), /* action to add/
change /delete/retrieve an invoice */
    @invoice_no            int,
    @customer_id           int,
    @invoice_date          char(20),
    @total_amount          money,
    @total_taxes           money,
    @total_discount        money,
    @payment_method_code   int,
    @credit_card_type      int,
    @credit_card_no        char(20),
    @next_due_date         char(20),
    @items_open            int,
    @store_id              int,
    @employee_id           int,
```

```
    @detail1                 char(120), /* each
        /* each @detail x variable
          contains a string of
        concatenated invoice details. */
    @detail2                 char(120),
    @detail3                 char(120), /* The program
        parses this string */
    @detail4                 char(120),
    @detail5                 char(120),
    @detail6                 char(120)
)
as
 declare
  @return                int,
  @temp                  int
/* data integrity is maintained by the calling program—
generally from a client workstation */
/* validate function parameter */
if @function != 'RET' and @function != 'ADD' and
@function != 'UPD'
        and @function != 'DEL'
begin
    select -50    /* invalid function requested */
    return 0
end
/* process request for retrieval */
if @function = 'RET'
begin
    select 200
    /* there is a one too many relationship between
      the invoice and invoice_items tables */
    select invoice_no, customer_id, invoice_date,
      total_amount,
          total_taxes, total_discount,
            payment_method_code,
          credit_card_type, credit_card_no,
            next_due_date,
          items_open, store_id, employee_id
      from invoice
        where invoice_no = @invoice_no
  if @@rowcount = 0
  begin
    select -200 /* invoice not on file */
    return 0
  end
```

```
   /* invoice is on file, select the related details
      from the invoice_items table */
   select 300
   select invoice_no, sequence_no, product_code,
          amount, pst, other_taxes, discount,
          due_date, date_returned
        from invoice_items
          where invoice_no = @invoice_no
   if @@rowcount = 0
   begin
      select -300       /* no invoice details on file */
      return 0
   end
end
/* process insert request */
if @function = 'ADD'
begin
   /* Verify that the invoice_no is not on file
      otherwise the request should be to add/update */
   select 250
   select @temp = invoice_no
        from invoice
          where invoice_no = @invoice_no
   if @@rowcount != 0
   begin
      select -250 /* Invoice is already on file, use
                     Update function. */
      return 0
   end
   insert invoice
   (
     invoice_no,
     customer_id,
     invoice_date,
     total_amount,
     total_taxes,
     total_discount,
     payment_method_code,
     credit_card_type,
     credit_card_no,
     next_due_date,
     items_open,
     store_id,
     employee_id
   )
```

```
values
(
  @invoice_no,
  @customer_id,
  convert (datetime, @invoice_date),
  @total_amount,
  @total_taxes,
  @total_discount,
  @payment_method_code,
  @credit_card_type,
  @credit_card_no,
  convert (datetime, @next_due_date),
  @items_open,
  @store_id,
  @employee_id
)
/* if there are details, the first position in the
   @detail variables is nonzero */
if convert (int, substring (@detail1, 1, 1)) != 0
   exec @return = parse_invoice_details
   @invoice_no, @detail1
if convert (int, substring (@detail2, 1, 1)) != 0
   exec @return = parse_invoice_details
   @invoice_no, @detail2
if convert (int, substring (@detail3, 1, 1)) != 0
   exec @return = parse_invoice_details
   @invoice_no, @detail3
if convert (int, substring (@detail4, 1, 1)) != 0
   exec @return = parse_invoice_details
   @invoice_no, @detail4
if convert (int, substring (@detail5, 1, 1)) != 0
   exec @return = parse_invoice_details
   @invoice_no, @detail5
if convert (int, substring (@detail6, 1, 1)) != 0
   exec @return = parse_invoice_details
   @invoice_no, @detail6
end
/* process delete request */
if @function = 'DEL'
begin
   delete invoice
       where invoice_no = @invoice_no
   if @@rowcount = 0
   begin
       select -200     /* invoice is not on file */
       return 0
```

```
    end
    /* delete related invoice items */
    exec @return = delete_invoices @invoice_no
    if @return < 0 /* error message already returned from
the called procedure */
        return 0
end
/* update invoice */
if @function = 'UPD'
begin
    update invoice
      set customer_id          = @customer_id,
          invoice_date         = @invoice_date,
          total_amount         = @total_amount,
          total_taxes          = @total_taxes,
          total_discount       = @total_discount,
          payment_method_code  = @payment_method_code,
          credit_card_type     = @credit_card_type,
          credit_card_no       = @credit_card_no,
          next_due_date        = @next_due_date,
          items_open           = @items_open,
          store_id             = @store_id,
          employee_id          = @employee_id
      where invoice_no = @invoice_no
    if @@rowcount = 0
    begin
        select -200 /* invoice number is not on file */
        return 0
    end
    /* delete all items on file belonging to this
       invoice, and re-insert the new items stored in
       the @detail variables again */
    exec @return = delete_invoices @invoice_no
    if convert (int, substring (@detail1, 1, 1)) != 0
       /* check if first position is nonzero */
        exec @return = parse_invoice_details
        @invoice_no, @detail1
    if convert (int, substring (@detail2, 1, 1)) != 0
        exec @return = parse_invoice_details
        @invoice_no, @detail2
    if convert (int, substring (@detail3, 1, 1)) != 0
        exec @return = parse_invoice_details
        @invoice_no, @detail3
    if convert (int, substring (@detail4, 1, 1)) != 0
        exec @return = parse_invoice_details
        @invoice_no, @detail4
```

```
    if convert (int, substring (@detail5, 1, 1)) != 0
        exec @return = parse_invoice_details
        @invoice_no, @detail5
    if convert (int, substring (@detail6, 1, 1)) != 0
        exec @return = parse_invoice_details
        @invoice_no, @detail6
end
return 0
go
drop proc delete_invoices
go
/* Procedure_name: delete_invoices                    */
/* Description:                                        */
/*      This procedure receives an invoice_no from */
/*      the caller and deletes all records in the  */
/*      invoice_items table having this invoice_no */
create proc delete_invoices
(
    @invoice_no              int
)
as
    delete invoice_items
        where invoice_no = @invoice_no
    if @@rowcount = 0
    begin
        select -300    /* invoice items are not on file */
        return -1
    end
return 0
go
drop proc parse_invoice_details
go
/* procedure_name: parse_invoice_details */
/* Description:                          */
/* This procedure parses the @detail     */
/* string into invoice items fields      */
/* and inserts them into the             */
/* invoice_items table.                  */
/* The format of the detail record       */
/* is:                                   */
/*    @sequence_no     5 characters      */
/*    @product_code    5 characters      */
/*    @amount          6 characters      */
/*    @pst             5 characters      */
/*    @other_tax       5 characters      */
/*    @discount        5 characters      */
/*    @due_date       20 characters      */
```

```
/*    @movie_id          6 characters      */
/*   total length is 57 characters         */
/* There are two occurrences of this       */
/* string in each @detail record.          */
create proc parse_invoice_details
(
    @invoice_no              int,
    @detail                  char(120)
)
as
declare
    @return                  int,
    @counter                 int,
    @sequence_no             int,
    @product_code            int,
    @amount                  money,
    @pst                     money,
    @other_tax               money,
    @discount                money,
    @due_date                datetime,
    @movie_id                int
select @counter = 0
while @counter < 2
begin
    /* each invoice_items record has a unique sequence no
*/
    select @sequence_no = convert (int, substring
(@detail, (@counter*57 + 1), 5)) /* each invoice_items
record has a length of 57 characters */
    select @product_code = convert (int, substring
(@detail, (@counter*57+1)+5, 5))
    select @amount = convert (money, substring
(@detail, (@counter*57+1)+10, 6))
    select @pst = convert (money, substring (@detail,
(@counter*57+1)+16, 5))
    select @other_tax = convert (money, substring
(@detail, (@counter*57+1)+21, 5))
    select @discount = convert (money, substring
(@detail, (@counter*57+1)+26, 5))
    select @due_date = convert (datetime, substring
(@detail, (@counter*57+1)+31, 20))
    select @movie_id = convert (int, substring (@detail,
(@counter*57+1)+51, 6))
    if @sequence_no = 0
        return 0    /* there are no more details to
    process in this @detail record */
    insert invoice_items
```

```
        ,
    (
      invoice_no,
      sequence_no,
      product_code,
      movie_id,
      amount,
      pst,
      other_taxes,
      discount,
      due_date,
      date_returned
    )
    values
    (
      @invoice_no,
      @sequence_no,
      @product_code,
      @movie_id,
      @amount,
      @pst,
      @other_tax,
      @discount,
      @due_date,
      "Jan 01 1980 00:00"
    )
    /* examine the next occurrence in the @detail
       record */
    select @counter = @counter + 1
end
return 0
go
```

20.8   CREATING TRIGGERS

Create a trigger by following the steps in this section.

♦   create triggers.syb

```
use video
go
drop trigger open_items
go
```

```
create trigger open_items
on invoice_items
for update
as
/* select firing open_items trigger*/
if update (date_returned)
begin
    update invoice
        set items_open = items_open - 1
        from inserted
            where invoice.invoice_no =
            inserted.invoice_no
    if @@rowcount = 0
    begin
        print 'impossible condition'
    end
end
go
```

- /* compile the trigger into the data dictionary */
     isql -Usector -Psector -itriggers.syb
  Note: Test the trigger by updating
        the date_returned field in the
        invoice_items table
        i.e., 1> update invoice_items
                  set date_returned = getdate()
              where invoice_no = xx
                and movie_id   = yy
            2> go
      where xx and yy identify one
             record in the invoice_items table.

20.9   DUMP TRANSACTION

Activities cause transactions to be written to the transaction log (syslogs table). This table will eventually get full. When this occurs, Sybase will no longer accept commands that cause records to be written to the log (e.g. **insert**, **delete**, **update**, **compile** stored procedures/triggers). This situation can be solved by dumping the records in the transaction log by using the following command:

- dump transaction video with no_log
  go

20.10   CREATING A TEST SCRIPT

The following **exec** will run the **invoice_function** stored procedure. This **exec** can be included in a batch script or typed interactively. Typing it interactively will be frustrating unless the reader is an exceptionally accurate typer and only wants to run this stored procedure with this data once! The author recommends typing the following code into a batch file (i.e., call it **exec_invfnc.dat**) and running it using the command:

Note: the data is fictitious, so the user can examine the parse_invoice_details procedure to map test data to the fields in the database in order to create additional test scripts. The reader should notice that the long strings corresponding to the details are parsed according to the following mask:

chars 1–5: sequence_no.

chars 6–10: product_code.

Next 6 characters are amount. Next 5 characters are PST. Next 5 characters are other_tax. Next 5 characters are discount. Next 20 characters are due_date. The next 6 characters are movie_id. This pattern repeats for the rest of the detail.

```
isql -Uvideo -Pvideo -SSYBASE -
  iexec_invfnc.dat
use video
go
exec invoice_function
"ADD", 14, 1, "Nov 29 1993 12:43", 30.00, 10.00,
0.00, 1, 0, "",
"Nov 30 1993 17:00", 3, 1, 15,
"10001222223333334444455555566666Nov 30 1993 16:00
12345610002222222333333444455555566666Nov 30 1993
16:00   123457", "0", "0", "0", "0", "0"
go /* do not forget this go */
/* the reader should adjust this script with other
test data. The return codes after execution can be
compared with the source code to interpret their
meaning. In general a positive number signals success
and a negative number signals that something went
wrong. */
```

20.11   CREATING A VIEW

A view can be created for users to access specific information, without having to be concerned about the total picture.

♦ create movierule.syb

```
use video
go
drop view getmovies
go
create view getmovies
as
  /* find movies that have been rented */
  select due_date, name
    from movie, invoice_items
       where movie.movie_id = invoice_items.movie_id
          and due_date > getdate()
go
```

♦ sp_helptext getmovies
♦ /* use the view as a table */
  ```
  use video
  go
  select * from getmovies
  go
  ```

20.12   CREATING A CURSOR

```
/************************************************
 * ProcName:     browse_cust                    *
 * Author:       Sanjiv Purba                    *
 * Date:         Oct 1993                        *
 * Filename:     brcustom.sql                    *
 * Purpose: This program uses a cursor to step  *
 *      through the customer table in the        *
 *      video database.                          *
 ************************************************/
use video
go
drop proc browse_cust
go
create procedure browse_cust
as
    declare @input        int,
            @last_name    char(30),
            @first_name   char(30),
            @home_phone   char(15),
            @status_sw    int
```

```
    declare browse_customer
            cursor
      for select last_name, first_name, home_phone from
customer
    open browse_customer
    select @input = 1
    select @status_sw = 1
    while @status_sw = 1
    begin
      fetch browse_customer into @last_name,
@first_name, @home_phone
        if @@sqlstatus = 2
        begin
          select "no more rows to fetch"
          select @status_sw = @@sqlstatus
          break
        end
        else
        if @@sqlstatus = 1
        begin
          select "unknown cursor error"
          select @status_sw = @@sqlstatus
          break
      end
      select @last_name, @first_name, @home_phone
      select @input = @input + 1
    end
    select 'records read: ', @input
    return
go
*******************************************************************
```

The reader should compile this stored procedure into the video database using the following command:

♦   isql -Uvideo -Pvideo -ibrcustom.sql

(Assume that video is a valid user/password combination.)

If the compile was successful, the cursor can be tested by using the commands in the following list:

♦   isql -Uvideo -Pvideo
♦   use video
♦   go

- ◆ select db_name() /* should show video database name */
- ◆ go
- ◆ sp_help /* display list of objects, look for browse_cust)
- ◆ go
- ◆ exec browse_cust
- ◆ go
- /* a list of customers and related information will appear on the screen. */
- ◆ exit /* quit SQL Server */

Note: if there are no customer records in the customer table, try writing a script to add a few, and re-run the **browse_cust** procedure. An example of a script that adds a few sample customers is included here:

```
/* Type the following script into an ascii file named
addcustomers.sql */


/************************************************************
 Filename:      addcustomers.sql
 Author:        Sanjiv Purba
 Date:          Nov 1993

 Purpose:       This batch script inserts customers into the
                customer table.

 Maintenance Log:
************************************************************/

use pubs2    /* change this to video */
go

insert customer
(
 customer_id,
 last_name,
 first_name,
 middle,
 address1,
 address2,
 city,
 state,
```

```
zip_code,
home_phone,
office_phone,
credit_card_type,
credit_card_no,
drivers_licence,
discount_percent
)
values
(
1,
"Sector",
"Neil",
"P",
"123 Tobos Avenue",
" ",
"Asgirus",
"New York",
"901234",
"555-555-5555",
"555-555-5555",
1,
" ",
" ",
10
)
go

insert customer
(
customer_id,
last_name,
first_name,
middle,
address1,
address2,
city,
state,
zip_code,
home_phone,
office_phone,
credit_card_type,
credit_card_no,
drivers_licence,
discount_percent
```

```
)
values
(
 1,
 "Flanders",
 "Marsha",
 "P",
 "123 Tobos Avenue",
 " ",
 "Asgirus",
 "New York",
 "901234",
 "555-555-5555",
 "555-555-5555",
 1,
 " ",
 " ",
 10
)
go
```

20.13 SUMMARY

This chapter provided tested examples of creating a complex stored procedure, triggers, cursors, and views. A command to clear out the transaction log (something that needs to be done in times of heavy activity) was also provided.

Readers are encouraged to design, build, and test stored procedures to manipulate data in the other application tables that were created in Chapter 19.

Summary of SQL Server 10 Enhancements

Sybase SQL Server 10 is an enhanced version of SQL Server 4.x. In some cases, new features have been added to SQL Server; in others, existing functionality has been improved. This section discusses some of the major enhancements in the latest release of this product as discussed in the Sybase manual, *What's New in Sybase SQL Server Release 10?*, and the author's testing and research.

1. Several new databases have been added to SQL Server. These are:
   - **sybsystemprocs** (holds system procedures)
   - **sybsecurity** (holds tables used to support auditing)
   - **sybsyntax** (provides help documentation for Sybase features and stored procedures)

2. Backup and recovery tended to be relatively time-consuming in previous versions of SQL Server. SQL Server 10 is packaged with a **backup** server that appears to be faster. Users can continue using the previous backup/recovery commands.

3. A **threshold manager** monitors transaction log space and executes specified stored procedures when free log space drops below a threshold amount.

4. Security has been revamped in SQL Server. Although this makes a developer's job a bit more difficult, the new facility makes logical sense. The **sa** role in earlier versions of SQL Server is now performed by the following three types of administrative staff:

- **System Administrator (sa)**
  The sa is the most powerful administrative role, having the ability to create a database, change the Sybase environment, and so forth.
- **System Security Officer (sso)**
  This role manages the system security procedures.
- **Operator (oper)**
  This role manages backup/recovery procedures.

5. Cursors are now supported by the SQL Server engine, whereas previously they were supported only by some versions of Open Client. Cursors are a helpful feature in applications that require a "one record at a time table browse" ability inside stored procedures.
6. Table-level constraints can be attached to a table as it is created to enforce referential integrity and perform other services.
7. Features in views have been enhanced.
8. Several new datatypes are available in the latest release, among which are:
   - IDENT
     A table can only have one field created with this datatype. IDENT fills the related field with a sequential number whenever a record is inserted into the table.
   - double precision, real, dec, decimal, numeric
9. Transaction rollback capability has been enhanced.
10. Stored procedures had a maximum size limitation of 2 to 4K in previous versions of SQL Server. This limit was easily reached and required some creative solutions. System 10 has increased this size limitation dramatically, to 16MB.
11. "Chained" transactions are supported to allow a wide range of SQL commands to be considered implicit transactions.
12. "Isolation levels" are supported to prevent dirty reads, nonrepeatable reads, and phantoms reads of database tables. By default, "isolation level" = 1, or prevent dirty reads. "Isolation level" can be changed by the **set** command to prevent either of the other two types of reads from occurring.
13. SQL Server will now track computer usage costs for users through several system procedures.
14. New system procedures and built-in functions are available.
15. New system tables have been added to the **model** and the **master** databases.

Miscellaneous changes and improvements have been made to "create index", "set", "dbcc", "kill", "tempdb", "shutdown", "raiserror", "query optimizer", "keywords", and "subqueries".

Bulk Copy (BCP) Utility

BCP is a Sybase utility that allows data to be copied to Sybase databases and out of Sybase databases into files. These files can be transferred to other applications or loaded into other Sybase databases. This is shown in Figure B.1.

While select commands can also move data to tables and into files, BCP has better performance if there are no indexes or triggers on the tables being processed. BCP also does not write records to the transaction file for data inserts in this case. (Note: ensure that "select into/ bulkcopy is on" using the **dboption** command.)

Copying Data out of a Table

Syntax

```
bcp database..table out new_file flag
```

Examples

1. ```
   /* -c flag copies data in character format */
   bcp video..customer out cust.dat -c
   ```

2. ```
   /* -n flag copies data in native format */
   bcp video..customer out cust.dat -n
   ```

Copying Data into a Table To use this option, an input file containing structured data must exist before running bcp.

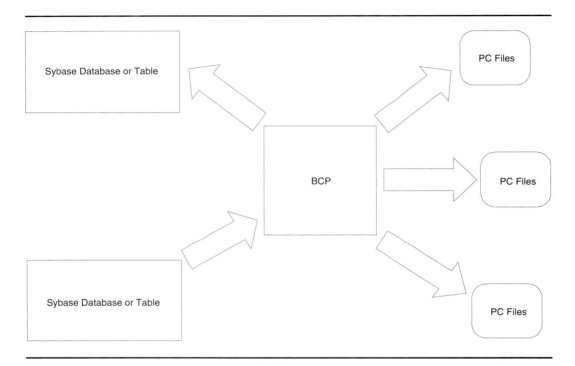

Figure B.1   Bulk copy utility (BCP).

Syntax

```
bcp database..table in in_file flag
```

Examples

1. `/* -c refers to character, t is tab character for field delimiter, r is newline for record delimiter. */`
   `bcp video..customer in cust.txt -c -t \\t -r \\n`
2. `bcp video..credit_card_type in cred.txt -c -t \\t -r \\n`

The format of the cred.txt file to support example 2 is shown in Figure B.2. Notice that the fields are separated by a tab character, while the records are separated by new line characters.

```
1       American Express
2       Mastercard
3       Visa
4       Diner's Club
5       Visa Gold
6       Canadian Tire
7       Imperial Oil
```

Figure B.2   Layout of the cred.txt file.

Performance
Considerations

Some simple considerations to improve the performance of a Sybase SQL Server application accumulated from various experiences are included in this section.

1. To optimize performance, ensure there is enough free main memory (RAM) when SQL Server is started. It is at this time that SQL Server makes a request for a specified amount of memory (indicated by the sp_configure memory environment option).

2. Use BCP with no indexes or triggers to insert large volumes of data (i.e., drop the indexes and triggers, run bcp, and rebuild the indexes and triggers). This is the fast version of BCP.

3. There is an overhead in invoking stored procedures from a client application that accumulates with every "exec . . ." issued from the program. This performance penalty (due to communication over the network) can be minimized by *reducing* the number of calls to stored procedures. A guideline to take advantage of this is to call a stored procedure only once for every function request. Instead of making multiple calls to different stored procedures from a client platform, it is better to issue a single request to a stored procedure that subsequently calls the other stored procedures.

   Client applications should be designed to complete validations and calculations as far as possible before communicating with SQL Server. The application should then collect all information that SQL

Server requires (this could consist of data to validate or data to save in SQL Server) into a series of parameters that are combined into a single call, as shown in Figure C.1.

A stored procedure must be designed to parse the parameters and call the other parameters without returning control to the client platform until all back-end work is finished.

This design returns results from multiple selects to the client application's DBRESULTS buffer. The client application must be capable of distinguishing between the results of different selects in the stored procedures. This can be done by coding stored procedures that return some type of code (either numeric or alpha) with the information. The client application must parse the code and/or check the number of columns in the batch to understand the information

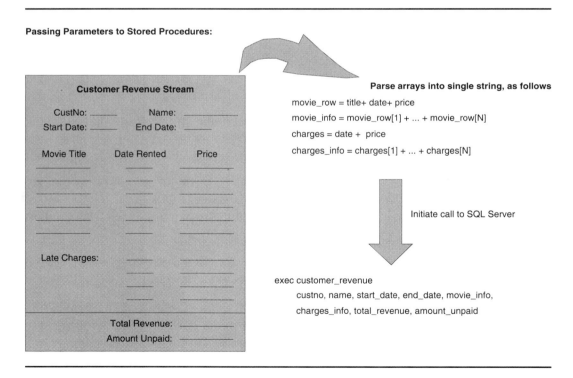

Figure C.1   Improving performance through streamlined stored procedure calls.

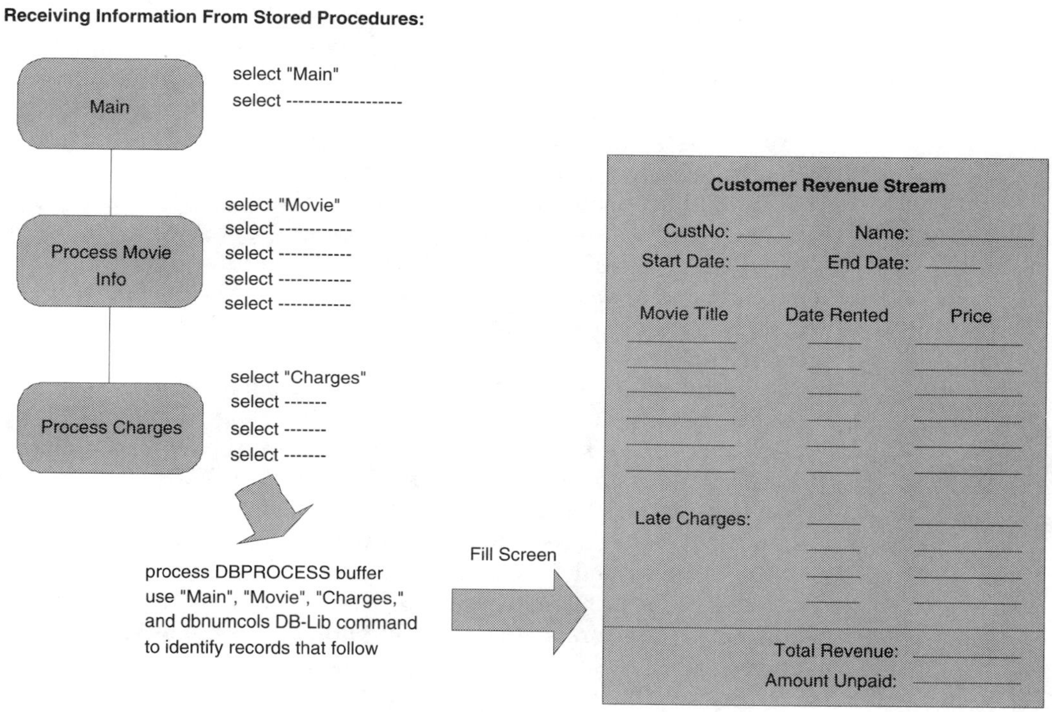

Receiving Information From Stored Procedures:

Figure C.2   Improving performance through streamlined stored procedure returns.

that follows. When the code changes, the application knows that a new batch of information follows, shown in Figure C.2.

This suggestion can improve system response time by an order of magnitude (e.g., reduce it from 5 seconds to .5 second).

The general steps to follow can be summarized as follows:

a) Request user to enter information into a form.

b) Complete all editing possible, using local data (perhaps downloaded from the server at an earlier time) and the host application language.

c) Collect all information that was entered and parse together, as shown in the previous figures.

d) Issue call to SQL Server stored procedure.

    e) Stored procedure should be designed to validate and return all information to the client in a series of batches without returning control to the client until all back-end work is completed.

    f) The client application should parse information returned in DBPROCESS and validate, calculate, and display information.

    g) The user may issue a confirmation message to the database. In this event, a group of information fields can be parsed as before and sent to the server with an appropriate flag to indicate that SQL Server should update the appropriate tables.

    A general design guideline for client/server systems is to design applications to do as much work as possible in the current location before communicating with another platform. These steps will be sufficient for most business cases.

4. Structure applications to avoid deadlocks and livelocks. Lock records for a minimal amount of time. This will have a great impact on the performance of a heavily used application. Minimize the number of instructions inside a BEGIN TRANSACTION..COMMIT block.

5. Background processes that run against online tables should be designed to avoid large table sweeps (e.g., select * from table where x>3), as these can lock large volumes of data and cause serious response time problems for online users. Read the tables one record at a time using cursors to avoid locking records that are required by online processes.

6. Some types of record updates result in two records being written to the transaction log—one delete of the old record, and one insert for the new record (resulting in an update).

    To avoid this situation, do not allow NULL values to be stored in tables and do not define fields with varchar attributes, (any variable attributes, really). Updates should also affect only one record at a time. Ensure that no update triggers fire as a result of the record update operation. The value being updated should not be part of the index. These suggestions will avoid writing two records to the transaction log, and will also allow an in-place update to occur in the affected table.

7. Trigger logic should be kept simple and involve a minimum number of tables. Triggers should be examined carefully. If too much (i.e., more than one table is accessed) is being done, move the code to a stored procedure instead. For better performance, avoid using triggers to change data in the table that is responsible for firing the trigger in the first place.

8. The Order By and Group By clauses can be slow because of their use

of temporary tables. It is sometimes better to use nonclustered indexes in their place to establish the order.

The cost of using an Order By or a Group By is incurred at the time the command is executed. Alternatively, the cost of using indexes is spread over their ongoing maintenance and retrieval costs. Based on this, indexes are preferred in time critical applications.

9. Position the transaction log on a separate device (with a separate disk controller) for improved performance and full data recoverability.

10. Use of temporary tables can be slow because of contention with other users and Sybase commands that use the same space. It is better to create tables, if their use can be predicted in advance, and to empty them out with the **truncate table** command after use.

11. While it is easy to add space to databases and transaction logs, the reverse is not true. If too much space has been added to a database or transaction log, it will be necessary to recreate the objects with the correct size parameters and to copy the old data from a backup copy (i.e., a conversion).

12. Avoid creating and dropping tables from inside stored procedures, as this can be inefficient. It is preferable to apply the recommendation given in the point above (i.e., use **truncate table** on a permanent table instead).

13. Network architecture can be a bottleneck. Eliminate unnecessary data flow across the network wherever possible. Let the server minimize data volume before sending it to the client and vice versa.

14. Streamline application performance by replacing joins and subqueries with individual selects and cursors in stored procedures. Make this decision after benchmarking an application because joins and subqueries offer their own advantages.

15. Eliminate situations where many users contend for the same data, thus risking deadlocks or lockouts. One common hotspot is the use of sequential code fields (e.g., invoice number). This can occur when an application needs a code that increases by one every time a user makes use of it. SQL Server 10 introduces a datatype called IDENT that automatically creates a new sequential number when a record is inserted into a table. Another approach is to allocate a pool of available codes to a group of users. Fewer users then contend for the same data page on the same table at the same time.

16. When users break out of Sybase without logging off properly, they often leave "sleeping" processes. These can be seen by logging on and using the **sp_who** procedure to see the processes. Some of the processes will be marked as sleeping. Eventually, as these accumu-

late, SQL Server slows down and can hang. These processes can be removed by using the **kill** command, as follows:

Syntax

```
kill process#
```

Examples

```
kill 5
kill 10
```

Some versions of Sybase also offer a rare command: **syb_terminate**; however, it is best to talk to Sybase Technical Support before using this command to verify that it will not cause side effects.

17. Only use indexes where there is a performance improvement. In some cases, using no index is as fast or faster than using an index. In general, small tables should not be indexed because the time taken to traverse the index is more expensive than scanning the entire small table ("table scan"). The Sybase Optimizer attempts to use statistics stored in the sysindexes table to determine when it is more efficient to use a table scan or an index.

18. Accessing data using clustered indexes is faster than using non-clustered indexes because the data in the former (clustered) case is contained in the leaf page of the index. Data is also physically stored in the sequence of the clustered index. Clustered indexes have a higher probability of being selected by the Optimizer than non-clustered indexes.

19. Examine the fillfactor option in index creation to leave enough free space for table growth. Minimize page splitting by leaving enough space. fillfactor is only relevant at the time an index is created.

   fillfactor is also useful in helping to avoid contention among many Sybase users, all going against a small table. Since Sybase performs page-level locking, small tables suffer when many users are trying to gain access to data on the same page, to the point of becoming bottlenecks. By using fillfactor to position a single record on a page, it is possible to spread records in small tables so that users do not lock several records at the same time, as shown in Figure C.3. This situation is generally less of a problem in larger tables because data is scattered over more data pages.

20. Another side effect of Sybase's page-level locking is experienced when a high volume of records are inserted into a table by multiple

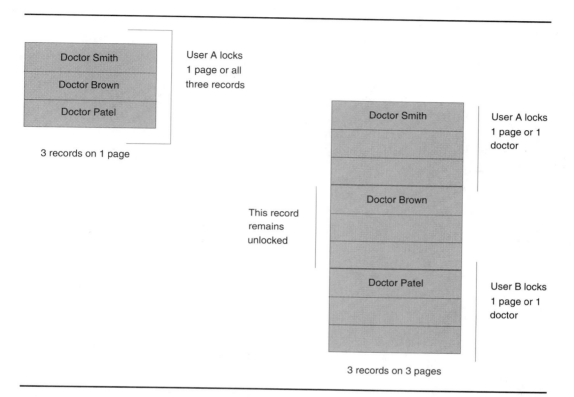

Figure C.3   fillfactor and locking.

users—contention. It is desirable to increase the probability that different users will lock different data pages for record insertion. If the key distribution of the inserted records is random (i.e., records are not coming in with sequential key values - 1, 2, 3, etc.), this situation can be improved by building a clustered index that scatters the inserts to different pages. Recall that a clustered index matches the physical sequence of the records in a table; thus all new records are not necessarily inserted on the last page of the table.

If the records to be inserted have a sequential key, they will still end up being inserted on the last page of the table, regardless of the clustered index. In this case, the *Sybase Administration Guide* suggests building a clustered index on some other unique field (e.g., user_name + sequence_number) that will cause the records to be scattered throughout the table.

21. Avoid table scans when using a table with multiple indexes. Always supply the highest order field in the index in a **where** clause. A table scan is selected by the Sybase Optimizer to sequentially process a table when it determines that using an index will not increase the probability of finding a record more quickly (calculation is based on input/output effort). The Optimizer is not always correct. Suppose there is a compound clustered index on the invoice_items table, namely, invoice_no + sequence_no + product_code. A select should use a **WHERE = invoice_no** to force using this index explicitly.

    To determine whether Sybase is performing a table scan, use the showplan option as follows:

Example

```
set showplan on
go    /* this go is necessary */
select invoice_no from invoice where date < getdate()
go
/* don't forget to turn it off, when the plan is no
longer desired to be shown)
set showplan off
go

/* to see the cost of running a command, use the
STATISTICS command as follows: */
set showplan on
go
set statistics io on
go
```

a. ```
1> select name from sysobjects
2> go
```
b. ```
1> sp_helptext sysusers
2> go
```
c. To turn these performance monitors off, do the following:
```
1> set statistics io off
2> go
1> set showplan off
2> go
1> select * from sysusers
2> go     /* notice that statistics are not dis
             played */
```

22. Statistics for optimized table access using indexes on a table are calculated and stored when the indexes are created (e.g., dpages column in sysindexes). If the key field distribution changes, or after heavy table inserts, the statistics should be recalculated as follows:

Syntax

```
update statistics table_name
```

Examples

a. ```
update statistics invoice
go
```

**b.** ```
update statistics invoice_items
go
```

Ensure that all triggers and stored procedures use the new statistics to access the table (i.e., recompile them using **sp_recompile**).

23. The **update statistics** command is much faster than creating an index on a table.

24. Using more than about four tables in a join may force a table scan. Experiment to get the best performance. Be prepared to split the join into individual selects. If this cannot be done, be aware that the order of the table names inside the join statement can also have an impact on performance when there are more than four tables being used.

25. There is an undocumented feature that was used with success in pre-System 10 versions of SQL Server that forces Sybase to specifically use one of a number of alternate indexes, bypassing the Optimizer.

Syntax

```
select * from invoice index# where invoice_date <
getdate()

index# = the invoice number of the index, relative
to the order in which they are created following
the "create table" command.
```

Examples

a. ```
select * from invoice (2) where invoice_date <
getdate()
```

**b.** ```
select * from customer (1)
```

c.
```
/* notice the change in sort order by using differ-
ent indexes */
1> use pubs2
2> go
1> sp_help salesdetail
2> go
/* if there are not 2 nonclustered indexes on this
table, add them */
1> select * from salesdetail (2)
2> go
1> select * from salesdetail (3)
2> go
```

Again, use the set showplan on to test how efficiently Sybase is accessing the table in question.

26. Use unique indexes instead of nonunique indexes to get faster performance.

27. Avoid using NOT conditions in where clauses (e.g., salary != 10000). The Sybase optimizer will select a table scan assuming it is more efficient than using indexes. Same situation can occur when using other operators like >, <, and so forth. Avoid using variables with different datatypes in where clause statements.

28. Recompile stored procedures if objects they access change (**sp_recompile**).

29. Instead of using **select * from invoice**, it is better to explicitly select the columns that are desired, as follows:

```
select invoice_no, cust_no, invoice_date from invoice
```

This approach will isolate the programming code from changes to the **invoice** table and reduce data volume.

30. The **truncate table** command does *not* log as much information as the **delete table** command. The latter writes every record that is deleted to the log file to allow full recovery, while the former (truncate) only logs space allocations. "truncate table" will consequently be a faster operation.

31. Transactions that do not complete normally can hang without rolling back or committing. These can be identified using the **sp_who** command (they are marked "sleeping"). These types of transactions can have a nasty effect on a transaction log. Since only the inactive portion of a transaction log is truncated or dumped, an incomplete transaction can make it impossible to remove completed transactions. The "inactive" portion of a log is defined as all committed transactions up to the first incomplete transaction. Transactions that were committed after an incomplete transaction are not considered to belong in the inactive portion. The **kill id** command can be used to remove sleeping processes (as described earlier). If this does not remove the sleeping process it may be necessary to shut down and restart SQL Server, at which time incomplete processes will be rolled back or committed.

32. Commands that do a lot of logging should be divided into smaller ranges to avoid having the transaction log fill up before the command is finished.

33. Sybase SQL Server versions 4.8 and greater support symmetric multiprocessing (SMP). In System 10, anywhere from 1 to 32 processors or engines are supported. The **sp_configure** "max online engines" command allows the system administrator to specify a number within this range. SMP can be implemented without requiring application-level changes, so the number of engines that are running is invisible to the application. SMP performance benchmarks typically show performance improvements with increasing data volumes and throughput. It is important to experiment to find the optimal number of CPUs for an application, at different peak times during the day.

Sybase SQL Server and Microsoft SQL Server: the Same Engine

Some readers may be wondering about the differences between Sybase SQL Server and Microsoft SQL Server. There are not many.

In 1987 Sybase, Inc and Microsoft Corporation entered into an agreement to co-market SQL Server. Consequently, both Sybase SQL Server and Microsoft SQL Server distribute the same database server engine.

Microsoft SQL Server is aimed at the PC Windows environment and is compatible with such networks as OS/2, Microsoft LAN Manager, Novell NetWare, IBM LAN Server, and Banyan VINES.

Sybase SQL Server is focused on the mini to large database environments. This version is tuned for use with Unix, VOS, NetWare, and VMS.

Both Sybase, Inc. and Microsoft Corporation have publicly committed themselves to maintaining consistency between the SQL Server engine marketed by the two companies. Recent developments, however, may change this relationship. Only time will tell.

Overview of System 10
Architecture

FEATURES AND COMPONENTS

Sybase, Inc. has aimed System 10 directly at organizations that want to build and deploy enterprise-wide mission-critical, online transaction processing (OLTP) application systems in competitive business environments. System 10 is designed with the following features:

Feature	Description
Scalable	The systems environment is flexible and will grow seamlessly with business requirements. System 10 solutions are leveraged and built for the long term.
Interoperable and Open	Vendor-independent. Systems from multiple vendors (Sybase, Ingres, Oracle) are transparently accessible to users.
Availability	24 hour/day, 7 days/week system availability. Backups, restores, recovery, referential integrity checking are performed while system is running with minimal impact on users.
Autonomous	Data and hardware independence from other corporate systems.

Feature	Description
Performance	Fast response time and high throughput. Degradation of these measures should be predictable and linear with increasing user and work loads. This is also true as data volume grows.
Portability	Applications are easily portable across server platforms, client platforms, and network protocols and network software.
Database Integrity	Database integrity is enforced by a Database Server (and associated servers). This must also hold true in distributed environments that involve multiple servers and geographically separated clients.

An improved version of Sybase SQL Server is at the core of System 10. The other products in the lineup support SQL Server and are identified below (Note: Sybase, Inc. has not released final details of a "Meta Server" product at the time of this writing).

Component	Description
Open Client 10	Application Programmer Interface (API) that is installed on a client platform. Allows clients to access a database server across multiple communication protocols, hardware, operating systems, and application software.
Open Server 10	Allows access to other SQL servers and database servers from other vendors. Supports remote procedure calls (RPCs).
Embedded SQL	Client languages such as C, COBOL, and Visual BASIC can incorporate calls to a database server using this component. Embedded SQL commands are translated in a precompiler step.
OmniSQL Gateway	SQL commands can access/modify data in nonSQL databases, flat files, ISAM files, and so forth.
Backup Server 10	Fast backup/recovery of Sybase SQL databases. Minimal impact on a running SQL Server.
SQL Monitor 10	Used for performance monitoring in a distributed, client/server environment.

Component	Description
Configurator	Used for capacity planning and database design.
SQL Debug	Source code debugger for SQL.
SA Companion 10	Used for system administration in a distributed, client/server environment.
Replication Server 10	Ensures enterprise-wide data integrity. Replaces a two-phase commit used in SQL Server versions earlier than System 10 and in Oracle Version 7.
Navigation Server 10	Supports application scalability.

Relationships are shown in Figure E.1.

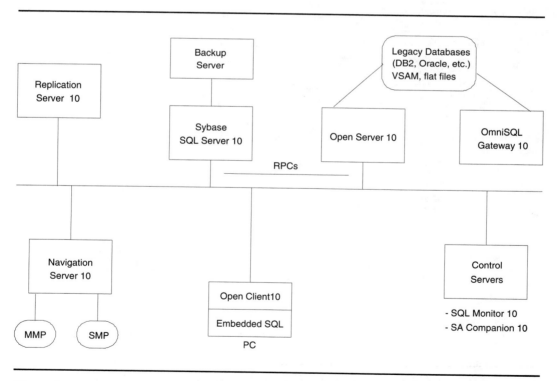

Figure E.1   System 10 components.

EXAMINING THE ENTERPRISE CLIENT/SERVER MODEL

A view of integrated enterprise architecture containing Sybase System 10 products, legacy systems, Microsoft SQL Server, and several gateways is shown in Figure E.2.

A brief description of these products is provided here in order to give readers a conceptual understanding of the enterprise model.

1. SQL Life Cycle Tools

The SQL Life Cycle Tools consist of the following toolsets: CASE Toolset, Operations Toolset, SQL Toolset, and Testing Toolset. These are described below.

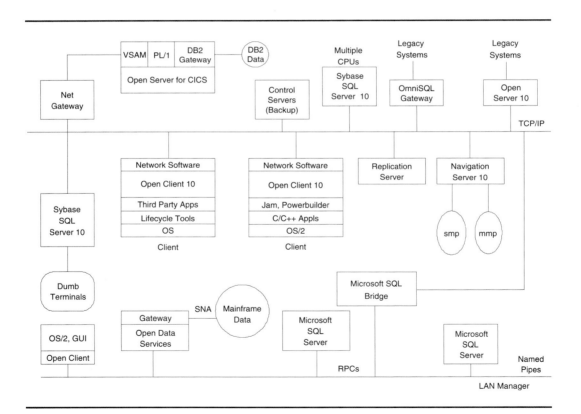

Figure E.2   Enterprise client/server architecture based on System 10.

CASE Toolset Deft is an Apple Macintosh-based CASE tool containing an integrated Data Dictionary and four editors (Entity-Relationship, Data Flow Diagram, Program Structure Diagram, and Forms). A Design Editor compiles the results of all the other editors into a single database design with screen layouts for a complete system. Through the Deft Gateway, the RDBMS-specific design can be uploaded to a variety of host environments and databases. Deft is not a Sybase-specific product and is only loosely integrated with the other Sybase products, requiring a file exchange from the Macintosh to the host platform.

Sybase Configurator is a CASE tool designed for application optimization. It accepts a variety of inputs such as database design and performance yardsticks (e.g., throughput, capacity, response time) and produces a proposed physical and logical database design. Configurator can also monitor an application.

Operations Toolset (SA Companion, SQL Monitor) SA Companion is a system administrator tool for managing the SQL Server configuration, database, users and devices. It supports, through a windowing interface, the automation of repetitious management tasks and the creation of scripts.

SQL Monitor is a performance tuning tool for the analysis of client and server behavior and resource usage. It consists of distinct menus for the Client Monitor, the Server Monitor, and a remote server management tool, the SA Monitor.

SQL Toolset (APT Workbench, Data Workbench, Embedded SQL, SQR) APT Workbench is an interactive, 4GL application development tool for online applications. It includes screen generation and formatting for standard database maintenance and supports rapid prototyping. Products in this class are APT-GUI, APT-Execute, APT-SQL, APT-Build, and APT-Edit.

Data Workbench is a collection of three components that provide easy access to the database. A Data Entry component generates simple table maintenance screens for browse and update of database tables. A Visual Query Language supports relational database queries for users not having a knowledge of SQL. A Report Workbench provides a basic report generator using default formats with an interactive editor for modifying the report layout. Products in this class are Report Execute, utilities, Report Workbench, Data Entry, Interactive SQL, and VQL.

Embedded SQL supports the use of 3GL (C, FORTRAN, COBOL, Ada) application programs through a standard interface to the database. Embedded statements are translated in a precompiler step (just as CICS calls are in a COBOL program).

SQR is a full-featured, 4GL report writer for programmers. It supports a number of procedural and other features providing considerable control over the execution and formatting of the reports. Some of the features include **if-then-else** and **do-while** statements, variable substitution and parameter passing, support for three-dimensional arrays, and in-memory table lookups.

Testing Toolset (SQL Debug, SQL Advantage) SQL Debug is a full-featured source code debugger for SQL. It provides the programmer and designer with detailed information on each execution step, including display of the value of variables, naming or definition inconsistency, execution timing statistics, and optimization plan analysis.

SQL Advantage is a three-component (SQL Edit, SQL Code Checker, SQL Help) development environment for use in mixed RDBMS sites. It assists programmers in debugging SQL procedural code.

SQL Edit is a flexible source code editor that emulates some of the more common editors, such as VI, Brief, EMACS, and EVE. One of its more useful features is the ability to submit all or part of a file being edited directly to the database for execution.

SQL Code Checker provides the programmer with detailed information on the specific source of SQL errors, variable definitions, object references, and coding practices.

SQL Help expands the usefulness of SQL Edit by supplying information on the database and its objects, SQL syntax, and other related documentation from within the editor itself.

The lifecycle tools are integrated through the Sybase **master** database. They are not themselves fully integrated, nor are they yet available on all development platforms.

2.   Database Remote Procedure Calls (RPCs)

Sybase uses a comprehensive messaging system for communication among servers on a network and between clients and servers, enabling calls to any programs on the network.

3.   SQL Server

The database engine, SQL Server 10, is available in three flavors or forms:

- Sybase SQL Server—for UNIX, VMS and VOS environments
- Secure SQL Server—a version of the SQL Server to address government security standards (to level B1)
- Microsoft SQL Server—for the OS/2, NT environment

This is the core of the System 10 suite of enterprise-wide products.

4.   Open Interfaces and Gateways

System 10 supports interoperability by offering a large selection of open interfaces and gateways to build an enterprise-wide application system that allows seamless communication between products from different vendors. These products are described as follows.

Open Client The Open Client interface provides transparent access to a variety of networks for the client application program, allowing developers to program a general solution that can be used in many environments. It contains two products, Net-Lib and DB-Library (DB-Lib). Net-Lib is an API supporting specific network protocols and software. DB-Lib is an API or DLL containing functions that allow access to SQL Server. Applications can be ported to alternate architectures simply by replacing Net-Lib or DB-Lib with a version suitable for the new architecture.

Open Client for CICS The Open Client for CICS component enables application programs (running under CICS on a mainframe) to access, including for update, the Sybase SQL Server through the regular CICS interface. The mainframe becomes a client to the SQL Server database.

Open Server The Open Server component provides an interface for any data source, including other RDBMSs, to communicate with other database servers or client platforms that are attached to the network. Open Server also allows execution of programs written in 3GL languages.

Net-Gateway The Net-Gateway provides SNA access to all IBM mainframe data, thus maximizing the use of data in existing legacy systems.

Open Server for CICS The Open Server interface for CICS, together with Net-Gateway, enables a CICS application on the mainframe to act as a server for any client. The server converts the database queries into CICS transactions known to the mainframe application.

Open Gateway for DB2 The Open Gateway for DB2, with Net-Gateway, provides access for third-party tools and applications to DB2 data and applications through SQL Server commands.

Open Gateways for Oracle, Ingres, Informix, Rdb, RMS Through the Open Server interface, Sybase applications can access data stored on one or more non-Sybase databases as if they were part of the SQL Server database.

OmniSQL Gateway OmniSQL Gateway is based on the Open Server API and is designed to offer application interoperability and portability. The Gateway allows developers to build applications that integrate databases from multiple vendors. Programmers can develop entire applications using Transact-SQL (the programming language of Sybase SQL Server), including functions that access other databases (e.g., DB2, Oracle, ISAM). OmniSQL Gateway parses Transact-SQL calls and translates them into a language compatible with the database being accessed. The command is sent to the appropriate database or file structure. The results are translated and returned to the calling platform. OmniSQL Gateway allows remote databases to be queried or updated. A database can also be migrated freely to any number of database environments without requiring changes to the application code.

Not all databases or file structures are supported by OmniSQL Gateway. Currently SQL Server, DB2, Oracle, RMS, and ISAM are supported. By the time this book is published (1994), other data formats (e.g., Ingres and Informix) may also be supported.

The reader should notice that while OmniSQL Gateway frees developers from having to learn multiple database languages, its existence adds a different level of complexity. The Gateway itself must be programmed to contain a variety of information, for example, different data sources, physical locations, and a global catalog. This role can fall on the DBA.

Microsoft SQL Bridge This product is used to bridge TCP/IP or DECnet protocols used by Sybase SQL Server to the Named Pipes protocol used by Microsoft SQL Server. Microsoft SQL Bridge allows Sybase and Microsoft client/server products to operate in an integrated enterprise environment. Client platforms on the Sybase network (i.e., under TCP/IP) can connect to a Microsoft SQL Server (i.e., under Named Pipes), while client platforms configured for the Microsoft SQL Server can connect to a Sybase SQL Server.

Open Data Services This product consists of a set of routines that access a variety of data structures (i.e., DB2 database). The first component of Open Data Services is a customized call (i.e., written in C language) to a specific Gateway. The second component consists of the Gateway itself. Open Data Services are an important tool in giving applications a wider reach.

5. Sybase Navigation Server 10

Navigation Server supports scalable client/server-based solutions in terms of hardware, software, and data storage components. Symmetric multiprocessing (SMP) and massively parallel processing (MPP) are both supported. With Navigation Server, applications can be initially deployed on single-server, single-processor systems and later scaled to multiserver, multiprocessor systems using multigigabyte databases—without requiring changes to application code.

The secret to Navigation Server is the physical partitioning of data between multiple SQL Servers while providing a single logical view to application users; this virtually removes data capacity limitations and has the added advantage of allowing requests to be processed in parallel. Applications that require additional storage capacity, better response time, or higher throughput can be configured to include additional Database Servers. Sybase Configurator can be used to build optimized configurations.

6. Sybase Backup Server 10

In earlier versions of SQL Server, database backup and recovery was slow and noticeably affected system response time. In some instances, users opted to use customized solutions instead, such as making direct copies of database files. Sybase, Inc. has responded to customer suggestions by building Backup Server and packaging it with SQL Server. This is one of the Control Servers[1] in System 10.

Backup Server is a remote solution that can make parallel database backups of running SQL Servers. It can also restore or load data into databases. Backup Server reduces load that would otherwise fall on SQL Server.

---

[1]Control Servers are: Backup Server, SQL Monitor, SA Companion, and The Configurator.

7.   Sybase Replication Server 10

This tool allows geographically separated locations to have access to corporate application data in near real time. Pre-System 10 versions of SQL Server employed a two-phase commit process to manage distributed sites. In this process, a transaction is not considered complete by SQL Server at a primary site until all physical locations involved in the transaction successfully apply it at their sites. Locations can be separated by vast geographic distances (e.g., oceans, cities) and involve LANs, WANs, and other networking architecture. This provides the opportunity for many problems to occur, such as networking problems, power failures, and computer downtime. In such instances, the two-phase commit backs out of a transaction and either does not commit it at the remote site or abandons it altogether at the primary site.

Replication Server is a more efficient method of ensuring data integrity because it is not dependent on the operational success of all sites involved in a transaction. Sites that do not commit a transaction are logged, but the transaction itself is applied at any sites that were successful. When an unsuccessful site becomes active, the Replication Server ensures that it receives the data updates (as recorded in a transaction log).

Appendix F

Testing Considerations

Applications and programs should be carefully tested prior to implementation. All features in a system should be carefully tested, fixed, and retested to ensure that there are no surprises or hidden areas in the application. This can be done by employing a series of testing phases managed by a committee of users and developers.

PRELIMINARY PHASE

In this phase, users and developers participate in identifying test cases. This must be a rigorous effort designed to validate all aspects of a business environment. This information can be captured by the test team and recorded on a form similar to the one shown in Figure F.1. These "Test Case Sheets" should be developed primarily at the function or screen level. There is no hard rule to dictate this breakdown. Every feature in the system must be captured on the sheets, and it is up to the project team to agree how these cases should be grouped. Each tester should use this form as a guide for testing, being careful to record observations and discovered bugs. These should be summarized and given to the testing manager on a frequent basis.

The value of this technique is directly proportional to the thoroughness of the test cases. A good strategy is to build these test cases over a period of time so that a time crunch does not occur in the testing phases. Testers should not limit themselves to only these test cases. They should learn to do things that have not been thought of before, while being

```
Setup
1. Run test.v12 script to re-establish database for
   testing.
2. Download current application from server to testing PC.
3. etcetera.....

 Tester
   Test Case                    Expected Results
 Observations
 1. Print Invoice              - printed invoice
                               - customer's amount owed
                                 should increase by amt.
                               - inventory should change
                                 by # of movies rented &
                                 products purchased.

 2. Invoke Customer           - Customer  information
    name search                 should appear on screen.

 etcetera.
```

Figure F.1   Test Case form.

careful to be able to reproduce the observations. Another powerful tool that will assist testers is to build test scripts that bring a database to a predefined state. This allows observations to be repeated.

An "Outstanding Bug List" should be created (presumably empty to start with) in a shared location (e.g., a file on the server). All discovered bugs should be added to this list. Fixed bugs should be moved to a different file, or a different part of the file. This list will prove invaluable for keeping up to date with the project status and will be a powerful audit trail for lessons to be learned. A format for this list is shown in Figure F.2.

UNIT TESTING

Programmers should learn business requirements and test every program by themselves. They may choose to do this without using the "Test Case Sheets."

SYSTEM TESTING

System testing is a structured approach that involves developers and users on the team. Complete days should be set aside for system testing to be done using the "Test Case Sheets." A small team of four or five is a good

```
/* Outstanding Bug List for Video Rental Store System */

Next Available Bug Number: 2
------------------------------------------------------------------
/* Copy the following skeleton to OUTSTANDING. When closing the bug,
change the status and move it to the CLOSED section in this file. */

Bug Number: nnnn
Date Reported: dd/mm/yyyy
Status:     OPEN
Problem:
Reported By:
Assigned To:
Description:


Closed By:
Closed Date:
Closed Comment:


------------------------OUTSTANDING BUGS------------------------

Bug Number:  1
Date Reported: 14/11/1993
Status:    OPEN
Problem:   Invoice Printing
Reported By: Sanjiv Purba
Assigned To:
Description:

When printing two invoices for the same customer, paper does not position
properly for the second invoice. Totals for first invoice do not print
out due to the second invoice.
```

Figure F.2   Outstanding Bug List.

size; however, this number is affected by the size of the application. This phase involves close communication with the development team. Discovered bugs should be fixed and thoroughly retested, as shown in Figure F.3.

INTEGRATION TESTING

Integration testing involves testing an application in conjunction with related systems. This could involve looking at what is being sent to the

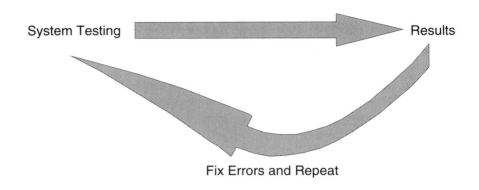

Figure F.3   System testing.

application and what is being sent to other applications. This phase could involve running several complete cycles to simulate the system running for several weeks.

ACCEPTANCE TESTING

This is the final opportunity to capture remaining problems in the application. The test team should consist mainly of users who will need to test the system thoroughly. The successful completion of this phase is tantamount to accepting the application.

BENCHMARKING

Divide the application into physical and logical components. Look for bottlenecks. Test throughput and online response time. Test the time required by the application, the time taken by the network, and the time taken by the critical stored procedures. Benchmark the main transactions. There are several benchmarking tools on the market; however, it may be necessary to develop your own.

IMPLEMENTATION

A final meeting should be held with senior management to obtain implementation approval. Results of the testing phases should be summarized and reported. Benchmarking results consisting of system performance with various loads (peak times, nonpeak times) should be available.

Despite the success of the testing phases, a backup plan should be developed to remove the new application and to revert to the old way of doing things if a problem is encountered after implementation. This plan should be kept available for some time even after successful implementation.

These techniques have been successfully used on many different mission-critical implementations.

ADDITIONAL CONSIDERATIONS FOR CLIENT/SERVER SYSTEMS AND SYBASE SQL SERVER

Client/server applications generally consist of multiple components and products from different vendors. The application is developed to run among these and not in isolation. Consequently, the test plan should attempt to isolate these components and test the pieces individually and then together.

It is sometimes necessary to bring a variety of players into the testing process as results are uncovered. In the client/server universe, nothing operates in isolation. For example, SQL Server runs on a variety of platforms (e.g., DEC, NCR, IBM, Sun, Stratus). While the SQL Server engine is the same across the platforms, in each implementation there are customized hooks that were developed by the different vendors for their platform and operating environment. The reader who is running SQL Server under DEC should try to involve technical staff from DEC as well as Sybase in evaluating test results and making improvements that are unique to that configuration. The same is true for other combinations of hardware/software.

In several previous projects in which the author was involved, it was necessary to bring several players into the same room on frequent occasions (this included the application developers, the users, the hardware vendors, the database server vendors, and some other highly specialized consultants) throughout the project development cycle. *Human communication* between all parties is the key to successful client/server development. It is important to keep every vendor aware of all key deliverables and milestones in the application schedule.

Due to the distributed nature of client/server applications, it is necessary to test all unlikely, fringe conditions such as network problems, localized power outages, and component breakdown. Test the backup and recovery process. Have you ever tried to do a complete recovery from the tapes? How long do backups take? How long does recovery take? Conduct regular consistency checking. How long does it take? Test for deadlocks. What happens when user load increases?

Schema for System Tables

This appendix contains a schema for the different system tables in the **master** and **Model** databases. This information can be obtained by running the following commands in SQL Server to see one row of information, as well as the column names of each of the system tables (Sybase SQL Server Release 10.0 **System Administration Guide** contains comprehensive information about each field and value for the following information):

```
/* signon as system administrator */
 1. use master
 2. go
 3. sp_help syslogins
 4. go

 1. use model   /* or any other database */
 2. go
 3. sp_help sysobjects
 4. go
```

Master Database Exclusively

1. *syslogins*
   (suid, status, accdate, totcpu, totio, spacelimit, timelimit, resultlimit, dbname, name, password, language, pwdate, audflags, fullname)
2. *sysservers*

```
(srvid, srvstatus, srvname, srvnetname,
srv_conn_level, sensitivity)
```
3. *sysprocesses*
```
(spid, kpid, enginenum, status, suid, hostname,
program_name, hostprocess, cmd, cpu, physical_io,
memusage, blocked, dbid, uid, gid, tran_name,
time_blocked, network_pktsz)
```
4. *sysconfigures*
```
(config, value, comment, status, sensitivity)
```
5. *sysmessages*
```
(error, severity, dlevel, description, langid,
sqlstate)
```
6. *sysdatabases*
```
(name, dbid, suid, status, version, logptr, crdate,
dumptrdate, status2, audflags, deftabaud, defvwaud,
defpraud, maxhold)
```
7. *sysusages*
```
(dbid, segmap, lstart, size, vstart, pad,
unreseredpgs)
```
8. *syslocks*
```
(id, dbid, page, type, spid, class)
```
9. *syscharsets*
```
(type, id, csid, status, name, description,
definition)
```
10. *syscurconfigs*
```
(config, value, comment, status, sensitivity)
```
11. *sysengines*
```
(engine, osprocid, osprocname, status, affinitied,
cur_kpid, last_kpid, idle_1, idle_2, idle_3, idle_4,
starttime)
```
12. *syslanguages*
```
(langid, dateformat, datefirst, upgrade, name,
alias, months, shortmonths, days)
```
13. *sysloginroles*
```
(suid, srid, status)
```
14. *sysremotelogins*
15. *syssrvroles*
```
(srid, name)
```
16. *sysdevices*
```
(low, high, status, cntrltype, name, phyname,
mirrorname)
```

System Tables That Are Present in All Databases (Including the Master)

1. *sysalternates*
```
(suid, altsuid)
```

2. *syscolumns*
   (id, number, colid, status, type, length, offset, usertype, cdefault, domain, name, printfmt, prec, scale)
3. *syscomments*
   (id, number, colid, texttype, language, text, colid2)
4. *sysdepends*
   (id, number, depid, depnumber, status, selall, resultobj, readobj)
5. *sysindexes*
   (name, id, indid, doampg, ioampg, oampgtrips, status2, ipgtrips, first, root, distribution, usagecnt, segment, status, rowpage, minlen, maxlen, maxirow, keycnt, keys1, keys2, soid, csid)
6. *syskeys*
   (id, type, depid, keycnt, size, key1, key2, key3, key4, key5, key6, key7, key8, depkey1, depkey2, depkey3, depkey4, depkey5, depkey6, depkey7, depkey8)
7. *syslogs*
   (xactid, op)
8. *sysobjects*
   (name, id, uid, type, userstat, sysstat, indexdel, schemacnt, sysstat2, crdate, expdate, deltrig, instrig, updtrig, seltrig, ckfirst, cache, audflags, objspare, maxhold, minhold, owner_curread, curread, curwrite, maxread, maxwrite, minwrite, cert_status)
9. *sysprocedures*
   (type, id, sequence, status, number)
10. *sysprotects*
    (id, uid, action, protecttype, columns, grantor)
11. *syssegments*
    (segment, name, status)
12. *systypes*
    (uid, usertype, variable, allownulls, type, length, tdefault, domain, name, printfmt, prec, scale, ident, hierarchy)
13. *sysusermessages*
    (error, uid, description, langid)
14. *sysconstraints*
    (colid, spare1, constrid, tableid, error, status, spare2)
15. *syslabels*
    (master_slid, db_slid, type, hostlabel)
16. *sysreferences*
    (indexid, constrid, tableid, reftabid, keycnt,

```
      status, frgndbid, pmrydbid, spare2, fokey1, fokey2,
      fokey3, fokey4, fokey5, fokey6, fokey7, fokey8,
      fokey9, fokey10, fokey11, fokey12, fokey13, fokey14,
      fokey15, fokey16, refkey1, refkey2, refkey3,
      refkey4, refkey5, refkey6, refkey7, refkey8,
      refkey9, refkey10, refkey11, refkey12, refkey13,
      refkey14, refkey15, refkey16)
```

17. *sysroles*
    ```
    (id, lrid, type, status)
    ```
18. *systhresholds*
    ```
    (segment, free_space, status, proc_name, suid,
    currauth)
    ```
19. *sysusers*
    ```
    (suid, uid, gid, name, environ)
    ```

The following script file can be used to retrieve the system table schemas from Sybase:

```
/* type the following commands into a script file and
compile using the isql command */

use master
go

sp_help syslogins
go

sp_help sysservers
go

sp_help sysprocesses
go

sp_help sysconfigures
go

sp_help sysmessages
go

sp_help sysdatabases
go

sp_help sysusages
go
```

```
sp_help syslocks
go

sp_help syscharsets
go

sp_help syscurconfigs
go

sp_help sysengines
go

sp_help syslanguages
go

sp_help sysloginroles
go

sp_help sysremotelogins
go

sp_help syssrvroles
go

sp_help sysdevices
go

sp_help sysalternates
go

sp_help syscolumns
go

sp_help syscomments
go

sp_help sysdepends
go

sp_help sysindexes
go

sp_help syskeys
go
```

```
sp_help syslogs
go

sp_help sysobjects
go

sp_help sysprocedures
go

sp_help sysprotects
go

sp_help syssegments
go

sp_help systypes
go

sp_help sysusermessages
go

sp_help sysconstraints
go

sp_help syslabels
go

sp_help sysreferences
go

sp_help sysroles
go

sp_help systhresholds
go

sp_help sysusers
go

/* the reader can add other tables or system tables
to this script. as desired */
```

The Temporary Database (tempdb)

OVERVIEW OF TEMPORARY TABLES

Temporary tables reside on the tempdb database discussed in Chapter 3. They serve two purposes:

1. They are temporary storage for a database application. The table disappears when the session ends.
2. They are shared storage for any running applications and are accessible by multiple users. The table disappears when the server is rebooted.

Temporary tables are often used to store a subset of a larger table for record-by-record manipulation. Another frequent use is to select another table's contents into a temporary table, as shown in Figure H.1.

A stored procedure can manipulate the data in the temporary table freely and without affecting other users that may be using the invoice table (which could be being used at the same time in an online high-performance application system).

CREATING TEMPORARY TABLES

Temporary tables can be created from any database, but are stored in the *tempdb* database. They exist until they are dropped by the user, or until the session ends (in the case of nonshareable temporary tables) or until SQL Server is restarted.

```
a. 1> use tempdb
   2> go
   1> select * into temp_table from pubs2..stoves
   2> go
   1> select * from temp_table
   2> go
b. select * into temp_table1 from pubs2.dbo.stores
   where
   state = "MA"
```

Figure H.1   Selecting into a table.

To create temporary tables that last for the current session only and that are not shareable with other users, use the following syntax:

Syntax

```
create table #table_name
(
   fields         datatypes
)
```

Notes

1. The # (pound sign) prefix is necessary when creating the table while logged into a database other than *tempdb*.
2. temp_table_name must be twelve characters or less.
3. Sybase SQL Server creates an internal representation of the table name so that it is unique between users. This means that two users running the same code at the same time will create two different tables with the same logical name but a unique internal name.
4. The # temp table can be created while any database is established as the default.

To create a temporary table that can be shared with other users, use the following syntax:

Syntax

```
create table tempdb..invoice_db
(
```

```
    fields      datatypes
)
```

This command will create a temporary table in the **tempdb** database with the name invoice_db. This is the name other users can use to access the table. The data in this table is lost when the server is restarted because the table is removed.

Examples. Some examples of creating and using temporary tables are provided below.

1.
```
create table #invoice_db
    (
        invoice_no          int,
        customer_id         int,
        invoice_date        char(20),
        total_amount        money,
        total_taxes         money,
        total_discount      money,
        payment_method_code int,
        credit_card_type    int,
        credit_card_no      char(20),
        next_due_date       char(20),
        items_open          int,
        store_id            int,
        employee_id         int
    )
    go
    /* the table disappears if the user signs off and
    back on again to look for it */
```

2.
```
create table tempdb..invoice_db
    (
        invoice_no          int,
        customer_id         int,
        invoice_date        char(20),
        total_amount        money,
        total_taxes         money,
        total_discount      money,
        payment_method_code int,
        credit_card_type    int,
        credit_card_no      char(20),
        next_due_date       char(20),
```

```
        items_open                int,
        store_id                  int,
        employee_id               int
    )
    go
3.  use pub2
    go
    select * into tempdb..temp_table3 from stores
    go
    select * from tempdb..temp_table3
    go
```

GENERAL CONSIDERATIONS

Temporary tables have overhead in their use that can affect online performance of a system. Careful consideration should be made before making use of them in an application that is mission-critical and response time-sensitive. In many instances, it is possible to do without them by doing some of the work on a client platform, dividing work between stored procedures and passing parameters using the output feature, or using local variables in a stored procedure.

The temporary database is also used by certain Transact-SQL commands such as the **Order By** and **Group By** clauses for intermediate processing. Depending on the number of users on the system and other factors, it can make the use of this clause unattractive because of potentially slow application response time. An index may be preferable to using either of these clauses.

The contents of the *model* database are copied to **tempdb** when Sybase is rebooted. For this reason, **tempdb** will be a mirror of the **model** database at bootup time.

Because **tempdb** is a common database among many users, its transaction log can get filled up relatively quickly. In order to avoid this, do one or more of the following:

1. Make the transaction log very large.
2. Frequently dump the transaction log.
3. Avoid explicit use of **tempdb**.

The author prefers the third choice due to performance reasons.

Appendix I

Locking

Locking issues in SQL Server become relevant in applications that have multiple simultaneous users and high database activity. Applications should be designed to consider the impact of locking from the start in order to avoid the problems identified in this appendix.

It is important to have locking capability in database systems in order to preserve the integrity of the data stored in a database. Some common situations that can occur in multiuser or multiprocessor systems can easily corrupt the data. Consider the following situations:

1. User A is looking at a record in a table and is making changes. User B begins to look at the same record with the intent to make changes. User A saves the changes. User B is still looking at the old record, unaware that the original record has changed.

2. User A is looking at a record in a table and is in the process of making changes. User B updates the table before User A finishes. When User A saves changes, User B's changes are lost.

3. User A is looking at a record in a table with the intent to makes changes. Meanwhile, User C deletes the record. When User A is ready to save the record, it is no longer in the database.

4. User A is waiting for User B to finish before continuing. User B cannot continue, because it is waiting for User A to finish. Neither can continue. This common occurrence in online systems is called a "deadlock." When a deadlock occurs, the second user is automati-

cally aborted by SQL Server. Although it is very difficult to prevent deadlocks from ever happening, it is possible to reduce their occurrence. A log of deadlocks should be actively maintained (especially in production systems); it is valuable in supporting tuning efforts of a production application over a period of time.

These are some of the problems that can confront users of multiuser, online systems. Sybase SQL Server supports sophisticated locking techniques and processing to prevent the occurrence of these problems and others. While locking prevents data corruption, it can cause occurrences of contention, slow response time, and deadlocks. Developers must build applications that use locking effectively to prevent data corruption, but allow fast response time when many users are active at the same time.

SQL Server can lock data at the page level or the table level. This decision is made automatically, depending on the query plan that is generated. Different types of locks are available, depending on the level.

At the "page level" SQL Server supports "shared," "exclusive," and "update" locks. Shared locks permit multiple users to access the same page. Exclusive locks lock the page and prevent other users from accessing the page until the lock is removed by SQL Server at the completion of a transaction. Update locks are not as severe as exclusive locks in that shared locks are permitted so long as a transaction is not changing data.

At the "table level" SQL server supports "intent," "shared," and "exclusive" locks. An intent lock identifies the types of page-level locks that are active in a table. A shared lock at the table level also permits multiple access to the data in the table. An exclusive lock at the table level prevents access to the entire table while the lock is active. Clearly, it is desirable to avoid this type of lock on tables that many users need to access in an online production environment (e.g., an invoice table in a department store application).

To minimize contention, applications should be designed with the following factors in mind:

1. An application should hold a record for a minimum amount of time.
2. begin transaction..commit blocks should contain the fewest number of commands possible.
3. Use indexes to randomly scatter data in a table so that users are likely to access different data pages.
4. Prevent table locks by using specific select where clauses (e.g., = instead of > type operators) and traversing indexes.

5. Avoid bottlenecks, such as tables that contain sequential key values (e.g., invoice_no) that all active users need at the same time (use IDENT datatype or possibly allocate a pool of key values to different users).

The sp_lock procedure shows a list of locks held by users at the time of invocation. A sample display is as follows:

spid	locktype class	table_id	page	dbname
6	Sh_intent Non Cursor Lock	384004399	0	master
8	Sh_intent Non Cursor Lock	455672671	0	video
8	Sh_page Non Cursor Lock	455672671	212285	video
9	Sh_table Non Cursor Lock	653245382	0	pubs2
11	Sh_page Cursor Id 393218	1932533918	58323	account

This information shows the type of lock that is in effect on a table within a database. For page-level locks, the corresponding locked page is also shown.

The sp_lock command is assisted by the sp_who command in determining which users are locking resources. The sp_who command retrieves the following information:

spid	status	logname	hostname	blk	dbname	curd
2	sleeping	NULL		0	master	NETWORK HANDLER
3	sleeping	NULL		0	master	MIRROR HANDLER
4	sleeping	NULL		0	master	AUDIT PROCESS
5	sleeping	NULL		0	master	CHECKPOINT SLEEP
6	running	video	FIRST	0	video	SELECT

The sp_configure "locks" variable establishes a runtime limit for the maximum number of locks allowed at any one time. The default limit of 5000 is adequate for starting development and can be changed as an application becomes more complex.

List of System Procedures

This appendix contains a list of Sybase SQL Server system Procedures (prefaced by sp_) categorized by the function they satisfy. The reader should note that some of the procedures require the user to have a specific role (e.g., system administration). Users who do not have the required role will find that the system procedure will not execute but will instead display a meaningful message. If this happens, the user should sign on with the appropriate role or permission. Also note that some of the procedures could be grouped into more than one category; however, the author has chosen the closest one based on experience.

Help information can be retrieved for the following functions by using the **sp_syntax** system procedure, as follows: sp_syntax procedure_name.

```
a.  sp_syntax sp_syntax
    go
b.  sp_syntax sp_addauditrecord
    go
c.  sp_syntax sp_help
    go
```

Another good source to get detailed information about the system procedures is the Sybase manuals.

This appendix is intended to serve as a checklist of the system procedures. It is doubtful that most readers will need to use them all; however, it is helpful to know which ones are available and where to get additional information about them.

AUDITING

sp_addauditrecord
sp_auditdatabase
sp_auditlogin
sp_auditobject
sp_auditoption
sp_auditsproc

BACKUP AND RECOVERY

sp_volchanged

BINDING

sp_bindefault
sp_bindmsg
sp_bindrule

CURSORS

sp_cursorinfo

DEVICES AND SYSTEM SPACE

sp_addtype
sp_addumpdevice
sp_addsegment
sp_diskdefault
sp_extendsegment
sp_logdevice
sp_placeobject

DROPPING

sp_dropalias
sp_dropdevice
sp_dropgroup

sp_dropkey
sp_droplanguage
sp_droplogin
sp_dropmessage
sp_dropremotelogin
sp_dropsegment
sp_dropserver
sp_dropthreshold
sp_droptype
sp_dropuser

ENVIRONMENT

sp_checkreswords
sp_configure
sp_dboption
sp_dbremap
sp_monitor

HELP

sp_help
sp_helpconstraint
sp_helpdb
sp_helpdevice
sp_helpgroup
sp_helpindex
sp_helpjoins
sp_helpkey
sp_helplanguage
sp_helplog
sp_helpremotelogin
sp_helprotect
sp_helpsegment
sp_helpserver

sp_helpsort
sp_helptext
sp_helpthreshold
sp_helpuser

INDEXES

sp_indsuspect

INFORMATION REPORTING

sp_clearstats
sp_depends
sp_displaylogin
sp_estspace
sp_getmessage
sp_reportstats
sp_spaceused
sp_syntax
sp_who

KEYS

sp_commonkey
sp_foreignkey
sp_primarykey

LANGUAGE

sp_addlanguage
sp_setlangalias

LOCKS

sp_lock
sp_locklogin

RENAME

      sp_rename

      sp_renamedb

SERVER

      sp_addserver

      sp_serveroption

STORED PROCEDURES

      sp_procxmode

      sp_recompile

      sp_remap

THRESHOLDS

      sp_addthreshold

      sp_modifythreshold

      sp_thresholdaction

UNBINDING

      sp_unbindefault

      sp_unbindmsg

      sp_unbindrule

USERS, SECURITY, AND PRIVILEGES

      sp_addalias

      sp_addgroup

      sp_addlogin

      sp_addremotelogin

      sp_adduser

      sp_changebowner

      sp_changegroup

> sp_modifylogin
> sp_password
> sp_remoteoption
> sp_role

CATALOG SYSTEM PROCEDURES

> sp_column_privileges
> sp_columns
> sp_databases
> sp_datatype_info
> sp_fkeys
> sp_pkeys
> sp_server_info
> sp_special_columns
> sp_sproc_columns
> sp_statistics
> sp_stored_procedures
> sp_table_privileges
> sp_tables

Bibliography

Aaron, Harold, "Who's Afraid of Big Bad Client/Server," *Database Programming & Design*, June 1993, pp. 52–56.

Date, C.J., *A Guide to DB2*, Addison-Wesley, Reading, Massachusetts. 1984.

Bozman, Jean S., "Sybase System 10 answers user pleas," *Computerworld*, November 23, 1992, p. 60.

Epstein, Dr. Robert S., "A Matter of Focus," DBMS, September 1993, pp. 36–78.

Galland, Frank J., *Dictionary of Computing*, John Wiley & Sons, Windsor, England. 1982.

Glass, Robert L., *Building Quality Software*, Prentice-Hall, Englewood Cliffs, New Jersey. 1992.

Kernighan, Lynn R., "Are You Ready for ODBC?" *DBMS*, October 1992, pp. 60–66.

Kersell, Monty, "Sybase, Inc. launches its System 10 products," Direct Access, June 4, 1993, p. 5.

Khoshafian, S., Chan, A., Wong, A., and Wong, H., *A Guide to Developing Client/Server SQL Applications*, Morgan Kaufmann Publishers, San Mateo, California. 1991.

McLachlan, Gordon, "The Road to Client/Server Nirvana," *LAN Computing*, April 9, 1991, p. 17.

Microsoft SQL Server Product Documentation:

Microsoft SQL Server Programmer's Reference for C

Connecting to Enterprise Data

What's the Smart Way to Bring Users and Information Together?

Nath, Aloke, *The Guide to SQL Server*, Addison-Wesley, Reading, Massachusetts. 1990.

Ricciuti, Mike, "Sybase Steps Up to the Enterprise," *Datamation*, July 1, 1993, pp. 18–22.

Ricciuti, Mike, "DBMS Vendors Chase Sybase For Client/Server," *Datamation*, July 1, 1993, pp. 27–33.

Roti, Steve, "SQL Server times two: Microsoft and Sybase cover all the mini- and microcomputer bases with SQL Server," *DBMS*, January 1993, pp. 91–92.

Sybase SQL Server 10 Documentation:

Sybase Installation and Operations

Sybase SQL Server Reference Manual Volume 1: Commands, Functions, Topics

Sybase SQL Server Reference Manual Volume 2: Stored Procedures

Transact-SQL User's Guide

System Administration Guide

What's New in Sybase SQL Server Release 10.0?

DB-Library Reference Manual

Sybase Open Server

Sybase Marketing Materials

Sybase SQL LIfecycle Tools

Sybase Open Interoperability

Sybase Products and Services

The Road Map to Enterprise Client/Server Computing

Conversations with Sybase

System 10: The Foundation for Enterprise Client/Server Computing (April 1993)

Technical Paper Series: Achieving the Benefits of Client/Server Computing

Technical Paper Series: Enterprise Client/Server Architectural Issues and Options

Tsichritzis, Dionysios, C., and Lochovsky, Frederick, H., *Data Models*,
    Prentice-Hall, Englewood Cliffs, New Jersey. 1982.
Ullman, Jeffrey, D., *Principles of Database Systems*, Second Edition,
    Computer Science Press, Rockville, Maryland. 1982.

Index

References to figures appear in italics